Copy Number 2345 of 2500 copies

THE HUNTER'S ALASKA

Roy F. Chandler

Iron Brigade Armory
Publishers & Purveyors of Rare Books
100 Radcliffe Circle
Jacksonville, NC 28546
Tel: (910) 455-3834
www.ironbrigadearmory.com

The Hunter's Alaska by Roy F. Chandler,
Copyright © Katherine R. Chandler, 2005
All Rights Reserved
Printed in the United States of America, 2005

This volume includes excerpts from
Roy Chandler books titled:
    Alaskan Hunter
    Choose the Right Gun
    Hunting Alaska
    The Sweet Taste

No part of this book may be reproduced in any form or by any means without permission in writing from the publisher, *Iron Brigade Armory, 100 Radcliffe Circle, Jacksonville, NC 28546*, Telephone (910) 455-3834

Chandler, Roy F.
The Hunter's Alaska

1. Hunting 2. Fishing 3. Alaska 4. Outdoor Adventure
I. Title

ISBN 1-885633-08-4

The Hunter's Alaska
By
Roy F. Chandler

Reviewers have told us that *The Hunter's Alaska* is the most satisfying Alaskan hunting book ever written. We concur. Anyone who has hunted our largest state will say, "That is exactly how it is in Alaska."

Hunters hoping to, or dreaming of, hunting the "Great Land" will discover, probably for the first time, exactly how it is done, how it feels, and what they can hope for if they make it into the Alaskan wilderness.

This is a personal book by a hunter whose Alaskan travels span half a century—an author/hunter who does not pull punches or gloss over, a writer who has been there and has done all that he describes.

Little of this information has been conveniently assembled elsewhere, and the 190 photographs, taken over decades, prove the writing real; the experiences are powerful, and the opinions are pithy and often controversial.

Roy Chandler has written to entertain as well as inform. There is nothing boring in this book. Even those who rarely read will wish that there were more.

No one will toss aside *The Hunter's Alaska*. The book is a keeper that will be proudly displayed in studies, dens, and on library shelves.

About the Author

Roy Chandler has spent a lifetime gaining the experiences a man of his era believed important. He describes himself (it is already in place on his gravestone) as an *Author, Educator, Soldier, and Patriot*. He should add *Adventurer* because that is what he really has been.

As a writer, he has had more than sixty books published. As an educator, he held, among other positions, Head Teacher of the Birch School in the Fairbanks North Star School System. A soldier? He served twenty years in the US Army. Patriotism is part of military service, of course, and the author served in the Pacific during WWII and the Korean Conflict.

Roy Chandler (most call him "Rocky" because he lived on Alcatraz Island for four youthful years) rides Harley-Davidsons as most men drive their pickups. Adventuring? He is still at it, and . . . he just keeps going.

Front Cover: Vernon Gessna, of Lykens, Pennsylvania, took this magnificent ram while hunting with Master Guide Ray Atkins in the great Alaskan Range.

Back Cover: Rick Hyce, an Assistant Guide, with two fresh wolf hides.

A Few Overdue Acknowledgments And Explanations

Roy Chandler's books are produced via procedures rarely attempted in the publishing world.

The author writes, of course, and produces a quite legible manuscript. His work at that point is probably as professional as most scribblers.

Thereafter, things become more complicated, because both author and publisher do not wish to create what we call a "computer-driven" book. That means a book that looks like all other books produced these days of squeezing pennies and pumping text through accepted standardization and "correct" formatting.

We do not offer paperback books. We dislike and do not allow the photograph-packs that are stuffed into the middle of most books. A photograph, we believe, should appear near the text it is depicting—on every page if necessary. Additionally, our photographs are the often-amateurish efforts that we insist on because no one has professional pictures of exactly what we wish to show.

As if that were not enough, evaluate the paper we use. The pages of this book are 70-pound paper that is almost twice the weight of typical book stock. The same search for quality and durability applies to the book cover and the dust cover. We are willing to invest extra to have a book the way we want it.

Acknowledgements

Consider our type size. *The Hunter's Alaska* is printed in Times New Roman, 14 point—that is big print, and that means extra pages and added cost. We use larger print because it is more comfortable to read. Is there anyone who has not struggled with book print so small that perusal became tedious?

To juggle our requirements and still produce a book at a fair price, always on time, that is handsome and readable, and that will be valued and saved on library shelves, requires special people. We found that team of caring experts more than forty-five books ago.

Edwards Brothers, Printers of Ann Arbor, Michigan does our work. All of it. They are generous with their know-how, friendly to deal with, and corporately and personally tolerant of our often less than professional requests.

In all of the years we have been working together we have failed to formally thank the company or compliment individuals within *Edwards Brothers* for providing their extra-special, personalized service. We begin to correct that oversight, now.

The company is more than a business partner; it and the folks who work there are our friends.

This time around we wish to especially mention:

>Jim Edwards
>Mary Beth Bower
>Steve Benedict
>Jim Stovall

In our eyes, you are the best of the best. Many thanks.

Table of Contents

Acknowledgments:	v
Foreword:	1
Maps:	4
Introduction:	8
Chapter 1 History and The Golden Years	13
Chapter 2 Alaska	27
Chapter 3 Background	34
Chapter 4 Guns and Ballistics	40
Chapter 5 Proper Sights	65
Chapter 6 Stocks	70
Chapter 7 The Best Rifle	74
Chapter 8 Kenai Rifles	76
Chapter 9 Shooting Ranges	79
Chapter 10 Elmer Keith	83
Chapter 11 Double Rifles	87
Chapter 12 Pistols	93
Chapter 13 Bush Flying	102
Chapter 14 Mountain Goats	108
Chapter 15 Tough Goats	112
Chapter 16 Learning About Goats	118
Chapter 17 The Doc's Hunt	120
Chapter 18 Goat Hunting Details	125
Chapter 19 The Great Bears	132
Chapter 20 Grizzly Hunting	153
Chapter 21 Dall Sheep	166
Chapter 22 The Lordly Moose	187
Chapter 23 Moose Shooting	201
Chapter 24 Caribou	216
Chapter 25 Wolves	233
Chapter 26 Binoculars	242
Chapter 27 Camping	249
Chapter 28 The Tractor	267
Chapter 29 Fishing (for Hunters)	272
Chapter 30 Knives	280
Chapter 31 Hunting Philosophy	288
Chapter 32 Random Thoughts	293
Chapter 33 In Closing	311
Index:	313

Foreword

The first letter from Tok, sent to me sometime in the middle nineteen-fifties by my closest personal friend, Roy Chandler, began my introduction to, and my subsequent lengthy love affair with that incredible vastness of solitude and grandeur to the north called Alaska.

Later letters continued to prod me, and so, I too began leaving my tracks on the Alaskan tundra. Many of those tracks, many made decades ago, are still there, for that is the way it is in the arctic. Things change slowly; drop a match and the burned woods can be seen for years—seventy or more; kill a moose and it will be years before another bull survives the hostile environment to make it to trophy class.

If you should go to Alaska to hunt, try to be a guest. A truck full of caribou shot from the roadside as a herd migrates across, and road signs full of bullet holes, are not indicative of mature mentalities or much foresight. Alaska's breadth is the equal of New Jersey to California. It is a huge land, but the *total* big game count is only a third of Texas' white-tail deer herd. If we could quietly back out of Alaska and let nature take its course, The Great Land would be worth a thousand times more than all the resources it could ever yield. But, that is not the nature of man, and Alaska remains as one of the few places left where we could prove or disprove man's ability to coexist—with anything.

In a span of nearly fifty years Roy and I, and those we hunt with, have observed great changes in Alaska. Many of these changes, we are afraid, will ultimately prove to be not good. I hope to be gone and away to join the great majority before someone builds a waterslide into the grizzlies' fishing hole out by Bristol Bay.

You will like this book of Roy Chandler's. It is a book to enjoy vicariously those things that are now possible, and it is NOT, hopefully, a history of things soon gone.

Roy writes this book for everyone. As they read, those who have been to Alaska will enjoy again their own experiences, and those who would like to go will daydream as they too live these fascinating stories and learn how it is done in the great state of Alaska.

Arthur B. Troup, Jr.

Arthur B. Troup, Ph.D.

The author's hunting companion for many wonderful years, Doctor Troup, now retired, has been an educator, a professional photographer, and was the finest fixed-wing, light-aircraft pilot this author ever encountered. Wow, could Art fly! Troup is an instrument rated commercial pilot and a retired infantry officer.

Foreword

June in Alaska
The sun at midnight

During the earlier fall hunting seasons, a hunter can expect the light to be strong from about five in the morning until eleven at night. In the north, up in the Brooks Range, daylight is a bit less, but there is still more light than a hunter needs. Even the most dedicated have to sleep now and then, but a strange phenomenon takes over, in that, when it is light, hunters become less tired than when darkness closes in at early evening. I offer no explanations, but it is observably so.

Maps

There are problems with author-drawn maps. They are usually crude, and what the great writer thinks is crystal clear information may actually be a bit foggy. We resort to them because they are the author's work—as he drew them for hundreds of lurid descriptions of Alaskan hunting. They lend authenticity—or something.

Alaska is a discouraging land to sketch. Almost everything appears to be located in the southeast quadrant of the immense state. That is where the roads are, as is the populace (including most guides), and the mountains of that quarter are those most talked and written about—as well as the most hunted. Game and humans seek the best weather, and excepting the panhandle (where it rains an awful lot), southeast Alaska gets the attention. Those facts jam up a map, and unless one can realize the incredible size of the state it can seem as if hunters might be bumping against each other. Nothing could be further from the truth. It is more likely that a hunter will never encounter another group or individual in the field.

Take the Brooks Range of mountains far to the north. Within that magnificent range there are at least nine named mountain systems. A hunter could spend his lifetime among them and not explore it all.

This is BIG country—bigger than your imagination can allow.

To exemplify, we include a detailed sketch of hunting Area 20D, where the author spent years and speaks of often herein. The Granite Mountains as drawn include about 900 square miles but, on a map of the state, they do not rate even a dot. We locate them by pointing out nearby Fort Greely. (As this is written, Greely has become our nation's anti-ballistic missile center. My my, what must the sheep, bears, buffalo, caribou, and moose think?)

Maps

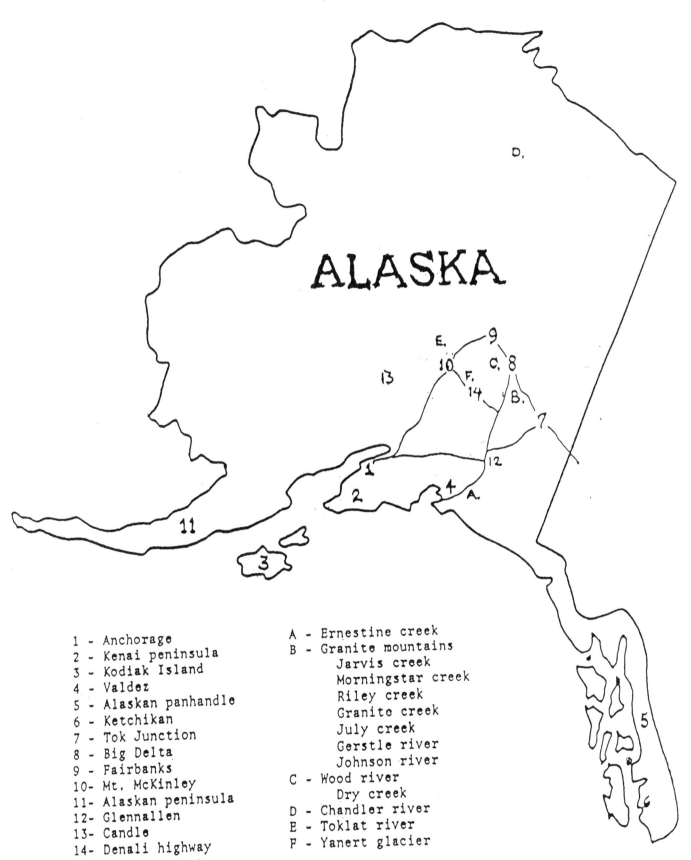

1 - Anchorage
2 - Kenai peninsula
3 - Kodiak Island
4 - Valdez
5 - Alaskan panhandle
6 - Ketchikan
7 - Tok Junction
8 - Big Delta
9 - Fairbanks
10- Mt. McKinley
11- Alaskan peninsula
12- Glennallen
13- Candle
14- Denali highway

A - Ernestine creek
B - Granite mountains
    Jarvis creek
    Morningstar creek
    Riley creek
    Granite creek
    July creek
    Gerstle river
    Johnson river
C - Wood river
    Dry creek
D - Chandler river
E - Toklat river
F - Yanert glacier

Much of Alaska is mountainous and, in lower elevations, there is hunting in most of those mountains, as well as on the vast flats between ranges. The question arises as to which areas offer the best chances, which can be reached, which include guide service (for those requiring such assistance), and what kind of game is to be found in a preferred hunting area?

This map can help orient the hunter to areas mentioned in this volume, and it indicates where the best of hunting has historically been found.

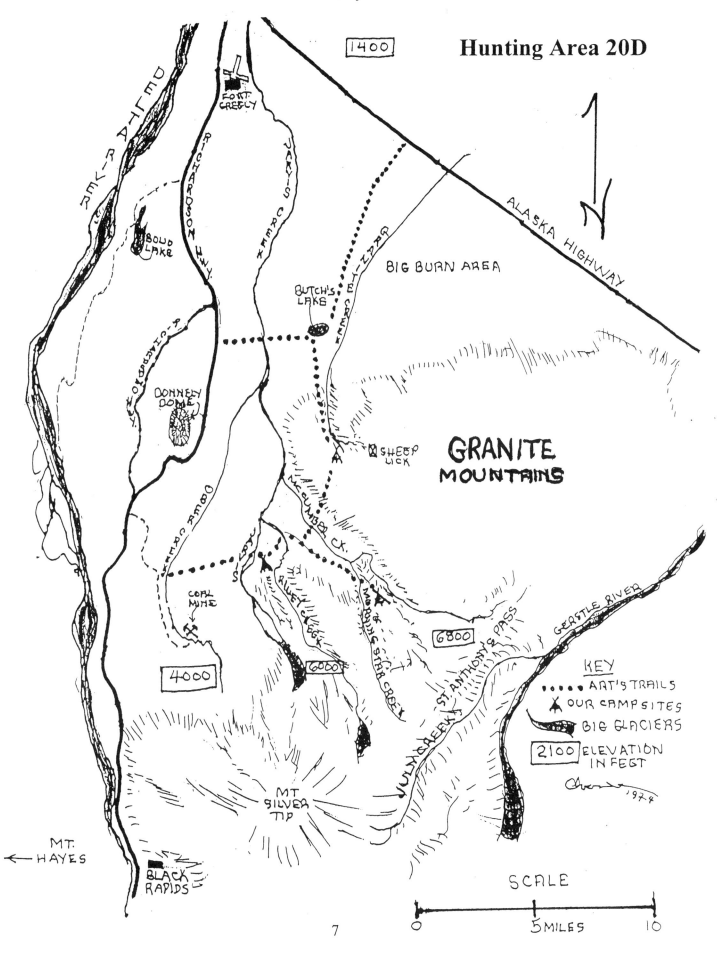

Introduction

Within some limitations, every book an author creates is a labor of love. Sometimes, however, knowing he can finish, the writing becomes drudgery and the author sags part way through his creation.

I have written and have had published more than sixty books on diverse subjects, and while finishing some of them I have experienced loss of interest. But not this one! Writing about the Great Land stirs half-forgotten memories and renews dimmed but cherished recollections.

I began hunting Alaska in the mid 1950s. Wow, fifty years ago! The first notes for my Alaskan hunting books were jotted down in 1959.

In 1977 I produced the book *Alaskan Hunter*, and a lot of what is in this volume appeared in that earlier tome. *Alaskan Hunter* was offered in a very limited edition and sold out virtually overnight. The book was so popular and so difficult to find that it was immediately stolen from almost every library in Alaska. As best I can tell, only the Valdez library still has copies. The book has never been reprinted, and a single copy has been sold for as much as $390.00.

That kind of popularity is uplifting, but the book was written for information passing and reading enjoyment, not as a collector's treasure.

Nearly twenty-eight years have drifted away since *Alaskan Hunter* appeared, and the stories therein need retelling to a wider audience. I believe that I have learned and experienced more worthwhile things during those

Introduction

hunting years. Certainly my opinions have firmed as evidence for or against my hunting and shooting beliefs have accumulated.

A few years ago an old hunting pal resurfaced after a forty plus year absence. My old buddy moved into my humble abode and became my dependent for ten wonderful days of reminiscing about hunts and travels long past—hunts, forgotten by all but he and me. We rehashed with imaginative tellings that required regular elaborations and additions by the listener.

June 2004. Aging Alaskan hunters, Jerry Rausch on the left and author Roy Chandler to the right, pose at the "Old Guide's" grave in Washington. Jerry's parents departed early and are still greatly missed. On the pages of this book, you will see them as they were in the early days. Jerry has his trusty pre-1964 .270 Winchester. The author holds Art Rausch's favorite Model 70 in 30/06.

To my great pleasure, his memories and descriptions matched mine, and his stories were the ones that I have told family and friends for decades without verification beyond my words. Now, here for all to hear, were the adventures of another hunter from an almost distant past who brought life and new meaning to the hunts I had fervently described. My friend was the previously unknown but immediately accepted expert who verified that I, the household head, really had climbed here, seen that, and shot the many game animals I have always claimed. My tales of great hunts in magical places were supported, in total—by a companion who was there. Vindication! Life was sweeter.

This would seem a suitable point to answer the reader's obvious wonder about, *"Who is this guy, anyway?"*

The question is valid. Few of us readers remember who wrote what. We are rightfully more concerned with what is written than who wrote it, and usually only those gun and outdoor authors who specialize in magazine articles become commonly recognized.

To describe myself I extract, and update, from a book I wrote titled *Choose the Right Gun* (1994).

I am a hunter of more than sixty years experience on three continents and a few islands.

Except for polar bear and desert sheep, I have taken (repeatedly) everything on our own continent. Polar bear are almost never hunted fair chase, so I do not participate. Desert rams have been thinned almost to extinction, so I will not assist in their decline. I patch over these "deficiencies" with the, by current bag limits, vast numbers of European and Asian game I have taken.

I have quotable experience in part because much of my hunting has been the real stuff and not the fly in, hop into a pickup, shoot, and fly out variety so commonly indulged in. But, while experience may be the best teacher, no individual can jam in enough hunting to do it all—thoroughly enough—to know everything. Therefore, I read and study.

Reading should be the frosting on a hunter's cake. Without it, a hunter can only hope that the guy filling his ear with alleged wisdom actually knows what he is talking about. Too often he does not because he also has not read. All that the information giver knows is his own limited experience and what somebody told him (right or wrong). Little read fathers teach little read sons, and dumb stuff as well as the good gets passed along.

Reading the experts can winnow a lot of the hunting foolishness, but even there you have to watch out. One might expect that before a publisher is willing to place his brand on a piece of writing he would make certain that everything was correct. Well, don't bank on it. A bunch of wrongheaded information gets into print. The advantage of reading over being told is that the reader has the opportunity to consider at length and reread if he wishes.

That this author is a *very* opinionated character with some cranky ideas that are not necessarily shared by the popular hunting community will be apparent in this volume.

I, of course, believe that what I write approaches gospel, and that if the reader will simply do as I suggest he will be doing things THE right way.

You will discover that I do not mince words or dance around many subjects. In most areas of hunting and shooting there arc best ways, and I have decided to my satisfaction (and I hope it will become yours) which ways are the very best.

Roy F. Chandler
Author
Life Member of The National Rifle Association

Introduction

The author on a warm Alaskan day in the 1970s

After all of these decades, I remember this photograph being taken. We had been out glassing moose. The bulls were still in velvet, and we had located two big old boys grazing near a distant pond. How big and how many points? We had to get closer.

We approached low, down on our praying bones, slow and careful, mostly hidden by the stuff around my legs. We liked to think we were clever—like wolves on the hunt—and we got close enough to see well or to shoot, if that had been our intent. Incidentally, it was before hunting season, and we did not have rifles. Jerry did not carry a pistol, and if he had skills with one he never displayed them, but my revolver added to the picture, and to tell the truth, I had worn the Ruger for so long that I was almost unaware of its presence.

When Jerry Rausch snapped this photograph we were about one hundred yards from the bulls. We stood up, and the moose just stood there. So much for our skillful stalking. They probably knew we were there all the time, and simply did not give a rap.

Chapter

1

A Bit of History
and
The Coming Golden Years

Every hunter visiting Alaska will be told that times have changed, and the great hunts are mostly behind. It will be claimed that freedoms have eroded, and that restricting state and federal regulations rule. Old timers will state with certainty that the caribou are thinned out, the moose are hard to find, and full curl rams are rare. Big trophy bears? Almost non-existent in most areas, they will complain.

Well, don't buy it. Although at times a bit thinned out, the game is still there. The great mountains, the moose pastures, and the goat meadows are unaltered. Still, the claims that the best times are gone bear looking into.

The most Golden Years of Alaskan hunting lasted about a decade, roughly 1950 through 1960. Before 1950 Alaska was hard to get to, and most prospective hunters came by ship and laboriously gained the Alaskan interior by train from Anchorage to Fairbanks. After 1960 over-regulation began intruding. Times were still good, but the best had passed.

The first road to Alaska, the Alcan Highway, was completed in 1944, but years were required to establish the gas stations, eating joints, and tourist cabins, and some log hotels that made driving the great road practical. By 1950 travelers of every ilk could safely drive from the contiguous forty-eight states and into the southeast quarter of Alaska. Many of those visitors were big game hunters.

Before about 1950 few of even the most seasoned resident hunters had barely penetrated the various mountain ranges that comprise Alaska's best hunting areas. Why would they? Hunters were few and game was plentiful in every neighborhood. To this day, dropping a moose or a caribou more than a mile or so from a road or track creates a brutal "getting it out" problem.

Because big animals are so difficult to pack out, and the law required saving all edible meat, Alaskan big game hunters rarely established the remote hunting cabins commonly found in the lower forty-eight where smaller deer-size carcasses are the norm.

Except for a countable number of long-established hunting camps (particularly on the Kenai and on Kodiak Island), most Alaskan hunters put up tents and used horse trains. Few went in deep. That meant that most Alaskan game had never seen a human. Of course, humans had never seen them either. For the most part, despite contemporary head shaking, the land of the 1950s and the game animals thereon were pristine.

Sheep hunting in the Brooks Range

In the distant Alaskan past, game animals could be taken and sold at market. Sport hunters and even subsistence hunters (Residents who took game only to feed their families.) had little chance as indiscriminate slaughter by greedy market hunters butchered everything reachable. That ended in 1925. Market hunting was declared unlawful and wild game could no longer be sold.

Animals and birds taken by market hunters being sold in this circa 1909 often used, but out of focus, photograph. We see moose, caribou and a flock of geese being offered.

Note: Please bear with us when you encounter ancient photos like the one above. Old pictures show how it used to be, but they can never be duplicated.

While market hunting has been responsible for virtually decimating species—the buffalo come to mind—sport hunting has never endangered a species and never will. Alaska has an enlightened game department that will continue to put the welfare of the animals ahead of human hungers to hunt. That is as it should be, and no one need fear that Alaskan game will again be thinned to the vanishing point.

Before 1900, a man became an Alaskan big game guide by announcing that he was one, but always remember that in those days almost nobody lived up here. The entire population of the Territory of Alaska (that was twice the size of Texas) numbered less than 300,000 sturdy souls.

Ninety or so years ago, the few professional guides were hardy characters most of whom managed only marginal livings finding trophy animals for well-heeled patrons who could afford a hunt's expense and the time commitment required.

In 1908 a series of Territorial laws began licensing Alaskan guides, but early qualification to be a registered guide required only "Being a good and honorable man"—willing to pay $25.00 for a license.

Most Alaskan hunting guides are remembered only during their lifetimes and within the memories of those they guided. How many of us recall Andy Simon from the Kenai who guided for fifty years beginning in the earliest 1900s?

A photo taken of Andrew Simon in the 1950s. If you wanted to hunt, say in 1911, you contacted Andy in Seward, Alaska. Simon guided famous and wealthy men who recorded their adventures in diaries and magazines. All gone and mostly forgotten now.

Does Oscar Vogel ring a bell? Not for many, probably, but Vogel was very successful and extremely well known from the 1930s through the 1960s. This is how the hardy guide looked in the late 1950s. (The author wonders where these ancient photos come from. I discover them in my files, but the sources—probably long gone, as are their subjects. I have no idea and can offer no credits.)

How about Slim Moore? Slim was guiding into the 1960s and was particularly proud of having guide license number one.

I took this photo of Slim in 1973 at his home in Anchorage. We reminisced about times past, and the occasions we had met sheep hunting in the mountains near Big Delta. Slim had hunted everywhere, and his mind was sharp—a good memory for me.

There is an old saying, "When you take your hand out of the water bucket, the hole disappears." That rule applies to even the most famous of us. We fade rapidly from memory, no matter how marvelous we may have been during our times.

Big game hunting took a terrific beating from the Great Depression of 1930 through The Second World War. Most American men were relatively poor and interest lay in making livings and in winning the most terrible war in our history. Sport hunting was out. Only subsistence hunting was in. That was a good era for the big animals with little human hunting pressure to add to predator harvesting.

A large percentage of the small, pre-WWII Alaskan population worked for the government and often had little interest in hunting beyond meat for eating. (Alaska remained a territory until 1959 and to this day retains a significant federal government presence.)

Being a miner or a logger did not automatically qualify a man to be a skilled hunter or a hunting guide. There were homesteaders struggling with subsistence farms, but most of them had grown up while living in other states. Their hunting skills were often limited to dropping a moose that wandered through or a bear that came too close. If caribou migrated nearby, men went hunting, but the Dall sheep and the high climbing goats were rarely threatened.

By the 1950s, Alaskan residents had been in place long enough to build and to accumulate. The permanent population had risen to about 350,000. The Alcan Highway was being continually upgraded and long-haul trucks were plowing their ways north in dramatically increasing numbers. A non-resident hunter had only to plunk down a fifty dollar hunting fee, and he could go out there and do his best on animals of his own choosing almost anywhere in the territory.

In those halcyon days, a hunting guide was not required. Whether they recognized it or not, cheechako hunters desperately needed guides, but for hunters skilled and knowledgeable, doing it alone added spice and adventure to their hunts.

At the war's end (1945), professional guides with experience and measurable qualifications began surfacing. Through the writings of men like *OutDoor Life* magazine's Jack O'Connor, sheep hunting became a new and accomplishable dream for ordinary red hat hunters of other states.

If you hunted sheep, many wondered, why not goats? And if you were up there doing that, why not seek out other mighty animals residing in our nation's game-rich northern climes? Conversely, if you went north, at great expense, to hunt the huge brown bears, why not try the high climbing game animals? Many did, and most enjoyed rugged if primitive wilderness hunts with remarkable trophies and unforgettable memories as their rewards.

A photo from the 1950s shows Steve McCutcheon holding on a brown bear. Mac was a famous photographer in Alaska (Mac's Photo™), and we have heard that he did not shoot this animal. We can sort of date the photo because Mac's rifle is sporting a Lyman Alaskan scope. No other sight that we know of had its adjustment turrets way out on the front of the tube like these are. The Alaskan had a skinny tube and a post reticle. Its power was 2 1/2X. Few continued to use these very excellent sights after the 1950s. It may be of minor interest to know that the author used this sight on his issue 1903A4 sniper rifle in the Korean War, and it was the primary scope used in his 1952/53 sniper school in Japan.

The bear guides of Kodiak Island wrote books and advertised in out-of-door magazines showing astonishing photos of gigantic bears with proud hunters crouched behind. Trophy hunters willing to pay handsomely for the chance to drop a big brown bear were becoming numerous and hunting thrived.

Do not misconstrue the above to imply that hunting guides have ever made big money. Rich guides are as rare as hens' teeth. Guiding is not a convenient route to worldly wealth. Professional guides of earlier times chose their careers because they liked what they did.

Guides owned packhorses and had learned how to reach territories theretofore too far from civilization. A select few had track vehicles that could carry immense loads and seemed able to go anywhere. Bush pilots increased in numbers, and those talented flyers opened valleys and rivers never before hunted.

Anchorage and Fairbanks had permanent taxidermy shops—*Jonas Brothers* (in both cities) was owned by and featured the three Klineberger brothers, Bert, Chris, and Gene, who racked up record trophies year after hunting year. The husband and wife team of *Haines and Haines Taxidermy* operated in Fairbanks. Gun shops and sporting goods stores were appearing in cities and a few larger villages. Game bags were huge and the seasons were long. In most areas, a resident's $7.00 hunting license allowed a brown or grizzly bear, a sheep, a goat, and three caribou, and there was a lot of game to choose from. *You got a fifty-dollar bounty for shooting a wolf.* The times were increasingly good for both resident and visiting hunters.

The best of hunting had arrived, and 1950 through 1960 was a hunting decade to remember.

It did not all end in 1960, but becoming a state brought changes to all Alaska, including our hunting regulations, and a never before recognized wolf-loving crowd suddenly exploded into a powerful political force that influenced predator control—unfortunately, to moose and caribou detriment. Ill-conceived wolf hunting restrictions have had brutal consequences on other species that should have been foreseen by the many wolf appreciators.

Over the decades, laws were passed requiring out-of-state hunters to use guides when hunting some of the great animals. That added expense, and the "looking over the hunter's shoulder" burden soured some mouths. Those and other restrictive regulations will never be rescinded or significantly eased. Non-resident hunters will always pay BIG for the privilege of hunting the Alaskan big four or five (depending on which animals you include).

How expensive? The 2005 guided hunt price list for Alaska's big five will run about:

Grizzly or Brown bear — 10 days	$9,000.oo
Moose — 7 days	8,500.oo
Caribou — 5 days	4,200.oo
Dall Sheep — 7 days	8,300.oo
Goat — 7 days	8,300.oo

Of course, that is not all. Today, a non-resident hunting license will cost:

Bear — (Grizzly or Brown)	$500.oo
Moose	400.oo
Caribou	325.oo
Sheep or Mountain Goat	425.oo

Free lunches are rare in Alaska.

It would be natural to wonder how expensive it was for non-residents back in the 1950s when this author began. Here is a listing from that era.

Grizzly or Brown	$500.oo
Moose	200.oo
Caribou	200.oo
Dall sheep	500.oo
Goat	300.oo

Prices from those special times can be even more startling. For example, you could purchase (legally from *Jonas Brothers*) a Grizzly open mouthed rug for $225.oo, or even a Polar bear for about $420.oo. The one-eared wolves we sold for $20.oo (probably to Jonas Brothers) could be bought from that firm, tanned and handsomely combed for about $55.oo.

We have to talk more than a little about professional guides because attempting to hunt Alaska without someone knowledgeable and experienced will most often prove frustrating and fruitless. Every mountain does not support game, and moose do not frequent every valley.

At the above rates, time is precious in Alaskan hunting. The Alaskan wilderness can also be dangerous. Beyond the obvious menace of unpleasant bears, the unwary can improperly negotiate glaciers and rockslides, even muskeg. Arctic streams can be underestimated. Boulder fields can be tricky. Mountains may look alike, hunters become lost, and unexpected weather changes can sometimes prove deadly. The cheechako should hire the best guide he can find and be pleased to have him.

In Alaskan hunting, stream fording is common. The author is shown crossing Ernestine Creek en-route to our favorite goat hunting camp. To get into the high end of the canyon, where the goats live, a hunter is forced to ford the creek about twelve times. It is rough country. Only an utter idiot would attempt crossing without a "third leg." Usually the hunter would face downstream with his butt into the current, but I wanted the best light for the picture. The stream bottoms are rough and slick as snake spit. Cut a willow pole, poke it a step ahead, plant it firmly, move one leg forward, plant the foot solidly, and then move up the second foot. It takes time to stay dry. The water in Ernestine is straight off the glacier—cold! It is clouded with glacial silt, and it runs very fast.

The Alaskan professional hunter (a guide) is not the casual hire of prior times. Alaskan guides these days are equipped and experienced. Many of them have airplanes. They have passed difficult tests, and they have had to produce for their clients or they would be out of business. Their association has an excellent magazine that can be subscribed to for $40.00 a year (as of 2005) by writing to *The Alaska Professional Hunter, PO Box 91932, Anchorage, Alaska 99509*. If you are seeking guidance or a guide for Alaskan hunting, the slick-papered magazine with its many descriptive ads and its astounding photographs will be money well spent.

Actually, the most dramatic change in Alaskan hunting arrived virtually unremarked early in the magical 1950s, and its acceptance changed the face of hunting the vast wilderness areas for all time.

Without being prompted, few would suspect that the dramatic increase in the popularity of big game hunting was, in large part, *due to the perfection and worldwide adoption of the telescopic hunting rifle sight.*

Suddenly, ordinary guys could hit what they aimed at. Older hunters with weakened vision could again shoot well. For the first time, big animals could be clearly seen and optically drawn into more certain hits. No struggling with sight alignment and sight picture, no having your front sight blade or bead cover half of the animal you were hunting. Shooting distances increased removing the need for more than a little skilled stalking. Now you could see clearly and often through brush or tall grass. Put the crosshair where you want and squeeze the trigger. That sounded easy to many a hunter who could not hit zilch with iron sights.

Of course, telescopic sights of diverse qualities had been around for decades, but they all came together and into common use during the 1950s with clear waterproof lenses and strong mounts. In 1952, variable power scopes appeared, and within the next few years a hunter could purchase almost every variation of telescopic sight that is offered these many years later. Those sights helped lure countless hunters into successful big game hunting. Many came to Alaska.

During that long past golden decade we had few restrictions, not too many hunters, astonishingly low licensing fees, lots of game, and . . . well, it was just a great time to be hunting the great land. This author began in Alaska back then, and those years provided hunting never to be forgotten.

Bitter facts are that hunters without access to aircraft are now struggling to find trophy moose and caribou where they can be harvested. And, as the marvelous decade of 1950 through 1960 is long past and virtually forgotten, what is this business about a coming *Golden Era*?

Fortunately, professional guides have become well organized and are able to push forward their wishes, knowledge, and experience.

Even more important, attitudes within Alaskan politics have shifted as never before. The current state governor is solidly pro-hunting and, unlike many before him, he has demonstrated the smarts, the will, and the ability to stand up to the well-funded and politically powerful Bambi crowd (both in the state and outside) who believe hunting to be a dastardly avocation no matter why the game is taken.

A short aside can mention that Alaskan tourism is big business (a very big business), and travelers visiting the state wish to encounter bears, moose, and caribou. Empty mountains are available in many states, but Alaska's bear and moose sightings always seem special.

Visitors returning to the lower forty-eight exclaim about the marvelous wilderness, but if they come upon a large wild animal, their cups floweth over—and they will describe and re-describe their thrilling encounter with anyone willing to listen.

Big animals entrance all of us, and tourism has long feared that increased hunting would reduce tourists' chances of stumbling upon the "real Alaska" of wild game animals. The fearful were and are wrong. New programs will immensely increase game herds while allowing more hunting with better trophies than has been possible for the last forty years. An explanation follows.

No one is more interested in the prosperity of the game animals than the professionals whose livelihoods depend on animal abundance. If the big bears and the full curl rams become scarce, or if the moose and caribou prove hard to find, wallets thin and businesses fail. The pros want a lot of game available and legal to hunt. For the guides and outfitters, conserving and growing the game herds are essential. They are the best game stewards that will ever be found, and therein lie the sea changes that are just beginning.

For decades, a management program entitled *Low Density Dynamic Equilibrium* has controlled Alaskan game hunting. That high sounding policy allows the animals to exist much as nature chooses. Most environmentalists prefer that kind of planning. Letting nature take its course sounds fair and perhaps sort of caring—but it is neither.

Under *LDDE,* predators accomplish more than eighty-five percent of the annual harvest of moose and caribou—and those are violent deaths. Ten percent more fall from sicknesses. If the herds are to be maintained at current levels, that system allows only five percent to be taken by humans. Seems like a pittance, doesn't it? And it is!

The Alaska state constitution requires that wildlife be managed as a *sustained yield program,* and that is good as a minimal standard. Governor Frank Murkowski sees beyond that basic requirement, and despite ill-conceived pressures from tourism and the anti-hunting crowd, he has adopted a better standard. It is called, *Managing for Abundance,* and this is the concept that is going to open the floodgates of good hunting.

A simply understood explanation of *Managing for Abundance* follows.

1—We want more moose and caribou available for hunting. We eat them, we mount them as trophies, and we like to see them.
2—Predators take so many calves of both moose and caribou that a less than satisfactory percentage of those animals survive to maturity.
3—Wolves and bears are the great game predators.
4—We also want more bears to see and to hunt.
5—Therefore, wolves must be radically thinned out to gain more shootable moose and caribou. (Explained and further justified in the Wolf chapter.)
6—**Complete number 5 and Presto!** Available game increases, probably by hundreds of percents, and hunting leaps ahead.

Of course, mature bulls with mighty racks will not instantly appear in every meadow, but they are coming. In Washington D.C. the Bush administration and congress as a whole, as well as the Alaskan delegation in particular, are supportive of the long overdue *Managing for Abundance* concept and it will roll forward this year.

The best of times are again on the horizon, and anyone wishing to hunt (or tour) in the great state should plan on encountering big heads with massive antlers. There will again be world records and of course astonishingly rewarding hunts for those who venture into the wilder country.

In closing this section we should point out that Alaska is the sole remaining geographical area where American hunters can hunt genuinely wild game as it roams freely and unfettered—and in most cases entirely unused to encountering human beings. In the lower forty-eight, game farms are everywhere, and the trophy deer, antelope, and elk are rarely on our limited Public Lands. Hunters down there hunt on someone else's acreage, and they often have to pay for the privilege of shooting animals little wilder than domestic cows.

How about Africa, that land of endless herds and gigantic trophies? There too, game farms are burgeoning. Let me describe a recent African hunt.

At stunning expense, my friend flew in and was provided with a rifle because it was far simpler to borrow or rent than to import his own beloved piece. He shot on a farm—a large farm, but still owned land with fences, and bag limits tightly controlled. He shot a zebra, and the unwanted guts etc. were dragged behind a range rover before hanging in a tree—bait for a lion, of course. As dark approached the "team" sat in the rover using a night vision device and examined whatever came to the bait. When an acceptable lion approached the hunter prepared himself, a six lamp light bar of a "skillion" watts was illuminated atop the rover, and the light-dazed lion was dropped at about thirty yards.

In most places, we call that *game shooting*, not *hunting*.

We do it a lot more fairly in Alaska.

A thousand word photograph. Mosquitoes had eaten me alive, and I was dead tired from bear hunting too many hours. The rifle has a bad scope mount (a see-under) and the stock sports a rollover comb. Dumb! So, is the plastic fore end cap. This was a good Springfield action that I remodeled more than a few times. This time around, I think the cartridge was a .375 H&H Magnum, but too many rebuilds and too long ago to be sure.

Chapter

2

Alaska

With good reason, Alaska's ancient name was Great Land. Our forty-ninth state is great in land area, great in its immense rivers and towering mountain ranges, great in living costs, and great in hunting opportunities.

Alaska is one-fifth the size of all other states combined. The sheer mass of the land is humbling. The state includes 586,000 square miles, which is more land area than Germany, Italy, France, England, Scotland, Ireland, and Switzerland combined.

Alaskan statistics are awesome. In the southern panhandle, Ketchikan experiences annual rainfall of 150 inches. The same area boasts over six million acres of timber. Giant bears live in those forests. Mendenhall Glacier has a snowfall in excess of 100 feet a year. In the center of the state, Mount McKinley soars over 20,000 feet and is the highest mountain on the North American continent.

The Alaskan brown bear is North America's largest land mammal. The Alaskan moose is the world's largest deer. Even the incredible yellow gold hordes that were washed and crushed from Alaskan soil are now dwarfed by black gold, as rich oil fields of northern Alaska deliver their shiploads. Vast oil reserves remain untapped within Alaska's Arctic National Wildlife Reserve.

Even approaches to the forty-ninth state are awe-inspiring. The Alaskan Highway stretches nearly sixteen hundred miles from Dawson

Creek in Canada's already remote Northern British Columbia. Driving the highway is an experience to remember. The Marine Highway, which is a luxury ferry from Washington to Alaska, meanders past fjords and bays that rival any in the world. (What other state has its capital unreachable by rail or automobile?) Even a plane passage to Alaska drones for nervous hours above snow capped mountain ranges that stretch alarmingly hungry fingertips toward the sky traveler.

Everything about Alaska seems determined to be either the biggest or the most numerous. In the right seasons, salmon run so thick in the streams there seems hardly room for the water. In their season, Alaskan mosquitoes excel in ferocity and numbers. Climbers on Mount McKinley report mosquitoes to 17,000 feet. One year at Wonder Lake I lay beneath a mosquito net so thick with mosquitoes that the sunlight was mostly blocked. Even with personal protection, they get in your food, coffee, and hair. Without screening and repellent, Alaskan mosquitoes can present survival problems.

No, Alaska is not all good things. The winter cold striking to sixty degrees below can be lethal. The wildlife also demands respect. It too can do in the unwary. Man challenges the harsher forces of nature only at personal risk.

Alaska continually offers a scent of danger, not imminent enough to cause fear, but a hint of risk that personally involves the Alaskan and adds the "touch of spice" that lends verve to living or hunting in the Great Land.

The people of Alaska possess a unique élan. The state has almost continual earthquakes, and the biggest recorded in North America hit Anchorage in the 1980s. That quake wiped out the village of Valdez (where the oil pipeline now ends) and a new town was constructed nearby. Alaskans face arctic rigors and dangers with an equanimity equaled only by their casual disregard for outrageous expenses. And, they spend with an abandon that often surpasses even their sometimes incomparably high salaries.

Alaskans seem to sense a mysterious "about to be" affluence. They seem to feel themselves always approaching some unidentified monumental prosperity. Although a family may reside in a decrepit trailer and subsist on salmon and beans, it almost certainly possesses the same expectations of impending good fortune savored by their most prosperous neighbors. Great expectations have been harbored in Alaskan breasts since gold rush days, and few real Alaskans doubt some personal mother lode will be somehow exposed.

Alaska is a land for people who enjoy and rise to the challenge and rigor of the outdoors. It has little tolerance for the timid or the foolhardy.

The arctic is rarely forgiving and can exact terrible penalties from those who fail to measure up.

Of course, there are also the warm months. August in Alaska may be the finest climate in the world. Imagine days just warm enough to wear sleeves at morning and late evening. Imagine a sun that rises about four in the morning and stays up until eleven at night. Imagine cloudless skies and mild breezes with all things growing their strongest. This author has traveled widely, but I have never found weather to approach Alaskan summer.

Alaskans are controlled by their land. They do not dominate it. The government notes, for example, that two thirds of all homesteading attempts failed, and there is a steady departure of hopefuls who could not adjust to the arctic wild.

Perhaps in the city of Anchorage, where nearly half of Alaska's population clusters, one can ignore the surrounding wilderness. There, man has insulated himself with civilization's niceties. But, that is not really Alaskan living. Out in the villages life is more real—more Alaskan, more exciting and, sometimes, just a touch hazardous.

Yet, Alaska defies these casual descriptions. She is too large and too varied. The rain forests of the panhandle cannot be compared to North Slope tundra. Civilization touches rarely across Alaska's expanse, and excepting the haul road (the Dalton Highway) to the northern oil fields, only the southeast quarter of the state even has roads. Anchorage is Alaska's only genuine city. Fairbanks and Juneau are just big towns. Ketchikan, Sitka, Haines, Tok, and Valdez are large villages. Kotzebue, Nome, and Barrow are native and tourist trading attractions. Those and a few others pinpoints of civilization mark man's limited intrusion on mighty Alaska.

The nonresident hunter need not overly concern himself with Alaska's size or climatic extremes. His hunt is carried out within a few square miles and usually under the direction of a knowledgeable resident guide. Additionally, most hunting is accomplished during relatively tolerable seasons of the year, and nature's worst at those times is rarely more than physical discomfort or poor hunting, not danger to life or limb.

Perhaps ninety percent of Alaskan hunting is done in the Southeast quarter of Alaska. Excellent guides do fly hunters to more remote areas including, of course the Brooks Range. It could be said, however, that the preponderance of big game lives where the weather is least severe, and our hunters mostly follow that game.

A quick rundown of likely and preferred game areas follows:

Caribou: South of the Alaskan Highway, also in the north as near to Anaktuvuk Pass as the law allows.

Dall Sheep: The best animals are in the Chugach, Talkeetna, and Wrangell mountains. The Alaskan Range has herds of sheep. The Brooks Range has fine sheep, but they tend to be smaller with tighter curls.

Mountain Goats: Along the coast between Ketchikan and Valdez in September.

Moose: Biggest are on the Kenai Peninsula, equaled on the Alaskan Peninsula, and followed by the Copper River. Not as large racks on the Tanana flats. September and October are prime.

Brown Bear: Kodiak Island and the Alaskan Peninsula are traditional. Also along the Southeast coast to Admiralty Island. September and October are best. April–May are second best.

Grizzly Bear: The Alaskan Range is best. Find smaller bears in the Brooks Range and on the North Slope.

Deer: Kodiak Island and the islands of the Alaskan panhandle.

Black Bear: All over Alaska.

There are game animals that come under special headings.

Elk: Have been imported and thrive on Afognak Island, just off the tip of Kodiak Island. (Why a lower forty-eight hunter would journey to Alaska to hunt an elk escapes me.)

Bison: Long introduced to Alaska, and there are two herds open to special lottery hunting. Again, this hunter hesitates to place the American buffalo in a sporting trophy class. My experience with bison shows them stupidly unafraid, much like Ernie's milk cows. But, Big Delta has the best herd—if you can get a permit.

Walrus: Hunting walrus also makes me uncomfortable. It should not. There are now more (far more) than are needed or desirable, and shooting those huge but hapless animals by non-residents will never become popular enough to endanger. Saint Lawrence Island is the place to go.

Polar Bear: Rigidly controlled by international agreement, but Kotzebue is best. Polar bears live on the ice. February is the right time. Bring your mittens!

Wolves: Very difficult to say. Trapping wolves is one thing, hunting them is quite another. Since airplane hunting has been limited, fewer wolves have been taken. Regulations shift with the popularity of the wolves or the desire to have more moose or caribou.

Musk Oxen: This will be the only mention of the Musk Ox. The so-called "Bearded One" is a valiant but not aggressive animal. He is surprisingly small. Although a big bull could go as high as 800 pounds, more are two hundred and fifty pounds. As there are only about ten thousand of these animals in existence any hunting is rightfully, carefully controlled.

A game-filled valley in the Chugach Mountains

It is a mistake to think of Alaska as a vast treasure land of big game. In reality, when compared with our more accessible and populous states, Alaskan big game is sparse.

Although Alaska does boast some 586,000 square miles, those miles are virtually empty of human presence, and much of the land will support only wide ranging game that browses or grazes and keeps moving around.

While a grizzly may be encountered on the vast tundra flats, there really are not significant numbers out there, and most of that land lies empty except when the caribou feed across it.

This is not to say that the land could support more game. Without nitpicking a few selected spots, it could not. Nature's balance is delicately poised in Alaska. The arctic does not tolerate undo meddling, or things will go to pot swiftly. You simply cannot put in more animals without some others suffering. Exceptions to this rule might be the elk placed on islands such as Afognak, or the reasonable and intelligently culled herd of bison around Big Delta. Those buffalo do not seriously compete. The buffalo is a grazer in moose country (moose mostly browse) and the Big Delta buffalo do not migrate long distances as did the mighty western America herds. Those are, so far, well-conceived experiments that are working.

Because of relatively few hunters, past hunting seasons in Alaska have been long. Thirty-five or so years ago we hunted bear for nine months of the year. We hunted caribou for seven months, and even moose were legally taken for three months. Such seasons in our lower forty-eight would have eliminated the game—too many people hunting down there.

All of Alaska, which remember is twice the size of Texas, has only about one million head of big game—that means all types. Texas has a herd of three million whitetail deer. California, which has only one fourth of Alaska's land area, boasts a mule deer population of one million, five hundred thousand animals. Obviously then, Alaska is not game crowded.

Potentially more critical, however, is the inability of Alaskan animals to survive in close proximity to man. Obviously, if humans multiplied, the great bears would be quickly gone.

When we hear reports of moose appearing in the streets of Anchorage we can lose perspective as to how quickly such animals could be shot out. The moose is about as difficult to locate as a milk cow and will always require enlightened protection.

Sheep and goats will no doubt survive in their lofty perches, if properly protected by wise game management. (Which I am quick to add, is the case in Alaska.) But the caribou with their need to migrate could fail quickly. Fences and highways could reduce and finally stop such great migrations. The caribou's innate curiosity could by itself hasten the herd's demise. A caribou simply cannot resist taking a look and a sniff. Anything strange is caribou appealing. Exit the caribou!

Alaska should never allow its wild animals to be reduced to token numbers, and in this author's eyes, it would be wiser to restrict human immigration to Alaska than to see the animals displaced by man's ticky-tacky civilization.

Sheep country in the Brooks Range, far north of the Arctic Circle. That means it is August or early September. The big point is, look at what Gary is wearing—a T-shirt, and there is snow all around him. By dusk, the temperature will have dropped nearly to freezing, and the mornings will be very brisk, but midday can be, as we see it here, very nice.

One might look at the sheer mountains and wonder what animal would be found living on such stark and forbidding terrain. Dall sheep is the best answer, and at times, the bears and wolves that hunt them. Hunting in such mountains can be extremely hard—in the physical exertion sense. Suppose that you glassed a marvelous ram on the peak behind the hunter, could you get there? If you could, would you try?

Chapter

3

Some Background

When I first jotted the notes now included, or during the intervening decades when I wrote magazine articles about Alaskan hunting and shooting, I reconstructed the format and content of *Alaskan Hunter* many times.

Originally, I was primarily concerned with the weaponry and ballistic data involved in taking Alaskan big game. Later, I thought to create a massive tome that would be the absolutely definitive work on Alaskan hunting.

Unfortunately, and predictably, the definitive volume promised to be not only a monumental undertaking but also a financial disaster that no publisher would attempt. My desire increased to provide hunters not familiar with Alaskan hunting with an informative and enjoyable volume that would be accurate in content, entertaining to read, and worth retaining as a reference.

Alaskan Hunter did all of those things, but in 1995 I became dissatisfied with the limited distribution the book had received, and I wished to report on certain hunting details in stronger terms. Using most of *Alaskan Hunter,* plus new information and a new title, I produced *Hunting Alaska*. That volume satisfied the itch to upgrade—for another ten years. *The Hunter's Alaska*? Surely this will be my last effort.

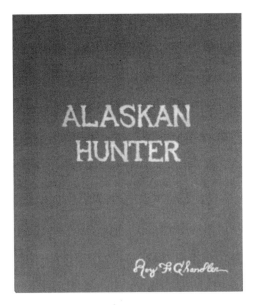

I fear that we who have been able to regularly stalk Alaskan game sometimes forget that to hunt The Great Land is the dream of most American big game hunters. To experience the Alaskan mountains, tundra, and the great trophy animals represents an ultimate hope for many "red hat" nimrods.

But, Alaska is a long and expensive distance from the stomping grounds of most hunters, and in recent years the fees for guides and licenses have become increasingly brutalizing expenses that ever fewer can manage. So, the great majority of those who dream of hunting the Brooks Range, Alaskan Peninsula, Kodiak Island, or the vast reaches of the Alaskan Range are destined to spend their days afield taking animals less exciting than the mighty brown bears or the lordly moose.

As one of the fortunate hunters who have been privileged to roam almost at will across the arctic wilderness, I have been able to hunt when I wished and explore to my heart's content. However, I am not wealthy with a secret gold mine deep in the headwaters of an unnamed glacial creek. Rather, I am a writer who lacks the driving energies and ambitions to discipline himself to spewing forth reams of profitable articles and books.

As this book goes to print, I have somehow survived to be eighty years of age. *Yeah, I am old, but I am not completely broken.* Because I have lived so long, I have generated a lot of experience and opinion. I have also produced a tall stack of books. A long life allows those accomplishments.

Unfortunately for my bank account, I would rather write a little and roam a lot. I still ride my Harley-Davidson to Sturgis and across our nation. Three years ago, I rode the Harley from Fairbanks to Maryland where I have a home.

There are times when I wonder if I have been a writer that hunts or a hunter that writes. If I had to sacrifice one or the other, the decision would be painful, and my world would lose much of its flavor. To be able to live among the great animals of Alaska and then be privileged to write about them seems to this author/hunter a nearly utopian existence. (Harley riding gets in there somewhere as well.)

I first hunted Alaska in 1956. At that time I feared that I was too late, and the great hunting was gone. I had been so warned by the many articles hammered out by then current writers.

To the old sourdough with his memories of an empty land, the freedoms of yore were no doubt diminished. But, in 1956, I found a land brimming with game and glowing with a pristine purity that whispered special rhythms to my ears.

Alaska sang of untrammeled barrens and unspoiled mountains. I heard the ripple of swift, icy streams and the rumble of moose belly. I listened to the roar of a great bear mixing with sharp winds funneling through deep gorges, distant wolves howled, and I knew I had found a land that fitted my visions of an outdoorsman's paradise.

As a hunter I swarmed over the land. During my first year in Alaska I took prime examples of every game animal in the territory, except the polar bear which we did not hunt. I have never considered the musk ox a game animal and so do not hunt them either.

As a writer, I began turning out magazine articles and even a Letter to the Editor of the *Fairbanks News-Miner* newspaper. If it had to do with hunting, I was somewhere in the middle of it. (More recently, I have written columns for *The Accurate Rifle* and *Precision Shooting* magazines.)

During my cheechako year, I was fortunate to have the friendship of the man I call, "The Old Guide." Art Rausch is dead now. He was never a registered guide, but he was a true woodsman. He was a naturalist, a hunter, and an unusual human being, and above all things, he loved Alaska and its untamed wilderness.

I doubt if Art Rausch owned a necktie. I like to think that he did not. If he had a sport coat or a pair of dress shoes, I never saw them. But, he had hunting clothes, guns, scopes, binoculars, and gear. He loaded his own ammunition. He had the finest arctic transportation I have ever seen. Together we used all of his equipment.

We roamed freely, Art and I. He gave me the roots of knowledge about Alaska upon which I have built since that first day in the early fall of 1956 when I knocked on his wanigan door and said, "Hi, are you Art Rausch the hunter? Well, I'm Roy Chandler, and I'm going to be your friend."

That is the way we met. Art gave me his friendship, and we spent days, weeks, and eventually years together looking at game, talking about hunting, shooting winter meat, and going together for the big trophies.

Arthur Rausch, my "Old Guide" in the late 1950s with his last Dall Ram. The rifle is a Model 70 Winchester in 30/06.

I remember the taking of this photo so well that I can smell and taste the brisk air, the sweat, the stink of sheep, and the sound of soft wind coming off the high ridges.

I can feel the texture of the ram's horns, and I can detect the excitement in our souls as we gloried in Art's success.

The victorious big game hunter beside his trophy—is there a more trite but as beloved photo in all of hunting?

The old guide suffered a heart attack while ice fishing and died on Christmas 1960. Even now, forty-five years later, I still miss his dry humor, his wisdom, and his companionship. In fact, sometimes on a fine warm afternoon, when I sit on one of the high spots from which we glassed game together, I hear him speak. Of course, I know it is my imagination, undoubtedly thought and memory patterns ingrained from a hundred repetitions of similar incidents. But, upon occasion, he has told me clearly where to look, and when I turned, there was the game, just as he said. Art Rausch was a grand companion to be with in the mountains. Much of what is written in this book came from Arthur Rausch's abundant knowledge. Here is an example of how good he was.

For over a week we had been successfully hunting goats down along the Copper River. On the way back to Big Delta I mentioned that I would like to get a grizzly. Art said nothing for a while and then sketched with his finger in the dust on the dashboard.

"We'll go out the day after tomorrow. There's a place where the trees grow in two bunches with a dry streambed between them. The grizzly will be right in there. I'll go in above and make a lot of noise. The bear will come loping out the bottom. You stand right here, where this little trail bends, look him over good and, if he is prime, get him when he crosses the path. The range will be about 100 yards, and you'll have to shoot offhand over the brush."

As scheduled, we went onto the flats along Ober Creek. Art went one way, and I took the stand he had described.

The bear came out! He was loping just as Art had predicted. The grizzly was a big, brown boar, sleek from fall eating, with a rich October coat. He seemed to reach out with his front paws and sort of pulled the ground back to him. He was not scared; he was just getting out of the way.

I put the Weaver K4 on the front of his shoulder and touched off the 300 Weatherby. The 180-grain Nosler struck just behind his shoulder. The big bear tumbled end over end like a rabbit hit with a load of six shot. He got his front feet under him facing back the way he had come, growled deep in his throat, nipped viciously at his side, and died.

Art strode up as I stood over the bear. He did not seem surprised. He said, "Roy-boy, what a year you're having."

I skinned out the big hide and retraced the bear's route to better understand and get the most from the hunt. The grizzly had been lying on top of a moose kill. What had brought the moose down, we could not tell, but little was left of the carcass, and the bear would have moved within a day or two.

About two weeks before, Art had noted a lot of recent bear sign further up the valley and had seen ravens circling the woods. He deduced a big animal was down and that a grizzly would find it. As usual, he was right. That's the kind of woodsman Art Rausch was.

Art knew a lot about bears. He was sharp as a tack on moose or caribou. I often thought he knew every goat in Alaska by a nickname. But on Dall sheep, Art was unlucky. He could put other hunters onto fine rams, but he never did get an ultimate sheep trophy for himself.

We all rooted for Art on his sheep hunts, but as his legs grew less resilient and the climbing became too tough for him our hopes grew dim that he would shoot a really big ram. The year before he died, Art nailed the sheep he is shown with in this volume. It is a good sheep, and the best he ever took.

It has always seemed strange to me that Art Rausch, who knew so much and hunted so steadily, was never rewarded with a magnificent ram trophy. As the years have passed, I have decided that it was good that he had not scored perfectly on the great sheep. It is good for a man to have something to work toward, and although it was also his frustration, getting a superior sheep was a living and active goal for Art until his own unexpected passing. Would that we could all have challenging goals still before us when our times come.

Any real hunter would have enjoyed knowing Arthur Rausch, and through the pages of this book readers may come to know many of the things he knew and vicariously experience some of the hunts he, and we, enjoyed.

Of course, that is not all. Alaska is an immense land, and our discussions and photos in this book will roam from the Brooks Range, to Haines, and west to the Kenai and the Alaskan Peninsula. My goodness, the memories those names conjure. Even reading them takes my breath away.

A Camp Robber

Jays are notorious for making themselves at home in your camp. The birds are noisy and almost fearless. They will steal anything eatable and sometimes things that are shiny. If you encourage them, they just might accompany you when you do not want them around—on a difficult stalk, for instance. I like them, the arrogant pains in the butt.

Chapter
4

Guns, Ballistics, and Other Interesting Stuff

Most hunters love to discuss guns and all the hardware that goes with them, and few subjects are more intriguing to hunters than an author's opinions on proper weaponry.

Yet, hunting guns are difficult to write about. Alaskan hunting conditions can vary so widely that generalities can become absurdities. Hunters differ in their abilities to handle recoil, heavy rifles, various sight combinations, and mechanical actions.

It must be added that, despite any difficulties inherent in evaluating hunting arms and calibers, there is little this author would rather write about.

In this portion of the book I would like to sort of roam across that subject matter. I would like to drift off a little now and then so that I can discuss that which I feel of immediate interest, rather than belabor until the reader is ready to holler "Uncle" just to get on to something (anything) else.

I cannot recall when I began shooting a rifle, but I was a small boy. Shooting, hunting, and the outdoors have remained unflagging interests. (God, those are trite sentences for a hunter to write. Most of us were like that growing up.)

Combine more than sixty-five years of gun and hunting experience with dedicated study and writing on the subjects and some pretty solid opinions are bound to develop. Having taken more than two hundred head of big game in Europe, Asia, and North America, I have formed some stern attitudes as to right and wrong in hunting weaponry.

There are other aspects to my weaponry experience. I was a combat rifleman in WWII and the Korean Conflict. During the latter war, I developed and operated an infantry division sniper school in Japan. I first came to Alaska as a US Army Arctic Test Board test NCO, including peripherally, what is now the M16 rifle. In later years, I coauthored (with my brother, Lt Col N. A. Chandler USMC (retired) seven books on military and law enforcement sniping. In particular, we had the honor of writing the USMC's master sniper, Gunnery Sergeant Carlos Hathcock's, biography. I have authored two novels on sniping and an eighteen-book frontier America series that is filled with hunting lore and vivid use of rifles in battle and hunting. I wrote the only published historical novel about Tim Murphy, our nation's first known sniper who was a hero of our Revolutionary War. If you read the magazines, you will have encountered my stuff in *Gun World, Gun Sport, Tactical Shooter,* and *The American Survival Guide* as well as the titles earlier mentioned. I could go on, but my point is that I have been involved in hunting and weaponry longer than many have lived. You can trust what I write to be thoroughly thought out and as accurate as I can manage.

Before getting in too deep, it might be advantageous to mention that, unlike many gun writers, I owe nothing to any firm or company and can therefore speak negatively about a rifle, pistol, or cartridge without endangering invaluable advertising that keeps my publications or writing career afloat. It is sometimes claimed that I am opinionated, and I had also better admit right-off-the-bat that a lot of experts do not agree with my conclusions. I do not complain about that. They have a right to be wrong.

As appropriate rifles, calibers, scopes, and bullets are delineated when discussing each game animal, we can deal here mainly with ideas, concepts, and philosophies of ballistics and the guns that create them.

That, for most of us, should be pure contentment. However, strangely enough, many Alaskan hunters are not gun buffs. Their pleasure is limited to the hunt and perhaps the kill with little attention paid to the weaponry involved therein. I have never completely understood such attitudes but suppose they are similar to my own disinterest in fine tents and downy sleeping robes.

I think that those fellows who know little more than how to load and sight are missing something. To a hunter who is also a gun buff, a rifle can become a treasured and beloved companion. An individual who loves guns but does not hunt is also missing out. The two go hand-in-hand. Personally, I admire a fine gun. I enjoy feeling of it and looking at it. I also like to use it.

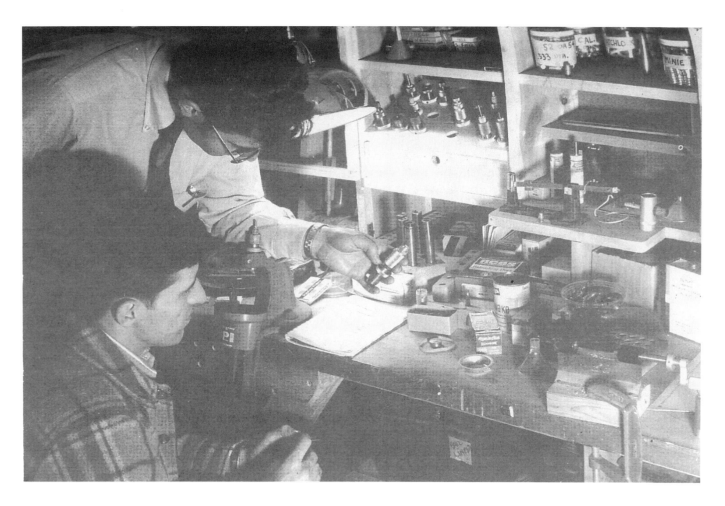

Young friends work at the author's loading bench.

While the vast majority of hunters have all they can handle using a scope-sighted rifle, a few are also pistol proficient. To become a deadly rifle marksman, and that includes being deadly on running and bounding game, requires both training and experience. To excel with a pistol is vastly more demanding. Errors tolerable in rifle marksmanship invoke gross inaccuracies with a short sight-radius pistol.

Few shooters possess the physical attributes mated with the dedication and opportunity to allow development of pistol skills comparable to Elmer Keith and wisely content themselves with rifles for most of their hunting. They reserve their pistols for self defense and occasional, selected game shots. It is a sensible and recommended compromise.

Perhaps my most basic premise concerning Alaskan hunting weapons should be immediately laid on the line. It is quite simply that most Alaskan hunters do not use a powerful enough cartridge. I can dramatize by saying that I believe that too many hunters get their game despite their choices of cartridge, rifle, and scope than because of them. There is a disgusting amount of wounding and blasting away at hurt and dying animals. While some of it is due to bum shooting, often at excessive ranges, too much can be placed at the door of too little gun.

Here is a short example of too light a rifle being used by Frank Cook when he took his world record Dall sheep in 1956, as printed in a publication of the time.

"The magnificent ram turned to the side and the first 130 grain bullet from Frank's .270 caliber King Sporter knocked the sheep down. It got back up. Another shot and the prize went down again . . . But champions die hard. After going down twice, Frank's target staggered up and started toward a steep slide area. Frank shot the big ram three more times before finally stopping it 10 feet from the edge of the slide."

How a hunter who uses a .30/06 on a 150-pound whitetail deer can rationalize that the same caliber is just the ticket for a 1000-pound moose (also a deer) escapes me. When we next include the duffers stumbling about Alaska with their .25/06s and .243 Winchesters—well, to put it kindly, it is irrational.

It would be foolish to suggest that small bores cannot kill. We recognize their lethality but question their ability to kill *quickly* and *cleanly* with great dependability on larger and tougher game animals. A lot of that doubt is because of personally observed, small diameter, hot bullet failures. Some doubts are because the ballistic tables, in which I have the most faith, demonstrate that small calibers do **not** cut the mustard.

"What tables are those?" you ask.

Well, not the ballistic tables you are used to, like those found in *The Shooter's Bible* and *Gun Digest*. Those most popular of tables are beloved by cartridge manufacturers and people who like high numbers. Those tables use an Energy column to demonstrate striking power. In this author's opinion, Energy does not accurately reflect a cartridge's performance on game.

Unfortunately, typical ballistic tables use the Newtonian formula to arrive at their Energy figures. The Newtonian over-emphasizes velocity. In fact, in that formula velocity is *squared*. Energy, which those tables depict as hitting power, is measured in foot-pounds and is referred to as Kinetic Energy. The formula is:

$$KE = [(V2 \div 7000) \div 64.32] \times BW$$

That impressive formula is very scientific and makes hot velocity cartridges look very good indeed. We need velocity, but there is another factor at least as significant, and the bigger the game and the farther away it is taken the more we need **momentum**.

Momentum is the stuff that pushes bullets through muscle, bone, too often wet guts, and two layers of very tough hide.

Momentum is provided in large part by:

BULLET WEIGHT

Here is a pair of empirical examples of the importance of bullet weight:

A Ping-Pong ball and a golf ball are about the same size. With which would you rather be hit? The Ping-Pong ball, of course, because no matter what its velocity, it is light and therefore will not hurt much. But a golf ball has weight. Weight provides momentum. Momentum keeps the ball going. The golf ball would hurt.

Here is another, perhaps more dramatic comparison. Which ball would you pick to have powerfully propelled at you, volleyball or a bowling ball? Same reasoning as above, the volleyball being light cannot do much damage. A bowling ball? Heavy, it will break your bones. Bullet weight does count, and there is a ballistic formula that gives weight more appropriate importance.

John (Pondoro) Taylor, a professional hunter of note, wished to best measure a cartridge's (bullet's) ability to put down game. He developed a formula that, unlike the popular Energy figure displayed in every magazine ballistic table, reduced velocity to a sensible value and better emphasized the importance of **bullet weight**.

Taylor called his formula **Knock Out Blow**.

While some have curled their lip, my experience indicates that Pondoro had it very close to right, and his formula is far superior to any other method of measuring hard hitting that I have encountered. Give his **KO values** consideration in your evaluation of all that follows.

One other point. No bullet has knock**down** power. No bullet! No bullet knocks down a whitetail deer, much less a moose. The impact of a bullet is too short in duration to move anything heavy. For example, only in the movies are humans tossed backward, through plate glass windows, to fall from tall buildings by bullet impacts. A rifle bullet moves nothing. A simple home test is to hang a heavy sandbag and shoot into it. A 150-pound bag struck by a .308-type bullet (at any velocity attainable) will barely twitch.

Taylor's Knock **Out** Blow means that the game is dropped and cannot run off. Impact can knock **Out**—meaning unconscious or incapable of movement. A punch in the jaw is a familiar if crude human example. Collapse follows, not bodily hurling aside.

Taylor was an African hunter who took thousands of head of big game while opening lands for settlement, protecting crops against animal damage, tsetse fly control, and while guiding the affluent from around the world.

This is not the place to delve into the ecological impact of removing those vast herds of animals. It was done, and at the time, seemed correct—perhaps inevitable.

Hunters like Taylor took game animals in numbers almost incomprehensible by modern measure. How does one equate the experience of a single man shooting hundreds of elephants, hundreds of rhino, lions, and leopards plus other hundreds of buffalo, and countless antelope with a modern hunter's accumulation of a couple of hundred head? To say the least, in comparison our experience comes off quite short.

Taylor does not date back so far that he had no experience with our modern high velocity (high density) cartridges. In 1948 he laid out his ideas in his definitive book titled *African Rifles and Cartridges.*

John (Pondoro) Taylor's comments on ballistic table Energy figures are pithy. Two examples follow.

1 — "Surely, the most misleading thing in the world, where rifles are concerned."

2 — "Gun and ammunition manufacturers invariably quote Energy figures because, particularly since the advent of the magnum, Energy is decidedly flattering to their weapons and cartridges. Personally, I take little notice of these figures. They are quite useless if you are

trying to compare any two rifles from the point of view of actual punch inflicted by the bullet. Muzzle Energy is far too dependent on velocity and tends to ignore bullet weight..."

Yet, too often we Americans conclude that the opinions of such men as John Taylor are suspect because they hunted non-Alaskan game, which somehow, it is alleged, makes their findings inapplicable. Any itemizing of African antelope alone will show size variations ranging from the twenty pound Dic-Dic through monstrous Élan that are moose size, with so many diverse species in between that they almost defy listing. We simply must acknowledge that Taylor knew his guns and his game.

This is John Taylor's Knockout Value formula:

(Bullet weight x velocity x caliber) ÷ 7000 = KO

Because the formula is simple, **KO** for any cartridge can be worked out using only our commonly available ballistic tables. Incidentally, although 7000 does indicate the number of grains in a pound, we believe that Taylor just needed a divider that would make his figures more intelligible. Dividing by 7000 results in conveniently low and understandable **KO** values.

By studying Taylor's writing, it can be deduced that he believed a bullet required a minimum muzzle **KO** of at least **22** to be acceptable on Alaskan-size game animals, and that when striking, the bullet must still retain a minimum of 17 **KO** value.

Here are some examples of popular American cartridges worked out at the muzzle and at 300-yard range to demonstrate how a man of Taylor's experience and perception rated striking power. There is a lot of discussion further on in this book about appropriate ranges to shoot big game animals. If a reader feels he needs figures for longer ranges, he can easily work them out by purchasing almost any gun or hunting magazine and using the tables normally included. The math is simple and the information gained will be enlightening and will probably encourage the huntsman to get closer to his targets.

To clearly observe the differences between use of an Energy figure and a **KO** value, I have included both the ever popular .30/06 and a current favorite cartridge, the 7mm Remington Magnum, neither of which I would recommend as a proper Alaskan cartridge.

Cartridge	Bullet Weight	Muzzle Velocity	Energy Muz	Energy 300	KO Muz	KO 300
.220 Swift	48	4110	1800	635	**6.2**	**3.6**
7mm RemMg	175	3070	3660	1750	**20.7**	**14.3**
.30/06	180	2700	2910	1660	**20.8**	**15.7**
.300 WinMg	180	3070	3770	2380	**23.6**	**18.8**
.300 Wthrby	180	3245	4201	2448	**25.0**	**19.0**
.338 WinMg	250	2700	4050	2090	**31.8**	**22.8**
.375 H&HMg	300	2550	4330	2230	**40.4**	**29.0**
.458 WinMg	510	2130	5140	2220	**69.8**	**45.9**

Writers on Alaskan hunting have for the most part suggested that the .30/06 is probably the mildest cartridge acceptable for Alaskan game and that the .30/06 can be used "in the hands of a good shot."

We often read,

"It is better to use a gun you handle well than to use a rifle that causes flinching."

Of course, but that line too often encourages a hunter to believe that his good old deer rifle is just fine for Alaska because he is familiar with it. Very often, the .30/06 is the rifle arriving with the hunter, and I have to state flat out, "A .30/06 is NOT an *ideal* Alaskan caliber."

I am, in fact, not certain that the vaunted 06 is the *best* for any particular hunting. In the lower forty-eight the .30/06 is often a darn good compromise, but for Alaska? Leave the old army caliber at home. It was designed to kill man-sized targets, not big animals.

In Charles Jacob's *New Official Gun Book* of 1951, Warren Page, shooting editor of "Field and Stream" magazine, wrote about the .30/06:

"The cartridge is not a true stopper ..."

At this time, Warren, one of our all-time great hunters, had already shot four grizzlies with a 300 Weatherby.

In the above chart, you will note that the .30/06 comes in just a bit short on John Taylor's **KO** value scale, and my experience demonstrates that is just right. Can you take everything in Alaska with an 06? Certainly, but you can also do it with a .222 Remington. Does that make either cartridge right? It does not!

Despite a bit of ritualistic grumbling, most readers can probably accept an 06's limitations. But look at the 7mm Remington Magnum. According to Taylor, that cartridge is less adequate than the .30/06.

Now everybody knows the 7mm Mag is a powerhouse of a cartridge, don't they?

No, they do not. The 7mm Remington Magnum has extremely flat trajectory and the kind of power useful for mule deer or whitetail deer hunting at longer ranges. Flat trajectory is the 7mm Magnum's strength, not hitting power.

It is ironic that the 7mm Remington Magnum is extremely popular among Eastern USA whitetail deer hunters. Ironic and absurd, I should add. 80% of Eastern whitetails are shot at one hundred yards or under, for heaven's sake. Of what value is flat trajectory in that kind of hunting?

In our examples, the 7mm Mag suffers from both a smaller diameter and a slightly lighter bullet—if compared to the venerable .30/06. The skinnier 175-grain 7mm bullet is ballistically better and will travel great distances. Unfortunately, it does not do as much when it arrives. Bullet weight can be jacked up, but in so doing, velocity takes a dramatic drop and, of course, trajectory then suffers. The 7mm can be a marvel on lower forty-eight deer-sized game out on the flat plains, but it is not the *best* on big stuff.

Since the perfection of good muzzle brakes there is no longer legitimacy in allowing hunters to use their old deer rifles in Alaska. Any decent recoil reducer will bring a .300 Weatherby down to .30/06 recoil levels, or a touch better, a brake can lower a .338 Winchester Magnum's kick to a comfortable shove.

As you will read, this author has used a .300 Weatherby more than any other cartridge for Alaskan hunting. I cannot fault the Weatherby, but I do not claim that it is the *perfect* Alaskan cartridge.

During 1948 and 1949 I began hearing a lot about Roy Weatherby and his hot, new magnums. I was at that time doing serious hunting in Europe, and while Weatherby's powerhouse magnums were not desirable on roebuck or hirsch, I even then thought in terms of Alaskan hunting. In short, Weatherby's added velocities, especially in caliber .30, seemed logical to me. It appeared obvious that if I could move my .30/06 bullet faster, the impact on the receiving end would be more devastating.

I did not buy the longed for .300 Weatherby until 1955. The rifle I chose then was a custom stocked FN Mauser action with a Buhmiller straight taper, 26-inch long barrel. I had a Weaver K4 scope mounted in a Redfield Junior mount and added a front barrel band to secure the forward sling swivel. There were no iron sights. This was to be a working hunter's gun. It was intended to last a lifetime. I took 29 head of Alaskan big game with that rifle (plus a bunch of lower forty-eight plains and mountain game). I retired the rifle in 1975.

For poking in the brush after a wounded brownie or grizzly, the .300 was too light—but not impossibly too light. I used it for that a few times. For some long and imaginative shots on sheep or goats, a heavier bullet (including greater diameter) would do a better job.

The .300 Weatherby shoots as flat as anyone could demand, and it packs enough wallop for most situations. The recoil is not as heavy as that of some of the bigger-bulleted cartridges but, as mentioned, recoil need no longer be worried about. Install a Packmyer Decelerator recoil pad and a muzzle brake and forget recoil for all time.

Staying with the .300 Weatherby for a moment longer, it should be noted that the .308 diameter offers an incredible assortment of bullets for the handloader, and every serious hunter really should load his own ammunition. To ignore that facet of the hunting sport is like a meat and potatoes meal without dessert.

A handloading hunter probably tries every bullet practical within his chosen caliber. I have used some lulus, some really lousy bullets, over the years, but I determined which one I liked best, and although I try others, **Nosler, 180 grain Partition Bullets** remain my favorite in .30 caliber.

When you examine cartridge ballistic tables and their trajectory tables you still cannot fault a .300 Weatherby for most situations. Flat shooting and hard hitting, a lot can be said for the .300.

A good cartridge requires three things.

It **must be accurate,** and I think we can set that requirement aside as all of our modern commercial cartridges do well in accuracy.

Velocity must be adequate. Many experienced hunter/writers have concluded that a bullet must start out at not less than 2450 feet per second muzzle velocity. Excepting a few of the really heavy cartridges such as the .458 Winchester Magnum, I concur and accept that figure as sensible.

The bullet must be effective. A bullet must expand sufficiently, yet penetrate deeply at the distance you are shooting—in my opinion completely through an animal from side to side.

Bullet performance is, in part, a direct result of its velocity. If that were not so, as Major John Plaster has written, "We could simply throw our bullets at our target."

The bullet must expand as it hits, but it must also hold together or it will not penetrate. Hunting bullets have been known to shed their jackets, to veer off course, or to explode. All are examples of poor performance.

We do not want any sort of "explosive effect." We should never "hope" that some unplanned separating bullet fragment strikes a lethal spot. We want the bullet to go where we aim it, expand as large as practical, continue in a straight line (no matter what it hits), and keep digging deep.

We must also note that "explosive effect" does not depend on *high* velocity. "Explosive effect" is a matter of velocity in relation to bullet design. Examples: A solid does not explode at any attainable velocity. A bullet designed to open well at 3500fps on groundhogs "explodes" on the side of a Cape buffalo. Want great "explosive" effect? Load a 405 grain Winchester .45/70 bullet full power in a .458 Winchester Magnum cartridge. You will get it with a vengeance because the velocity of the load exceeds the design speed of the bullet. Although we do not desire "exploding" bullets, consider that a .458 bullet "exploding" is more effective than say a .308 bullet also "exploding." Bigger bore bullets usually win.

The author's backyard chronograph setup about twenty years ago. Modern equipment is more simple to use, but probably not significantly more accurate. Since this time, I have farmed out chronographing, but calculations of old loads measure about the same on the new equipment as they did on the old.

To design bullets that expand but stay together within one small velocity range is rather simple. To develop bullets that will do the same from say, 3070fps at the muzzle to 1640fps at 500 yards is a lot tougher. That is the velocity range of a 7mm Remington Magnum. When we are encouraged to shoot at extreme ranges we might think a bit about what we are asking the bullet to do because—they are not always up to the task.

This is a Sierra, 180-grain boattail bullet that separated in a grizzly bear. There was great expansion, but the jacket stopped just a little way inside the bear, and the core went off in a weird direction. The bullet was used in one of my handloads for the 300 Weatherby. I loaded 79 grains of 4350 powder at that time. My 26-inch long barrel backyard-chronographed that load at 3200 fps. I often dropped to 78 grains, but I also loaded a few blocks of cartridges at 80 grains. In my rifle, the 80-grain loads seemed maximum, and although I did not spend time on the range testing them, the big powder charge kicked like a mule, and I thought the heavy loading shot less accurately.

The author's custom 300 Weatherby as it looked in the 1950s. The recoil pad has now been replaced and the plastic stock tip is gone—replaced by a rose wood tip. The white inserts at butt and grip cap are history. The Weaver K4 is still on the rifle. The 26-inch barrel is cut off in this photo.

This might be a good spot to compare three interesting cartridges, all of which have been claimed to be "good stuff" for Alaska by various hunting scribes.

First let's look at:

Trajectories

Cartridge	Bullet Weight	Range in Yards* 300	400	500
7mm RemMg	175	-8.5	-26	-55
.300 WinMg	180	-6.5	-19	-38
.338 WinMg	200	-8.0	-23	-47

*All are zeroed for 200 yards.

Using recommended Alaskan hunting bullet weights, the 7mm Remington Magnum falls short in the flat trajectory department. Surprised? Many are. To shoot as flat as a .300 Winchester Magnum, the 7mm has to shoot a light bullet. A 150-grain bullet is about right, to regain flat trajectory.

Trajectory

7mmRM	150	-6.0	-18	-38

The above 7mm Remington Magnum trajectory figures look much better, but look where the lighter 150-grain bullet would end up in hitting power—**KO** value, if you will. We again compare the three calibers.

KO Value

Cartridge	Bullet Weight	Range in Yards 300	400	500
7mm RemMg	150	16.9	13.1	12.5
.300 WinMg	180	18.8	17.8	16.2
.338 WinMg	200	20.9	18.9	17.1

I must ask why anyone shooting long distances would choose a 7mm Remington Magnum? I guess I go further. Why would anyone shooting any distance believe a 7mm Magnum to be the best?

My old .300 Weatherby Magnum, you ask? Well, the Weatherby does a lot better and, with the following figures supporting my conclusion, I can ask—Why would anyone turn their nose up at a 300 Weatherby, for any Alaskan big game hunting? Some do, but their reasoning is specious.

		Trajectory—to match previous scale:		
300 Wthby	180	-5.2	-14.5	-32

		KO Value—to match previous scale:		
300 Wthby	180	22.5	19.4	17.8

That is why I used a .300 Weatherby through more than a dozen seasons, but there are other aspects to be discussed before we all rush out to buy Weatherby magnums.

Bill Ramer at the bench. This is the only correct way to zero a rifle. If a benchrest is not available a hunter does what he must, but a bipod is not the best, nor is a sandbag, or even a sniper's pack method. If anything were better, accuracy buffs would use them and ignore the bench. The author has found this style, with three sunken-post uprights, thick rough-sawn plank top—cut away for both right and left-handed shooters with a chain saw—is one of the sturdiest, the cheapest, and the easiest benchrest to make.

Two subjects are bound to be controversial. The two subjects are: Big Bullets vs. Little Bullets and How Far Should You Shoot? I, as usual, take a contrary view. Neat stuff to examine. Let's begin with the bullet part.

When I was a youth and ardently supported the .30/06 and .270 Winchester as all-round game getters, I punched a great many holes in packed magazines, lumps of clay, and spaced one-inch boards. I suppose I arrived at special conclusions from those experiments, but I have long forgotten what they were. I have run similar tests on a lot of super-duper cartridges, and some unexpected results leaped out.

I was surprised, for example, that my .44 magnum pistol, loaded with a Keith type 240 grain lead bullet, cast pretty hard with tin and antimony, out penetrates my .300 Weatherby Magnum at 50 and 75 yards. (It is difficult to test pistol cartridges at much longer ranges, and I did not try.)

It was not surprising to find that my .458 Winchester Magnum blasted through about three times as much material as a 180 grain .30/06 hunting bullet and had twice the penetration of the .300 Weatherby; this also was at close range.

This is not new information. Consider the following.

In 1947, *Outdoor Life*'s **"Sportsman's Encyclopedia"** summed it up like this:

"Everything else being equal, a bullet traveling at 2000 foot seconds will go through brush more nearly in a straight line than one traveling at 2500 fps, and one with a muzzle velocity of 2500 foot seconds will do a better job than one driven at 3000. Other things being equal, the heavier bullet goes through brush better than a light one and the round nose better than the spitzer."

Nothing has changed since then.

Elmer Keith wrote in his *Keith's Rifles for Large Game* on page 34:

"I would far rather use a .45-70-405 grain smokeless soft point in close range timber shooting than any .30 caliber rifle made, regardless of how fast the bullet is driven."

If you want your bullet to carry powerfully a long way, or if you want deep and sure penetration, use a big, heavy bullet.

Some of the above raises the question of just how much penetration do we need, anyway?

Any reader of hunting stories will have noted that the "perfectly mushroomed bullet" is often found just under the skin on the far side of an animal. This is a common occurrence. Skin is tough and stretchy. A light bullet with most of its velocity gone often does not get through the second skin layer.

If a .300 Weatherby bullet (for example) punches clean through an animal, is it necessary that it bury itself in inches of ground on the other side?

Elmer Keith always said that a bullet should continue on through an animal and leave a good big hole on the far side to let air in and blood out. Sounds logical to me. The western scribe, Les Bowman, described shooting a big grizzly with a .350 Remington Magnum, and the bullet went clean through leaving a 2-1/2 inch exit wound. To me that sounds effective, and I have administered enough of those kinds of deadly wounds to large animals—including brown and grizzly bears—to believe in that kind of bullet performance. (See photo on page 181.)

But, there is a more commonly accepted concept that a bullet should expend all of its energy inside an animal because any energy left after the bullet leaves the game is wasted. Hmm, that also sounds good.

In the matter of lethality then, one wonders just what is proven by finding which is the most penetrating bullet?

I recall my service years in US Army research and development where penetration of a 3/4-inch pine board (called a one-inch board) was considered lethal penetration. While that may be good thinking on a human, it certainly does not indicate effective knock out punch or much of anything on an animal that may be five times the size of a man.

To judge a cartridge's effectiveness, I have settled on a rule touched on earlier but no longer remembered by most hunters. It is:

Choose a cartridge that will push the bullet completely through the animal from side to side—at the ranges you are hunting.

At the same velocity, that type of bullet will also plow through most of the length of the same animal if you take a raking or a from-the-rear shot. (We should remember that we get a lot of that kind of shooting.)

If your bullet will not completely penetrate your animal from the side, a shot taken from behind cannot be expected to range through hard muscle and all those wet guts to reach a distant heart/lung area. That means a hunter may not even realize he wounded a big animal, which can run off with a bullet in its belly that will kill slowly and painfully. I have recovered or come across far too many animals lost from such hits.

In wrestling with the problems of bullet effectiveness we are dealing with a terrific number of variables. This is what to do: Keep reading along until you find the author's recommendation for the all-around Alaskan rifle. Buy one and use it.

Now for an eye opener. **How far should we shoot?**

I suppose we have all seen some really long shots. Unfortunately we tend to dwell on the successful ones. Some background:

In the U.S. Army it has been found that beyond four hundred yards soldiers cannot estimate range worth a hoot. The problem is so serious that the military has given up the task. 400 yards (perhaps meters) is IT.

The military Sniper is another story. I know a lot about Snipers because my brother and I coauthor a book series called **Death from Afar** which digs deep into all aspects of USMC Scout Sniping. Those one thousand yard (and longer) experts with their 14-pound (and heavier) rifles and match grade ammunition (who have been trained to the limit) have little to do with conventional big game hunters.

Neither do shooters like the 1000 Yard Club down in Pennsylvania. Decades ago I used to sit with Al Hoyer, their master gunsmith in his concrete block shop above the Juniata River (Al often lived in a corner of the shop) and talk about those esoteric shooting distances. Those guys shoot off benches with huge rifles, using Battery Commander's range finders. (I remember that Al once took 20+ shots to get on and kill a black bear at the favored 1000 yards.)

I will begin range limitations with a quote from Clair Rees in his important book *Matching the Gun to the Game,* Winchester Press 1982, p. 236.

"The wise sportsman knows the limitations of both himself and his equipment. An honest 300-yard shot is a long one, and most riflemen would be well advised to limit their shooting to shorter distances."

I can sense the stuck out lips and squinted eyes. Yes, I have met a thousand liars who claim to have shot assorted game at incredible distances. I can recall about the same number of hunters who have missed or wounded at similar ranges.

I have also known many hunters who have legitimately connected at five hundred or more yards, but author Rees is correct. We should limit our shooting to 300 yards.

Here is a zinger for you to consider. I first wrote this in my book *Alaskan Hunter* in 1977. I still make the claim.

> "In all of my Alaskan big game hunting, I have never shot at game over 300 yards distant."

No one has to, not even in the open mountains—unless he is a lazy-assed pilgrim unwilling to actually hunt. Yet, I do not know a hunter who does not have a story about some completely bizarre, long range kill in their repertoire. Most admit their shot was pure luck, but—they took it, and that means that they probably took others that were not as successful and so are rarely repeated.

Many stories published in hunting/shooting magazines explain long shooting because "The open terrain made it impossible to get closer." If asked if they had attempted to low crawl—like an infantry soldier or a primitive Indian hunter—for a few hundred yards with the slowest and lowest motion possible, the answer would be, "No."

That is unfortunate, because a genuine hunter's stalk should also be part of the chase. Because you cannot conveniently walk up to a decent shooting distance does not mean game is beyond reach or that an imaginative shot is required.

I find it hard to remember an incident where, if I was on the same mountain as the game, I could not get within three hundred yards by getting on my belly and edging forward, often not directly at an animal, but always shortening the distance or changing the altitude. (It is usually an advantage to be above an animal but not always—see moose hunting section.)

Because I can be as lazy as the next guy, I remember many situations where I chose not to attempt a final and difficult creeping and crawling stalk that would put an animal within my self-imposed 300 yard limit, but I also passed up the long shots that unwillingness to hunt hard offered—those shots that are attempted by far too many.

A major point to limiting your range to 300 yards is that when you, or I, or any hunter squeezes a trigger, he should be astonished if the animal does not go down and stay down, not as most long shots are experienced—with surprise and pleasure if a good hit is made.

At longer ranges we miss and wound far too often. Animals are hit and disappear over ridges or into cover with the shooters believing they missed. We all know that to be true, and although it is tough to hold your fire when there is a target, not shooting beyond 300 yards is the sporting way.

I have heard every excuse and every possible exception declaimed as a legitimate reason for having to take that long and inspiring shot. I reject them all. I include in that rejection the famed *"last moment of the last day of the last hunt and a world class trophy."* Get close or stay home. The game deserves better.

I suppose that over the decades I have passed on shots I could have made. I am far better trained in long range shooting than most hunters (I operated that Sniper school in Japan in 1952), and I am still peripherally involved in training both law enforcement snipers (whose ranges are short) and military snipers (who sometimes shoot very long indeed), but I am just as sure that I also avoided wounding and losing animals because I shot at distances beyond sensible range estimating, probably beyond adequate bullet performance, and possibly beyond my actual ability.

During my better hunting years, I could lie on a known distance range and place most of my bullets within a ten-inch circle at one thousand yards. But, I had a special rifle, match ammunition, a perfect supported-prone position, and shooting conditions were ideal. In the hunt, my rifle has usually been subject to harsh treatment, I am using hunting ammunition which is inherently not as accurate as match grade, range to my quarry might be iffy (animals move around and so does the shooter), my shooting position is rarely Camp Perry and is sometimes simply terrible. Weather conditions? Every known rotten condition will be encountered if one hunts enough. Only occasionally will it be calm and bright. A hunter is also often physically stressed and geared-up emotionally. How well we shoot in practice has only limited bearing on how we will do in the field.

Limiting your shooting to 300 yards has some distinct advantages. The most interesting is often called

The 300-Yard Rule.

Although it has been around since the birth of smokeless powder, the 300-yard rule is even more practical with our modern flat trajectory cartridges. The concept is to choose a zero that will allow the shooter to hold dead on out to 300 yards without worrying about any ranges in between.

So, a .300 Win Mag using a 180 grain bullet could be zeroed to strike 3.6" high at 100 yards, 4.4" high at 200 yards, and on the nose at 300 yards.

Not bad really. A hunter could expect to lethally hit big game without holdover (or hold under) out to about 340 yards—which is beyond proper game shooting distance.

A better solution for the .300 Winchester Magnum, and the zero the men I hunt with settled on for almost all of our shooting was 1-1/2" high at 100, 2" high at 200 yards, and 2-1/4" low at 300 yards.

As you can see, the trajectory *appears* to flatten. We did our zeroing at 200 yards, getting the two inches high just right, but if only a 100 yard range was available, or for checking our rifles in the field, we settled for the +1-1/2" at 100 yards.

I used the same zeroing with my .300 Weatherby Magnum and obtained +1-1/8" at 100 yards, +2" at 200 yards, and −1-1/2" at 300 yards.

I suppose it is necessary to warn that trajectories can change with individual loadings and even with different rifles. You must check out your own, but your results will be close to those shown here.

We should never forget that at reasonable ranges our bullet's expansion will be more certain, its hitting power greater, and its penetration more sure than at extreme ranges. All are good reasons for staying at less than 300 yards.

Range estimating in Alaska can be extremely difficult. Part of the difficulty lies in the vast expanses being observed. When the air is more clear than most in the lower forty-eight ever see, details normally unobserved can stand out, and the game can appear closer than it is. The very size of the animals encountered in Alaska is also disturbing. Those used to estimating ranges to a whitetail or an antelope going 150 pounds may find their calculations thrown when checking out an 800-pound moose.

Generally, however, it is the natural features that give Alaskan range estimating a twist. A grove of distant trees I was once glassing suddenly sprouted the world's most enormous caribou. I had been conscientiously searching beneath the branches of the distant spruce looking for a betraying flash of light from an antler when suddenly there arose an animal so huge it towered three or four times tree height. Following an instant of blank astonishment, I belatedly realized I had been glassing a forest in miniature. I had been examining mature spruce that stood only three feet or less in height. The trees stood alone, probably a fourth of the distance away than I had believed them to be.

A similar incident occurred when three of us glassed a raccoon for some time before noticing its tail. We thought it was a far distant bear. Such gross misjudgments are embarrassing to admit, especially so for allegedly experienced hunters, but in Alaska, they happen.

Poor estimating can occur on the long or short side. In the 1950s Art Rausch gave me a rule for shooting that I have passed on to many hunters who found it useful—although some were at first skeptical.

The rule is simply this:

For your first shot, never hold over an animal. If you believe the range to be extremely long hold close to the top of the spine, but never hold above an animal's back, or something of that nature. **Always see hair in your scope.**

Using this rule means that you will never shoot over your target. If you were right and the range really is extremely long, your bullet will strike short of the target—it may even raise a puff of dust or a spatter of rock. If you miss, you KNOW that your bullet went too low.

Too often, I have seen hunters shoot and shoot until the game wandered out of sight. They could not understand why they missed as they had kept raising their aiming point higher and higher to compensate for the long range. The fact that they had gone over an animal's back with the first shot and increased their margin of error each time they held higher escaped them in the heat of action. (I have sometimes suspected that in the excitement of *the moment of truth* a lot of hunters' IQs drop to about fifty, anyway.)

Some fifty years after I first made a dummy of myself trying to estimate range in Alaska I still follow the rule. **Always see hair in your reticle.**

Notice that I wrote **reticle** in the above interpretation of the rule. That was no accident. The choice is a lead-in to discussion of sights for Alaskan hunting.

Using his latest experimental rifle, the author demonstrates the correct offhand hold for hunters. The cheek is welded to the stock with the head nearly upright without significant forward thrusting (limit stock crawl). The right hand grips with the thumb around the stock, never alongside the trigger finger. The right elbow is raised naturally without exaggeration (as is often taught in competitive marksmanship). The left hand is well out on the forearm, and the hand grips the stock to control its action. (Gripping with the front hand also helps control recoil.) The left elbow is *not* below the rifle; it is a bit off to the left—which makes a stronger position for following moving animals. The body is *not* turned completely sideward. The left foot should be well to the left of a line to your target. Think of a boxer's stance. The body has a slight forward lean, which can be increased to intensify concentration and balance. This is not Known Distance target shooting remember. Our shooting is one shot, possibly a couple of more, in rapid succession. To properly increase forward lean, have a wider than usual foot placement (further apart), bend the left knee strongly and bend at the waist—just a little. I learned the technique from a German Jaeger who shot game with uncanny certainty. Try it; you might make a discovery.

The sling? Although some suggest otherwise, I see the rifle sling as nothing more than a carrying strap. Of course, I learned how to use a sling in the US Army (whether we liked it or not), and in competitive marksmanship you need a sling, but in the field, hunting big game? Not in my opinion. Forget the sling.

The experimental rifle just mentioned is a Swiss army Schmidt Rubin, model 31, straight-pull sniper rifle modified into a hunting rifle. The rifle was barreled to the .358 Winchester, a cartridge that is an absolute hammer out to about two hundred yards. The scope is 2 x 7X with a custom *Premier Reticle* tapered crosshair. The stock is English walnut with 24 lines per inch checkering. The straight pull action is very fast, but there are difficulties in sporterizing the Schmidt Rubin. The huge ring on the cocking piece is less than attractive, and the magazine release seen on the side is a military monster. I like the gun and enjoyed developing it, but the cost was excessive (including having my name engraved and gold inlaid on the receiver ring), and I do not recommend anyone else taking on the task.

Hunting alone (photo taken with a timer) in the mountains west of Mount Sanford—many decades ago. I shot nothing on this trip, but it was adventurous, and I saw an exceptional moose, better than any I had shot, but the camera was in my pack and the bull did not hang around. I could have shot him and backpacked the antlers, but we did not do that kind of wasteful thing.

The Rifleman's Rifle™

The Pre-1964 Winchester Model 70

      If we never had a big game hunting rifle other than the pre-64 Model 70, Alaskan hunters would still be well served. The example pictured above is a stock, off-the-shelf rifle of the mid-1950s. There is no composite stock, no exaggerated stock shapes, no "snappy" plastic inserts or fore end tip, not even a thick, recoil-reducing butt pad. If you desired free floating, you had to do it yourself, but this, the most basic of rifles, never faltered. It came in every practical caliber, it was never sensitive, the trigger was excellent, the rifle held zero, and it shot like a laser. When a hunter held a model 70, he was confident that he handled the best. Excepting a telescopic sight, anything added merely gilded the lily. Nice, maybe, but not essential.

      The model 70 really was *The Rifleman's Rifle*, and all of us hunting at that time knew it.

      Winchester's disastrous decision to build a cheaper rifle doomed the justly famous Model 70 to decades of mediocrity. From 1964 until recent years, The Rifleman's Rifle had died, and there was no reason to choose a Winchester before dozens of other offerings by companies from across the world. Winchester's huge share of the bolt-action market dropped precipitously, and it should have. These days, it is almost rare to encounter a Winchester Model 70 in the field. Cheapening the Model 70 was almost unpatriotic, and we hunters would have voted to hang the bottom-line marketeers responsible.

      Of course, the controlled feed action is back in the Model 70, and Winchester is again producing a darn good rifle, but no hunting rifle will ever gain the mystique, or enjoy the prestige possessed by the pre-64. That was one hell of a good rifle and, if you harbor doubts, go to any gun show and check the prices on those forty-year old masterpieces.

Chapter

5

Proper Sights for Alaskan Hunting

If you were going to hunt primarily brown or grizzly bear in thick brush your very heavy caliber rifle should not have a scope. That tight in, you want an extremely short barrel, fast following shots, and nothing to catch on brush. That kind of hunting is discussed when we get to the great bears. For the rest of Alaskan hunting, only a telescope sight fills the bill.

I have hunted moose, bear, wolves, sheep and goats with iron sights, but that is not the most effective way. Only in thick brush against dangerous game can iron sights be better than a decent scope. What I use against "bear in the brush" is described later on. **Forget the iron sights. I no longer own hunting rifles with them attached.**

Scope application for Alaskan hunting can be short in description. *Choose a fine variable power scope of something like 1-1/2X to 9X—or as close to those figures as they make. Use the strongest mount made. Fasten it and the scope on as low as the objective lens and the bolt handle will allow and as tightly as you can wind the screws.*

When I went to Alaska in the middle 1950s, good telescopic sights were just being offered. There were any number of excellent fixed power scopes, and the top of the line variable power scope for that era was the Bausch and Lomb 2-1/2X to 4X. It was an excellent scope, but you sometimes wished for a bit more variation in power, and the scope's adjustments were in the mount—a system that was rarely satisfactory and has long been abandoned.

The only other variable power scope that I can recall was the Weaver KV 2-3/4X to 5X. I had one. It was a bummer. The scope changed zero with power adjustments, and it lost zero during firing, and no, it was not the scope mount moving around.

In 1957 Bausch & Lomb introduced their 2-1/2 to 8X Balvar 8. What a high price, $99.50 in Alaska. What a scope! A tapered cross hair reticle and super clear optics. I brought one of the first arriving in Fairbanks. One problem, however. The Balvar 8, like its cousin the 2-1/2X to 4X had its adjustment in the mount. In the field, the system rarely held the perfect zero a serious hunter demanded. I tried a Williams mount and that did better, but still ... it pays to stick with the "screw it down tight" rule.

This is Mark Kelley's sporterized Springfield 1903. The stock is probably from a Bishop semi-finished blank that Mark completed. The girder recoil pad was popular in the 1950s. The important point here is that the rifle mounts a Balvar 8 scope with the adjustments in the spring-loaded Bausch & Lomb mount—as described above. A great all-around hunting scope. A so, so mounting system.

The scope power I missed most in those earlier variable power days was 1-1/2X. Every time I took (or had to hold on) an animal very close in (less than seventy-five yards), I wished that I could eliminate all of the magnification and have only crosshair placement to worry over. Such scopes are now offered, and anyone who believes he might find himself in too-close proximity to game (a big bear, for example) should consider a variable power scope that goes all the way down.

During the days of the men whom I consider to be the great hunting writers, Jack O'Conner, Elmer Keith, Townsend Whelen, Ted Trueblood, Russell Annabell, et al, the experienced advice was always to choose a fixed low power scope because variable powers were unnecessarily bulky and were often undependable. For the time, the advice was sound, but products improve, and now an Alaskan hunter should choose a good variable. Excessive size and weight have been eliminated and variable scopes no longer falter in tough going.

I doubt that an Alaskan hunter shooting at intelligent ranges ever needs 9 or more magnification. He certainly does not if he observes the 300 yard rule. Laying 9X magnification on a sheep at 300 yards brings the animal in as if he were at thirty-three yards. Good heavens, do we need that?

Another point. Magnification over 9X requires use of a parallax adjustment. Why bother with that apparatus inside your scope when the high magnification is unnecessary?

For my own rifles I like a compact 1-3/4X to 5X scope. Remember, at my self-imposed limit of 300 yards, a 5X makes the game look as if it were at 60 yards range.

But, suppose a hunter is one of those wild guys who plunk away at animals five to six hundred yards away? Assuming we cannot just convince him to work closer or forget the shot, we can still realize that at, say, 550 yards a 9X places the game image at 56 yards, and even my little scope on 5X would bring him in to 110 yards. That is still close enough.

The *experienced* sheep and goat hunters that I know who use <u>fixed</u> power scopes seem divided between those sticking to an all-game power of 4X and those who use dedicated sheep and goat rifles with 6X scopes. Four to six power scopes are excellent choices for the high country.

I also have a few friends who dropped down to 2-1/2X dozens of years ago and use that power with complete satisfaction on all game. A point to these details is that double-digit scope powers are almost never the best. *My observation is that the more experienced the hunter, the lower his scope power is likely to be.*

We should keep in mind that the lower your magnification, the steadier your hold will appear. Unless you have a very solid rest, at higher magnifications you will have trouble keeping your crosshairs on your animal.

Magnification in telescopic sights of more than 9X require a parallax adjustment mechanism. A few scopes still use twisting of the objective lens to adjust parallax. The latest trend is to have a third adjustment knob on the tube of the scope that can be easily reached with the left hand. The best solution for hunters is to keep power below ten and not have to worry about parallax.

What to avoid in scopes and their mounting takes more space than describing what is good.

High-mounted scopes with those see-through mounts (so that you can use iron sights under the scope) are BAD. Unless you have a freaky looking high-rise stock comb, your cheek cannot rest solidly on the stock comb and still have the eye looking naturally through your scope's ocular lens. If a stock comb is high enough to provide a proper stock-to-cheek weld, the shooter trying to use the see-through iron sights must jam his face against the stock. See-through mounts are also less strong "engineering-wise" than low and tight scope mounts. I have more experience than I like to admit with such rigs. I have owned, built, and used rifles with high, see-through mounts. There is a photograph on page twenty-six that shows me with a .375 H&H Magnum so equipped. Note also the high, rollover comb on the stock. Ludicrous. Embarrassing.

Unfortunately, someone will say, *"I mount high so I can use my iron sights in an emergency."*

Emergency? That reasoning might have been acceptable forty years ago (but I doubted it even then).

Once, many decades ago, both mounts and scopes were shaky propositions that fogged and moved around, and it made sense to have iron sight backup. That need birthed swing-aside and quick detachable mounts. None were truly satisfactory, but the idea refuses to die and the foolish still sometimes succumb to such nifty sounding schemes. The idea of "quick detachable" has always amused me. No one I ever met in the hunting fields or on the mountains carried an extra scope that was zeroed and ready to go on his rifle.

Emergency? If you want an emergency, go afield with iron sights. I cannot recall a scope damaging accident that would not have knocked an iron receiver sight just as screwy. Iron sights can be really hard to keep in zero.

Hunters sometimes doubt that because no one can see well enough with iron sights to really zero them in the first place. The human eye cannot see exact zero at 100 yards. Iron-sighters are lucky to get three-inch groups at 100 yards. In the field, their sights get knocked askew, but they often never realize it and cannot hold tight enough to genuinely check. Scope users try to group within an inch at 100 yards. Most settle for a little more than that. Correctly tightened down, their scopes will stay in place, stay in zero, and take a ferocious beating.

I have a recommendation on tightening down scope mounts. Mount screws (bolts) are the weakest points in scope mounting. The best move you can make to secure your scope to your rifle is to have your friendly gunsmith open your receiver's threaded scope mount bolt holes from 6x48 to 8x40. Enlarge the holes in the scope mounts to match, and use 8x40 screws (bolts) touched with Loctite to hold the mount on.

A number 8 bolt has almost twice the strength of a 6 bolt. *Iron Brigade Armory, Sniper Rifles* (that really are the best in the world) are modified in that manner because it works. Military sniper rifles routinely absorb beatings that would demolish most hunting rifles. Thicker mounting bolts do make a difference, and we hunters should do our best to emulate a sniper rifle's inherent strength and durability. I must add that we cannot completely match sniper rifle unbreakability because few of us will be willing to pack the extra weight of a top-level sniper rifle.

IBA sniper rifles, by the way, use only one-piece scope mounts. In the past we have referred to such mounts as Redfield Jr.-type mounts, but *IBA* manufactures its own mounts that are light-years ahead of the old Redfield Juniors. One-piece mounts in general are sturdier than two-piece setups.

I wish to mention a superior scope mounting system called a Picatinny rail that hunters wishing to swap scopes on a rifle might consider. The idea is to have a one-piece scope mount with a laterally grooved bar on top (the Picatinny rail) to which your scope rings are clamped. Extra scopes will have their rings already attached and will be zeroed for use on the Picatinny rail. Scope swapping is only a matter of loosening the installed rings and tightening on the replacement scope's rings.

The idea of such a device would be for a single-gun hunter who might prefer a 3X x 9X scope for mountain hunting who could switch to a fixed power 2-1/2X or a 1-1/2X to 5X variable power scope for the flatland (shorter range) bears, moose, and caribou. The little known Picatinny rails were not popular because they added weight to a rifle. *Iron Brigade Armory* (Telephone: (910) 455-3834) has recently developed titanium Picatinny rails that are lighter and stronger than conventional mounts. The Picatinny can be a sensible choice.

Here is a little scope mounting trick I have been using and recommending the last few decades. If you use a crosshair or a dot reticle, rotate the scope ninety degrees counter-clockwise in your rings. That makes the elevation a windage adjustment and changes the windage knob into elevation. Once zeroed, hunters do not adjust sights other than to re-zero, so there is no inconvenience. The change opens up your cartridge loading area by removing the windage knob from the middle of it. It might interest anyone considering turning his scope ninety degrees to know that British military Snipers had their scopes built that way more than fifty years ago.

Chapter

6

Stocks

A few thoughts about Alaskan hunting rifle stocks should be inserted.

If you really like a wooden stock use one. Expect to beat the hell out of the finish, plan to recheck your zero with some regularity (particularly after rain), and make sure your front sling swivel is backed up by a plate on the inside of the barrel channel—or better yet have the swivel mounted on a barrel band. Swivels have been known to pull out of wood at inconvenient times.

A further point on sling swivels. I succumbed to the handiness of quick-detachable swivels forty years ago. However, I no longer advise selecting them. Quick-detachables have a record of failure—no matter who manufactures them. The USMC adopted QD swivels on their latest sniper rifle, the M40A3, and combat snipers in Iraq have suffered breakage and regret the change from solid swivels.

Conversely, I have never heard of a solid military-style fixed swivel letting go. Finally, I would ask, what good are QD swivels? How long, after all, does it take to remove a conventional sling and how often do we remove one? Keep it simple should apply to sling swivels. Make them solid and indestructible.

There is no need for an Alaskan hunting rifle to be pretty. I know hunters who use fiberglass stocks and paint their barrels and most of their receivers with Rust-Oleum™. The famed Alaskan Bear guide and widely published author Phil Shoemaker has recommended painting rifles for decades. The best sniper rifles in the world are first Parkerized then painted with an almost indestructible finish called "Manowar™." That finish has been Iraq and Alaska-proven. It is tough.

This is a thumbhole stock. I built the rifle in .264 Winchester for use on goats and sheep. Two mistakes! The cartridge is nothing special and thumbhole stocks do not belong in big game hunting. They are slow and awkward to use, and they offer nothing a normal stock does not.

By any practical measure, the composite stock users and the metal painters have it right. Rifles take hammerings in Alaskan hunting. They get tossed in trucks, in cross-country vehicles, in cockpits and in boats—and that is just in getting to the hunting. On the mountains and in the bush the rifles are regularly soaked, scratched from rocks and limbs, frozen, clanked together, hung on trees, and more times than we would like to admit, dropped.

Have a handsome rifle if you wish, but remember shine reflects, and animals notice those glints and flashes.

Do make sure that your stock fits. Use the rifle enough to make certain that it feels good. Be positive that the butt-plate will not slip on your shoulder. *It is better—far better—to have a stock a hint short than to have one even a hair too long.* Remember, you will not often hunt Alaska in your T-shirt.

I was brought up on the teachings of Jack O'Connor, and I have always liked his stock recommendations for hunting rifles. Jack liked handsome checkering and thin neat-feeling stock grips. He hated Monti Carlo cheek-pieces and things like Snobbles (gunsmith Clyde Baker's spelling) or plastic tips on forearms. I'm with him, but I do not claim all of those preferences are the most wise. Thin wrists on stocks are prone to breakage. Fine checkering does not grip as efficiently as rougher. A fine custom stock will probably have 24 lines per inch checkering. That is really too fine for best gripping under tough field conditions. I like twenty lines per inch checkering and have some rifles with eighteen lines. The "checkering" stamped into plastic stocks (like McMillan's) works just fine.

My recommendation would be to choose a stock that had the classic pre-64 model 70 Winchester shape in whatever material you prefer. Plan on it becoming scarred. Consider those wounds badges of honor. Enjoy the gun; do not worry about its looks.

A Model 95 Marlin in .45/70. This is a powerful combination, but with a cartridge handloaded to about 1800 fps, the .45/70 becomes a genuine bear dropper. On John Taylor's KO tables the cartridge's impact is raised from a hard-hitting 34.3 to a smashing 47.6. Note the low power and low mounted scope, a good set up for a brush hunter on Kodiak Island or on the Kenai Peninsula.

A Few Stock Thoughts

The **Kimber** is an excellent hunting rifle, and the composite stock's lines are graceful enough to use as a good example. The grip is small, but it could be smaller. To review Jack O'Connor's ideal stock description in his classic 1950, *The Rifle Book*, Jack wrote:

"The average hand is best fitted with a pistol grip of about 4 3/4 inches around . . . The (rifle's) pitch down should be somewhere between 3 and 4 1/2 inches, depending, of course, on the length of the barrel . . . The comb should be made as high as withdrawal of the bolt will permit. I believe also that the rifle to be used with scope sights only should be "straighter" with less difference in drop between comb and heel. I like only 1/2 of an inch difference . . . The cheek piece should be flat. It should be thick, projecting at the bottom of the stock about 1/2 to 5/8 of an inch . . . The fore end should be more or less pear-shaped in cross section, but even a perfectly round fore end is not bad. A fore end shaped like this that is about 1 3/8 inches in diameter is also surprisingly adequate, Possibly a fore end of that type 1 1/2 inches in diameter is a little better . . . "

We can add that stock length for an average hunter should be about 13 1/4 inches. Remember that we often wear heavy clothing in Alaska and a too long stock is terrible. Too short can be used very well.

The rifle we are showing comes close to those standards.

If you have a wood stock, you can modify to suit your tastes, but composite stocks are more difficult, and most hunters will have to accept what a company offers. Notice that within the photographs included in this volume that almost everyone used and still uses wooden stocks. Nothing like walnut to soothe the heart and feel good in the hands.

I now double-coat my wooden stocks with epoxy (I use WEST System™ epoxy that I learned to like during my boat building days) A stock properly epoxy-coated will not absorb a drop of moisture and will not move around on you—period. Of course, the finish looks different than a fine hand-rubbed oil finish, but there can be no argument about which finish is best. Epoxy wins hands down.

Chapter

7

The Best Rifle

Before leaving this part of the book it is right to commit myself to exactly what weapon I would choose for a single-gun Alaskan hunt for all large game. Despite what most write, I do not find the requirement particular treacherous or difficult.

Choose any good quality bolt-action rifle with a decently heavy 22-inch barrel.
Buy your rifle chambered for the .338 Winchester Magnum.

The only points to emphasize *at this stage of discussion* are, if your stock rifle's barrel is longer, and many are in magnum cartridges, cut it back to 22 inches. Eliminate the iron sights. Fasten on a top quality (I recommend 1-1/2X to 6X) variable power scope as **tightly** and as **low** as you can mount it and, if you are recoil conscious, have a muzzle brake let into the barrel.

Three excellent Alaskan big game cartridges

Of course there is no end to cartridges offered by hungry manufacturing companies and hopeful experimenters, many of which are alleged to do wonders but, if you used only these old stand-bys, your successful hunting in The Great State would be assured.

On the left: The awesome (for American game) .458 Winchester Magnum. The .458 is our premier dangerous game cartridge. For a bear in the bush, it could be the best. KO at the muzzle using a 500-grain bullet is a thunderous 60.8.

Center: The 300 Weatherby Magnum. With a 180-grain bullet at 3240 the KO is 25.7. Use a 220-grain bullet at 2845 and you have a KO of 27.5 at the muzzle.

To the right: The .338 Winchester Magnum. Using a 225- grain bullet at a muzzle velocity of 2940 fps, the KO value is 31.8, or go to a 250-grain bullet and up the KO to 33.8.

Chapter 8

Kenai Rifles, the .450 Alaskan
&
A bit about Garrett Ammunition

In the 1950's Harold Johnson produced his **Kenai Rifles** down on the Kenai Peninsula, not far from Cooper Landing. Johnson modified Winchester model 1886 and model 71 lever action rifles into his own specialty, the .450 Alaskan. Bill Fuller was Johnson's gunsmith, and until his death in 1988, Fuller would still make you a .450 Alaskan—if you provided the rifle.

To create a .450 Alaskan, Johnson re-barreled an 1886 or a model 71 in .458 caliber and chambered it with a reamer which was basically a .348 Winchester expanded at the neck to hold a .458 diameter bullet. The .450 Alaskan, as made by Kenai Rifles, had a 20-inch barrel and, it is claimed, the rifles kicked like wild bulls. Add a muzzle brake, I say!

Winchester 1886

Winchester Model 71

The rifles are shown in different scales, but the actions are almost identical and strong enough to hold the powerful .450 Alaskan. The .45/70 and the .348 cartridges are rimmed cases, therefore, the extraction and ejection systems required almost no modifications.

Initially, Johnson made his own bullets. He cut off a 30/06 case, and inserted a swaged, tight fitting lead slug into the remaining cartridge case. The bullet looked like a 1-1/4 inch fully loaded cartridge. Later, Frank Barnes made special bullets for the .450 Alaskan. Accurate ballistics for the .450 are difficult to obtain, but they went about like the following.

	Velocity			**KO**		
	Muzzle	**100 yds.**	**200yds.**	**Muzzle**	**100**	**200**
450 Alaskan	2000fps	1820	1502	51.4	43.8	38.6

In more recent times, efforts have been made to reintroduce the .450, but its time has passed. The model 1886 and 71 Winchesters are now collector's items, and the harder hitting .458 Winchester Magnum has appeared, but in its day, the .450 Alaskan was a powerhouse. Because of a lever action's fast follow up shots, the Kenai rifle has probably never been surpassed as a bear in the brush weapon.

Harold Johnson in the 1950s

This book concerns itself almost exclusively with bolt-action rifles because the bolt gun has proven itself to be the toughest, most readily cleanable, and usually the most accurate rifle out there. However, the almost forgotten lever action may also have its place. The remarkable .450 Alaskan was always in a lever gun. Guides loved it for its smashing power and fast follow up shots.

In some quarters, humming and hawing over facing dangerous game with a lever action persists (meaning grizzly and brown bear in Alaska). You do not find lever guns in Africa where really dangerous animals abide. Lever rifles are American, but no one that I ever encountered complained about their lever rifles jamming or failing to perform in any situation in any weather.

We might note that until the First World War and the sudden availability of cheap bolt rifles, the lever action dominated in Alaska, and the limited literature of those earlier times describes no examples of lever action failures. *It is also noteworthy that most lever action rifles can be reloaded while the rifle is cocked with a round in the chamber.* Bolt guns require opening the bolt, which might not feel comfortable if attempting to reload in a dangerous situation.

The modern Marlin lever action rifles are vastly superior to old time rifles. (They can, for instance, mount a scope directly over the bore where it should be instead of offset to the left—where it should not be.) The Marlin .45/70 should be considered because there is new ammunition that is apparently knocking the socks off the standard cartridge beloved by buffalo hunters that has proven itself over more than a one hundred year period.

The new ammunition for the .45/70 is centered on a *Garrett* hardcast bullet. The bullet is very heavy, almost flat-ended, nearly a cylinder, much like a wad cutter. The huge meplat imparts a tremendous blow that reportedly penetrates forever and flattens the biggest and toughest animals as if they were struck by lightning. At this time, *Garrett* bullets are sold only in *Garrett* cartridges, and I have not personally seen the dramatic results reported. If they are that good, as so many claim, a guide protecting his hunter should like them, and anyone digging a bear out of a thick stand should consider a lever gun in that caliber shooting that ammunition.

Chapter

9

Shooting Ranges

A few pages back I wrote that I never shoot animals at over three hundred yards. What follows could have been entered there in support of my opinion, but I wished the concept to sink in a little. Some supporting evidence of the practicality of the idea follows.

In September 1953, *The American Rifleman* magazine published a survey of professional Alaskan Guides that included the details of the taking of 321 head of Alaskan big game. That game included all of the Alaskan "big five," which are brown or grizzly bear, moose, caribou, goats, and sheep. Those, of course, are the major animals discussed in this book.

Of the 321 animals taken, only eight (8) were shot at ranges over 300 yards. Or to put it another way, if you shot 100 animals, which is a lifetime of hunting, only three 3 of them would be taken over 300 yards. These figures clearly demonstrate the rarity of long range shooting.

The survey further notes that 283 of the 321 animals were taken under two hundred (200) yards. This figure indicates that some 90% of our Alaskan shooting will probably be less than 200 yards.

Furthermore, 126 head, or 40% of the animals were taken at under one hundred (100) yards. Wow! That is pretty close in.

Breaking the longer range shooting down by game animal we find that:

Of 42 sheep included in the survey only three (3) were taken beyond 300 yards. Thirty of the remaining sheep, or 70% of them, were shot at less than 200 yards.

Shifting to goats, we find that of 45 goats taken, only two (2) were shot beyond 300 yards, and 34 goats, or 66%, were at less than 200 yards.

Surely, these statistics, which demonstrate that more than 97% of Alaskan hunting is done at less than 300 yards, should put to rest a hunter's concern over the need to shoot at extreme ranges.

Despite the above data, or any that will ever be published, big game hunters insist that they have to be ready to shoot at astoundingly long ranges, and most have a story or more explaining how some shot on something had to be taken at ranges so distant a Marine sniper would hesitate.

I doubt that a month goes by that I am not challenged by telephone or e-mail—often quite vehemently—by hunters propounding the need for and their expertise in dropping, in their tracks, animals so distant I am embarrassed to hear the yardages.

Those hunters and their almost certain attempts to kill at impractical ranges are major reasons for suggesting a big cartridge and a powerful scope for Alaska. If we could be certain that hunters would limit their ranges to the shooting I have recommended they could use less powerful rifles and lower magnification telescopic sights. That would be more satisfactory all around, but it is not about to happen.

So, what about those large cannon-like rifles that are alleged to drop elephants by their mere presence? There are so many calibers and cartridges available that one hardly knows where to begin, but it might be best to deal with a few of the old standbys—proven over decades and realize that the newer offerings are just as good—and in some cases a bit better—but that all of the largest cartridges are more than we will ever need—unless we are doing things that we should not be doing in our hunting.

We can use the popular .308 Winchester as a standard and measure a few larger cartridges in comparison, but I must add a disclaimer. Every ballistic table seems to differ from all others. Chronographs differ and recording systems are different. Therefore, in one place, using a certain ballistic table, the results shown herein for a specific cartridge may not be the same as the figures shown in another table—also herein. (Incidentally, the ballistic tables I am using at the moment list more than seventy .308

Winchester (7.62 NATO) loadings, each of which has a different energy and **KO** figure.)

I could even up all the figures (make them uniform), but it may be informative to notice how they vary with the publication the author is using at the moment. Rifles are not identical and may record different results, but most ballistic tables these days are calculations based on computer models. They rarely match, so use the figures included here or offered elsewhere for guidance, and do not consider them handed down from Mount Sinai.

Cartridge	Bullet Wt	Mz	Velocities & KO 300	500	Drop—zeroed at 100yds 300	400	500
.308 Win	180	2620	2117 **16.0KO**	1815 **14.7KO**	-8.9	-25.9	-52.5
300 Wthby	180	3240	2634 **19.1KO**	2271 **16.1KO**	-5.5	-16.0	-32.4
7mm Mag	150	3130	2320 **14.8KO**	1866 **12.3KO**	-6.7	-19.7	-39.8
.338 Win	250	2800	2250 **31.0KO**	1920 **22.1KO**	-7.8	-22.5	-44.9
.375 H&H	300	2700	1960 **28.7KO**	1540 **22.5KO**	-9.4	-28.0	-58.3
.458 Win	400	2380	1779 **46.0KO**	1430 **37.4KO**	-12.1	-35.3	-72.3

So, what can we deduce from the above data?

My first reminder would be that to enjoy shooting these powerful rifles demands weapons in the eleven-pound class. Hunters unhappy with carrying what many consider to be the excess weight of seven or eight-pound rifles should take note. These guns are heavy. When shooting game, recoil and sound make little difference because minds are focused on the hunt, but zeroing and practicing with a big rifle can be unpleasant and involuntary flinches can develop that are carried into the game fields.

Even with muzzle brakes, big cartridges have heavy recoil and the muzzle blast when using a muzzle brake can be uncomfortable. Never allow a companion to be beside or just behind you when you touch off a big Bertha using a muzzle brake. Ears can be permanently damaged. Don't be fooled. Big guns kick, whether you feel it or simply hear it. Never, by the way, fire a big rifle with a muzzle brake inside a building. The blast is enormous and can cause permanent hearing loss.

Note that bullet drop becomes serious as ranges increase. Which initiates the next rule.
If you insist on shooting animals way out there, buy, carry, and use a range finder.
The devices now on the market are reasonable in cost and light to carry. Examine the drop you are dealing with at 500 yards range and consider what those figures will be even further out.

Can you handle that kind of trajectory? If you have figured your bullet's drop from your zero at various ranges, using a range finder will greatly improve your chances of making too long shots. In my opinion, neither the .375 H&H or the .458 Winchester Magnum are suitable for extreme range game shooting, but—unlike most cartridges—if you do hit your animal way way way out there, your KO value will still be decent

Flat trajectory is most notable in the 300 Weatherby, but the .338 also does well. A point to consider is that the drop figures shown here were calculated for a one hundred yard zero. I have no idea why anyone would zero at point blank unless he was going into brush after bear or moose. Zeroing for a greater distance makes drop look less.

I believe that except for the .458 Winchester Magnum and the .375 H&H Magnum, two (2) inches high at 200 yards is perfect for Alaska. Remember that 300-yard rule?

Perhaps the figures shown above will support my contention that the .338 (or perhaps the 300 Weatherby) is the best all around cartridge for Alaska. Check those KO figures at 500 yards—they mean something.

Ah well, let us turn to the godfather of big bore weaponry, and if readers would listen and apply the teachings (preachings) of Elmer Keith, there would be dramatically reduced missing, wounding, ammunition wasting, and embarrassing shooting failures.

Chapter

10

Elmer Keith

I have mentioned Keith in regard to large bore cartridges. Elmer died in 1984, and some readers may not be familiar with his books and articles. I suggest that anyone interested in big game hunting, particularly in Alaska, should study Elmer Keith's works before believing that they understand hunting in general and cartridge and bullet performance in particular.

Doctor Art Troup's photo of Keith, shown here, was taken on one of our visits to Elmer's home in Salmon, Idaho.

Keith (as he was often called) hunted all over the world with both handgun and rifle. His vast experience taught him—as similar experience teaches most—that a big heavy bullet, in pistol or rifle, does a better job than a skinny light bullet. Elmer preached the big bore philosophy without reservation and was regularly chastised by most other scribes for his beliefs.

Until his death, Keith's was a lone voice decrying the use of small caliber, high velocity cartridges on big animals. Nearly everyone else was caught up in the high velocity craze and was swept along in that slick current. Keith stood like a rock in the channel, and more than a few writers and armies of biased readers ridiculed him for his contrary opinions.

Since Keith's death, no widely known gun/hunting writer has seized the big bore banner. Too bad, because Elmer was right. His opponents were and are basically wrong. *If you doubt, study Keith's books with an open mind.* Then read John Taylor's **African rifles** as a dessert. Your eyes will be opened, and you will probably agree with Elmer Keith—and a host of genuinely experienced but unpublished big game shooters that we should hunt with larger diameter and heavier bullets.

Recognition of Elmer Keith's importance to the shooting fraternity has been long overdue, and it is the author's hope that this volume and those that went before will help focus attention on Elmer's voluminous contribution to the arms and hunting fields.

In researching Keith, one could begin with his final book, *Hell, I Was There.* The title is odd, but really, Keith was there for so many significant incidents and occasions that the title fits.

Elmer Keith

This author's description of Keith would endeavor to show a hardy man of average physical stature with large hands and experience-blunted features. He was a proud man, confident of his abilities. He was friendly, yet wary of those who sought to ridicule his positions. Keith lived clean and simple amid the trophies and mementos of his accomplishments. He was concerned that his place in gun and hunting history be secured, and belated recognition of his outstanding contributions was balm to his soul.

Elmer Keith was a patriot who loved his country and its traditional freedoms. He feared for his nation's future as he saw the old ways crumbling around him (as so many of us still do).

Keith was a man who lived by his word. His handshake was his bond, and he was dismayed by actions that were less than straightforward.

Elmer enjoyed his Chivas Regal. He puffed on awful cigars. He loved a bull session with real men. As the years took their toll, his hunts shortened and he lived evermore in his memories. In that he was fortunate, for he had done much in his many years.

Yet, how can you adequately describe a man who has been bronc-stomped, dragged, and tossed, and who safaried in Africa shortly after incurring a broken back? The reader can try to visualize what manner of man this was that seemed physically indestructible while accomplishing rarely matched feats with six gun and rifle over a more than seventy year period.

But, unless you knew the man, you cannot get it right. Next best is to read Elmer Keith's stuff. From his writing you will gain at least a partial picture, and let me assure you ahead of time, when Keith said he did this or that, or made some marvelously improbable shot *believe what the book says*. Keith did not lie, and he did not exaggerate. His detractors could rarely understand that about Elmer Keith. Too bad for them. I hope my readers can examine the evidence more squarely.

I corresponded with Keith over the years, and his answering letters were always lengthy, unedited, and full of meaty information. We never discussed anything except guns, hunting, and conservative politics. When I visited Salmon, Idaho not long after Elmer moved there, our face-to-face conversations were exactly like our correspondence—a lot more salty, perhaps. (I had been a US Army First Sergeant, and Keith? Well, he was a man's man, and our subjects remained the same.)

When I began hunting with .44 Magnum pistols in Alaska, Keith became very interested. That was in 1956, and the cartridge was new and it was his baby. Our letter exchanges increased remarkably. I enclose one from 1977 because it concerns *Alaskan Hunter*, my first book on hunting up here. Consider the letter shorter than usual, but typical Keith.

Elmer Keith

GUNS&AMMO

ELMER KEITH, EXECUTIVE EDITOR • SALMON, IDAHO 83467

May 7th-77

DEar Chandler:

Thanks for the book and also for dedicating it to me but think you should have found someone more important for that post.

Due to the fact you agree exactly with Ted Fowler my old elephant- hunting partner and I o n suitable calibers I sent tour card down to him urging hiM to get a copy.

This is the best Alaskan book I have seen and am abo ut half way through it now. Only thi ng I have found so far o n which I cannot agree is a jacknife for heavy game. I done a damn lot of skinning in 30 years guid(.ing and also live stock as well and in the cedar level country of the lochsa you hav e tp bla..se out from ay kill or chance losing it especially if you get abig snow storm. Saw many hunters kill and hang their game over there andnever find it at all. Also for that country and most elk moose or big bear prefer at least a 5" blade and preferably my shape knife with 3/8" thick blade at back this so i can unjoint a front leg and hammer the blade right down through
brisket and pelvis and also blaze trees out as well as bend over small one sand hit them a crack with a knife then you can spotthem after a big snow storm whn blazes and everythi-ng else blotted out also like a good curved bladeat least 5" long for peeling heavy hides buffalo, elk,. moose or big bear and I been there on all of them.

At any rate want you to know I think it the best Alaskan book have seen, Made six trips up there myself one of them to the arctic from 1937 on and conditions sure have changed since that 1937 trip, Anbchorage then a small town dog pens a block from cenet er and òne board walk one side main and hotel room four bucks a day.Will Rogers had been there ahead of us and wanted to knww what he had to do to become a Sourdough. They told him Spend a winter in Alaska, kill a brown bear and sleep with a cluck. He replied " I will not' mind the winter in Alaska but will kill the Cluch and sleep with the brown bear" Nough said, Best and will write this book up for my column.

Sincerely
Elmer

Chapter

11

A Bit about Double Rifles

Heavy caliber double-barreled rifles are fine guns for bear and moose at closer ranges. You will rarely encounter double rifles in our hunting fields because they are themselves rare in this world and most are inordinately expensive. A new double rifle of Ferlach make will cost many thousands of dollars. Fine English rifles are nearly out of this world, probably costing twice the amount of a Ferlach gun.

Although I have owned a number of double rifles, all were used, and for this discussion we will examine only one as an example of what an Alaskan shooter might choose.

This rifle is interesting because it is a complete weapons system possessing four sets of barrels for the one action.

The double, side by side rifle barrels are in .486 caliber.

A second set of barrels combine one .486 rifled barrel with a 16 gauge shotgun barrel.

Third, is a pair of short, twenty inch shotgun barrels in twenty gauge.

And fourth is a pair of twenty-four inch, full choke sixteen gauge barrels.

As all barrel sets fit the same action, the shooter need familiarize himself with only one setup of safety, triggers, and ejectors.

My particular rifle has a partial history. It was spirited out of Germany while World War II drew to a close. The rifle lay unused for twenty or so years until a widow made it available for purchase. I happened onto the scene and snapped the kit up at a bargain price.

The rifle was built by Rausch, a German gunsmith about whom I know nothing—except that he was a master craftsman. The rifle was built about the time of the switch over from black to smokeless powder, and only the shotgun barrels are nitro-proofed. I normally shoot black powder in all barrels. Firing an old weapon is certainly the only time I can enjoy the rotten egg smell of burning sulfur, but every time I touch off the trigger on that fine double rifle, the sulfur stench seems almost a necessary part of the fun.

Mickey Weston tries out the double rifle on a target.

The .486 caliber is an odd one, and as with many foreign calibers, I had to work up my own loads. As there were no sample rounds with the piece, I made chamber castings and sent them to various companies for identification. I settled on .500 x 3 inch nitro cases which I necked down in a homemade swage to grip a .486 bullet.

Lyman mailed me a .509133 bullet mold, and we cast bullets in it and squeezed them through the .486 swage. The finished round, as shown here, was a deadly looking thing right out of a King Solomon's Mines movie. We were not sure, however, just how it would shoot.

A great amount of experimentation followed, and that is always enjoyable. An empty case held a comfortable 115 grains of black powder. Although wanting full power, we still had to arrive at a loading that would print both barrels together at about seventy-five yards.

We conducted experiments rating paper patched bullets against lubricated ones, and both against an odd type we worked up with a zinc washer screwed onto the base like the old Harvey Protex bore pistol bullets, and some even wilder rounds using epoxied-on felt and cork base wafers.

The bullets from our swage weighed 525 grains and were first made of Lyman #2 bullet metal.

In other experiments we tried pure lead and regular wheel weight metal. There was a severe problem in developing a bullet that would open up on game. Low muzzle velocity, plus a heavy, pointed bullet gave immense penetration, but the bullets did not like to expand. Hollow pointing the bullet with a lathe center drill helped—a little. A copper plug placed in the hollow point did no good. Finally, soft lead, a hollow point, and an epoxy on zinc base washer to scrub the bore gave us our best bullet.

Our final loading calls for 115 grains of FFG powder with a number 172 Berdan primer, pushing the zinc based bullet. Expansion occasionally runs to .700 caliber and penetration is awesome.

Why wouldn't it be? The old .45/70 with its 500 grain bullet and only 70 grains of powder was a powerful load fit for most game. The not as famous .50/100 with a 450-grain bullet and 110 grains of FG powder was a super-blaster.

Applying Taylor's **KO** formula we get a 525 grain .486 diameter bullet traveling at 1500fps giving a **KO** rating of 54.6, which is up there with the biggest ones.

Recoil in this rifle is kindly and might be favorably compared with any .50 caliber Hawken. The recoil is a sort of long shove without the jolt accompanying smokeless powder.

Only one moose and a fine bull caribou have been taken in Alaska with this .486 double rifle. Both animals expired on the spot with the bullet making complete penetration and little meat destruction due to low velocity. As we like to say, *"You could eat right up to the hole."*

Because this rifle is now an almost century old piece of gun-making history we no longer take it afield.

Experiments with the .486 cartridge included the cast bullets displayed here. The completed round shows an unwanted crimp a bit above the base that the author's full length resizing die insisted on leaving. Note that the bullet in the finished cartridge is a solid point. Solid tip bullets expanded poorly. If the nose was cast completely flat with an almost full .486 meplat, the lead bullet expanded, but penetration in our wet telephone books could be erratic.

The cork-based bullet was intended to scrub away bore fouling and to seal against escaping gas (a gas check). It was not effective, and screwing on the pad was ludicrously laborious. The hollow pointed bullet proved to be the most effective—if the hollow was huge and the bullet was made of pure lead. Hollow pointed alloy bullets still would not expand with certainty.

The bullet with a bit of brass rod inserted into the hollow point was a failure. It acted like a solid and did not expand at all.

The last bullet is a joke. The fuzzed end was created by feeding in the hollow pointer too swiftly. We called it the *Brush Point* and claimed it dusted the wound clean before entering.

Every double rifle this author has ever seen has been a quality piece. It should be safe to conclude that any double rifle of .375 caliber or more will prove satisfactory for flatland Alaskan game.

Double rifles balance about as perfectly as guns ever will. The balance is always between the hands with just enough muzzle weight to ensure steady holding. The guns come up fast and point naturally in the double barreled shotgun tradition.

Stocks are quite straight because double rifles are meant to be off hand weapons. Actions are glass smooth, and the triggers crisp with little movement. Many, as does our example, have individually adjustable triggers.

Safeties on double rifles are sometimes non-automatic. If the shooter desires to use the safety he must deliberately put it on. A hunter reloading against a charging or wounded animal might prefer to do without the extra move of snapping off a safety. Elephant and Cape Buffalo (perhaps bear) hunters may not want the unnatural sound of a safety being snapped off at a critical moment.

A scope on a double rifle has never proven satisfactory to this author. The tube destroys the symmetry of the rifle and makes it clunky to handle. Although the double rifle discussed here has a 3X scope, I never use it.

If the above descriptions and the following photographs are intriguing, do not be surprised. Double rifles are gorgeous pieces. Barring their expense, they have a lot going for them. So, if you own a chunk of ground on the North Slope with a pumping well or two, do not hesitate. Buy a few.

The photos that follow show how a double rifle can be fired four times quite rapidly—if the rifleman is as competent as Doctor Troup.

The technique is to hold two live rounds between the fingers of the left hand. After firing both barrels, the rifle is broken open and the spent cases plucked out with a fingertip. Automatic ejectors would remove this action, of course. The live rounds are then dropped into the chambers, the action closed, and the shooter is ready to fire. It is harder than it sounds! Those live rounds try to wander and avoid going where you want them.

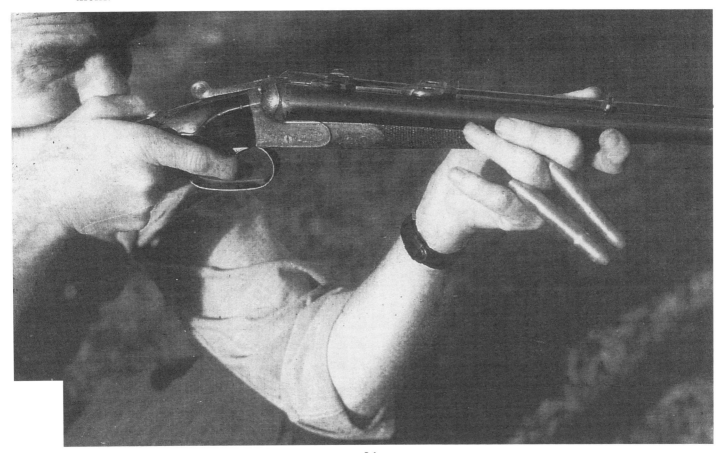

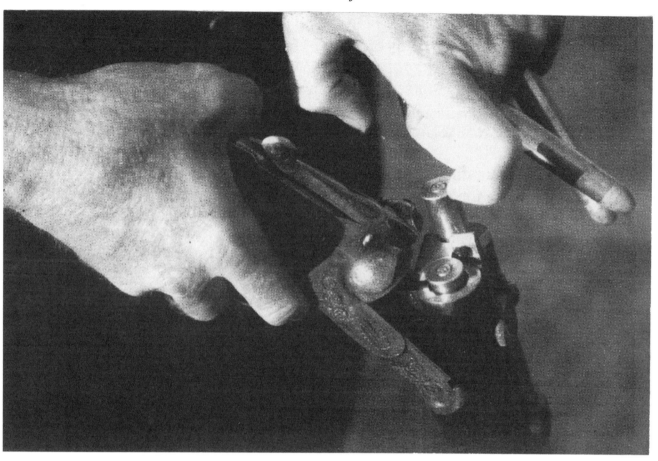
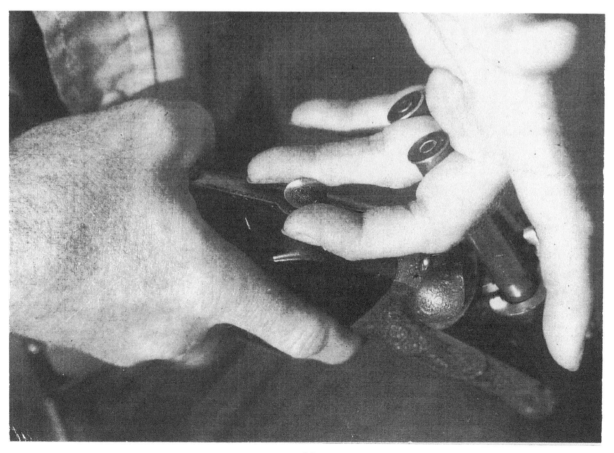

Chapter
12

Pistol Thoughts

I am not overly enthusiastic about hunting big game with a pistol. Some hunters have what it takes to kill cleanly with a handgun, but most do not. I know of no way to keep the poor shots from trying, and that is not good.

My personal philosophy on hunting with pistols was spelled out in a *Letter to the Editor* of the *Fairbanks News-Miner* on September 21, 1958. I find, these forty-seven years later, that my feelings have changed little.

The late Al Georg had just made his first splash as a pistol hunter and received some publicity in the paper. I thought little of it until I encountered a young man I knew out in the bush stalking grizzly bear with a .22 Colt Woodsman pistol. No joke here, my hair stood on end because the man was in grizzly country. The lad believed that he could take a grizzly bear by shooting both its eyes out when the bear came at him. Then he would "finish off" the bear at his leisure.

We discussed this concept at some length, and he quoted Al Georg's taking of a rather average Dall ram with a scoped pistol as his inspiration. I then wrote as follows to the *News-Miner:*

Dear Editor:
    I have been slightly perturbed by the publicity recently given an individual for shooting a Dall sheep with a .44 Magnum Revolver.

I shot and killed a running caribou with one shot through the spine from my Ruger .44 Magnum at 165 paces. I did not and still do not consider this a great feat. I personally know a number of pistol shooters here at Fort Greely who could do the same.

A disturbing aspect of all of the publicity given long range pistol kills is that it encourages unskilled hunters to try their luck with pistols and, too often, results in wounded game.

If it is necessary to publish stories concerning the feats of pistol hunters, it would seem correct to ALWAYS mention that the taking of big game with a pistol is for top pistol marksmen properly backed up by another hunter armed with an adequate rifle. Any big game animal deserves to be killed cleanly and suddenly, not wounded and lost.

It should be remembered and emphasized that the pistol should be carried as a defensive weapon, not as a game getter. Even the tremendously powerful .44 Magnum does not equal in energy the puny .30/30 rifle, which knowing hunters realize is not powerful enough for Alaskan game.

Sincerely,
Roy F. Chandler

Well, I would not word my thoughts quite that way anymore, but the lesson is still the same. Pistols take special expertise and should be used with discretion.

Some weeks after the letter appeared, I received a lengthy rebuttal from Al Georg which implied that I was full of hot air. I answered in the same spirit, and we insulted each other for a few letters until I almost became fond of Georg. He is long gone now, killed in a plane crash in Alaska.

The pistol, in the hands of an expert shot and hunter, CAN be an efficient game getter. Its primary value, however, lies in its handiness and effectiveness as a last ditch protector. A quick grab at the hip is far more efficient than a frantic scramble to reach a rifle lying across a pack.

In the practical sense, it can be argued that *extremely* few hunters or woods travelers are ever attacked by anything. Of the few who are attacked, most escape with only minor injuries. Quite naturally, those who do not escape with their lives are written and rewritten about so regularly that the occasions of attack seem far more numerous than actually occur. The fact is that a man will probably never need that heavy pistol swinging at his hip.

You will, however, note the use of *probably* in the foregoing statement. A pistol rubs, it scrapes, and it invited wise cracks, but if that rare attack occurs, the gun may be worth every prior bump, curse, and conceivable inconvenience.

If you are going to carry a defensive (or hunting pistol) for gosh sakes carry a .44 Magnum. The .357 Magnum is not enough. Consider these figures:

Caliber	Bullet Weight	Muzzle Velocity	KO Value
.44 Mag	240 grns	1470 fps	21.6
.357 Mag	158 grns	1410 fps	11.3

Obviously, the .44 Magnum has almost twice the power of a .357. When trying to stop an animal that could weigh seven hundred or more pounds, no one is so competent that he can willfully give away half the wallop his handgun could have.

Few would consider a .30/30 Winchester a proper weapon with which to face say a charging bear. But, the .30/30 with a conventional 170 grain bullet at 2220fps delivers a **KO** value of 16.6. That puts it ahead of a .357 Magnum, but well behind a .44 Maggie.

The self-defense pistol, as we apply the meaning to big game, has to not only kill the animal, it has to put it down RIGHT NOW! Thirty seconds after wounding could mean a badly mauled or stomped hunter.

Jeff Cooper, then Hand Gun Editor of *Guns and Ammo* magazine and one of the most knowledgeable in the pistol field, who is a confirmed advocate for the .45 ACP in police work, notes in the magazine's issue of April 1973 that in bear country he packs a .44 Magnum. No other pistol can cut the mustard on a big bruin.

To continue compiling similar commentaries by writing luminaries would be merely gilding the lilly. Accept the fact that if you carry a handgun to defend yourself against attack by Alaskan wildlife, it must be a .44 Magnum.

Most will be aware that there are more powerful pistols on the market than the .44 Remington Magnum. I do not discuss them because all are oddities that only a few could like and even fewer could shoot well. All kick like mules and, because of recoil recovery, all are extremely slow on follow up shots. Carrying defensive pistols physically larger than a .44 Magnum becomes a bit grotesque and inconvenient as well.

In 1973, I ran into Joe Benner, the Hall of Fame shooter, in *The Bullet Hole* in Sarasota, Florida. (I was outside seeking warmth.) Joe and I had, of course, fired against each other in matches around the country. I never recall threatening his scores on any course of fire. We posed for this photograph with my new .44 caliber Auto Mag, shown elsewhere in this chapter.

The Auto Mag attained fame as The *Executioner's* pistol in Don Pendleton's fiction series.

The pistol is easy to shoot, it is accurate, and it has little recoil. It is a good choice for those who hunt with a handgun. The Auto Mag is NOT a good self-defense pistol. It takes two hands to operate the slide, and the big pistol is really a two-handed affair to shoot properly. It is heavy and the balance is odd with the weight high in the hand.

As long as the author can remember there has been a lot of scoffing at long range pistol shooting. Having seen the average man trying to shoot a pistol, it is understandable why many cannot accept the claims of accurate shooting well beyond 500 yards. When a shooter has trouble finding where his bullet went while firing a scoped rifle at 200 yards, the same man dares not believe that another can HIT game at 300, 400, and 500 yards with an open-sighted handgun.

Well, most cannot shoot a pistol properly, and they cannot hit game at long ranges. Other men may be able to dot your eye at 50 yards but have never practiced at long range and find the concept improbable. Some give it an afternoon's try, and when they experience ignominious failure, are forever convinced that 600 yard hits are all talk.

I recall a *test* conducted by a pair of writers for a popular gun magazine. The two nimrods took a newly purchased Ruger Super Blackhawk in .44 Magnum to a sandy beach, set up a target and backed off a few hundred yards. They could not hit much of anything. They reported trying to aim high overhead at branches and things to give them aiming points, but they did lousy. Their article confirmed their belief that Elmer Keith, in particular, was talking through his big hat when he claimed he shot game way out there.

Those men were wrong. A pistol can be used for hunting at long ranges. *More correctly, a pistol can make hits on game sized targets at ranges out to 600 yards.* Perhaps a pistol can regularly hit game further than that. I have not practiced beyond that distance.

From this position, I could do real damage out to about 600 yards. Can you see the Mag-Na-Port below the front sight?

If a shooter intends to dispute this claim, he should prepare in a number of ways. He should first read the books on the subject. *Sixguns,* by Keith would be an excellent start. He should note, for instance, that sighting for extreme range is not done by holdover, but rather by raising the front sight while still holding on the target. If you do not do it this way, you will experience indifferent results.

Shooting positions should be studied. Flopping on your belly and straining your neck while half-expecting to have the recoiling Big Bertha plant a hammer between your eyes is not conducive to effective shooting. The author's favorite long range position is shown in an accompanying photograph.

After many months of diligent practice, one might then consider himself qualified to voice an informed opinion. And, one will then have nothing to expose, as one will be hitting targets at previously seemingly impossible ranges.

In his *Pistols, A Modern Encyclopedia,* Henry Stebbins notes that while practicing with the All Navy Team at Annapolis he shot his 9mm Luger at a 600-yard target. It took him two shots to get on the paper. Thereafter, all shots went on the six-foot square sheet with about a third of them within the twenty inch bull. He also notes that at 300 yards, using a Model 1911A1, he was able to put seven shots from his magazine into a twenty inch target spotter.

There are a number of interesting points here. First, not only Elmer Keith and I say it can be done. Also noteworthy is that neither the 9mm nor the .45 ACP is exactly ideal for such long range work, but it can be done even with such inappropriate pistols and cartridges.

My first years in Alaska, I fired and recorded over three thousand rounds from my .44 Remington Magnum, Ruger Blackhawk. This was the early Blackhawk with the fluted cylinder. Most of those rounds were fired at long ranges. I sat on the bluffs over the Tanana River and shot at rocks and flotsam. I perched on likely spots above Jarvis creek and the Delta River and drove hundreds and hundreds of bullets into unoffending stones and logs. I developed a strange callus on my second finger (the one below the trigger finger) where the trigger guard struck it—on both hands. I wore the full cock notch off the hammer the first year, and the ejector rod and housing regularly flew back over my head. Bill Ruger put the works back together for me, and I shot it all loose again.

Before I quit keeping records, I had fired over six thousand rounds through that old gun. Most were fired at long-range targets. Additionally, I wore that pistol on my hip nearly all day, *every day*, for over two years and less regularly for years thereafter. I still find my hand now and then trying to rest on the gun butt.

This is Elmer Keith's long range shooting position. The author's modified preference is shown on page 97. Keith's is steadier but, unless raised up a little, the author had difficulty shooting across *flat* land.

During all the shooting, I discovered I could hit with astonishing regularity at seemingly improbable ranges. I hit hat-sized stones at two hundred yards as a matter of course. I would say that once I got on at 600 yards, I could hit the side of a one-hole outhouse almost every time.

Of course, I also shot at game. I recall missing a coyote making time across Bolio Lake. I never caught up with him, but dusted him until I could not see him anymore. That was good for a rueful laugh, but it was the coyote's speed that got me, not the range.

I thumped a Harvey Protex bore, 220 grain bullet through a caribou at 165 long steps. The bullet passed completely through the animal, including breaking his spine. I used my favorite hump shot on that one. I took four caribou in two years with that pistol, but that was the longest shot.

Arguments over whether or not a good shot can hit big game at long range with a pistol should cease. It can be done.

Should it? I must ruefully join the camp of those who say it should not. Unless you hit exactly right, the pistol is not powerful enough for Alaskan big game. Unless you are a cool and deadly shot at longer than usual ranges you will wound and wound and wound.

After all, when I exclaim that *no one* should shoot Alaskan big game at over 300 yards with a **rifle**, it would be ludicrous to endorse similar shooting with a **pistol**.

I am embarrassed to say that in this case, *"Do not do as I have done; do as I tell you."*

Forget pistol hunting for Alaskan big game.

Which brand of sidearm should a hunter carry for self-defense? If we stick with American made pistols, our choice lies primarily between Ruger and Smith and Wesson. A Dan Wesson might get in there as well, but we will keep the explanation simple. I have carried my single-action Ruger Blackhawk for decades and my Model 29 Smith almost as long.

If I thought I was going to be attacked by a grizzly or an insane moose in extremely close quarters, I would go with the Smith and Wesson 29 for two reasons. The Smith is double-action. Pull the trigger and the gun fires. The Ruger must be cocked between rounds—not as inherently fast.

For me, at least, the Smith and Wesson recoils straighter back, more into my palm than rotating upward in my hand—as does the Ruger. If you are shooting two-handed, that might make little difference, but using one hand, the way one might in an emergency, straight back allows quicker recovery.

Finally, there is the matter of carrying. We carry a lot more than we shoot. I like the Ruger best on my hip. It feels like a pistol ought to feel, and I can haul it out more certainly than I can the Smith. For the first shot, there is little difference in speed. Thereafter, the Smith and Wesson pistol is better.

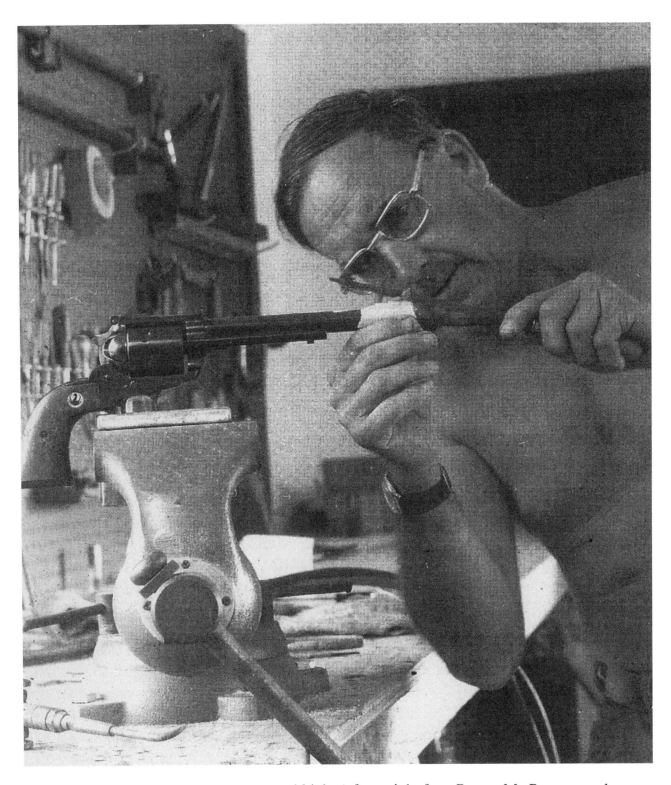

The author making a new (and higher) front sight for a Ruger. My Rugers, as they came from the factory, always shot high. On this sight I included a slanting ramp across which I inlaid silver bars. The idea was to use different bars at various ranges. This was Elmer Keith's idea, and it worked pretty well.

Chapter
13

Bush Flying

I learned to fly in Manhattan, Kansas. Kansas is parking lot flat. I flew my single-engine Cessna up the Alcan Highway to Fairbanks, but the highest point in that road is only a bit over 4000 feet. I learned little from the trip except how very far Alaska is from Kansas. Navigating the Alaskan Mountains, on the other hand, provided many learning moments. Some of them were frightening, as an example will demonstrate.

I had been told a hundred times never to fly UP a canyon. *Always fly down a canyon.* The down-canyon rule is basic, and breaking that rule can find you unable to climb steeply enough to clear the rising ground.

On a handsome July day in the late nineteen fifties, Jerry and I flew UP the Gerstle River to examine sheep along the canyon edges. We saw a lot of rams, and more than a few were worthwhile with more than a full curl.

Admiring sheep, I paid too little attention to how far upriver we had proceeded. Belatedly, I realized that the ground was rising rapidly; the canyon was narrowing, and ahead rose the intimidating height of Mount Silver Tip. We were far below the canyon rim, and it appeared dicey whether I could climb fast enough to get above an edge before I ran out of air.

On came full power, down went the flaps, and up came the nose. Slow flying at the edge of a stall, my eyes glued to the altimeter, we leaned forward in our seats straining to help the slightly underpowered 170 Cessna to rise beyond its expected capabilities.

Approaching steeply rising ground, a pilot can expect either a lift from rising air or exactly the opposite (which would wipe out any chance we had of getting above the cliffs hemming us in on either side). The situation was so desperate that I was considering pointing the nose straight down and diving while racking the plane into a 180 degree turn and trying to drop toward the river as I built up air speed and pulled out heading back downstream. I might make it, but if the wind were wrong, I would be attempting a low altitude, downwind turn, and that is most often deadly.

Almost as I considered the drastic maneuver, we got a tremendous lift from wind blowing toward the mountain. As if on an elevator, up we went, and over the ridge to the right we flew. Trapped one instant, free and clear the next. Scared the hell out of me!

Do not misunderstand, I never considered myself a "genuWine" bush pilot. Those "fly anywhere, almost anytime" pilots have skills beyond those most of us acquire. Few hunting guide pilots are actual bush pilots. Guides fly in and out, weather permitting, but they do not brave the arctic month in and month out delivering and picking up precious cargo. Still, any flying in Alaska can be hazardous as most landing strips are informal affairs, and only the largest commercial airports have control towers and weather advisories.

There are dirt landing strips all over Alaska, and in the old days we used to land on the highways. However, if they find game, hunting guides and other bush pilots land in some hugely unlikely places. In the winter they land on strange snowfields. In warmer months they drop onto gravel bars and flatter tundra. A popular landing technique is to fly low and slow over a chosen "strip" looking closely and judging the wind. On the next pass you hold flying speed and lightly drag your wheels or skis over the surface. If everything feels good, in you go on the third pass.

Gravel bars along rivers are popular landing spots. Most of the named rivers and larger streams in Alaska have wide flats along them and some are braided rivers, meaning that the river divides itself into entwining channels. Those rivers or creeks are sometimes half a mile wide and many offer safe landing.

Many pilots shift their landing gear from fat, balloon-tire wheels, to floats for the countless lakes across Alaska. In the winter, everyone not flying from or to conventional airports has skis.

During one of my first years in our state, I was given a set of fat-tire, tandem wheels by the US Army Arctic Test Board that had finished fooling with them. The idea was to be less committed if a wheel fell into a hole, but they slowed the plane and made taxiing less friendly. I used them for two summers, as best I can recall.

This is a typical Alaskan bush landing strip. This one is a flat along the Johnson River. It is well up toward the glacier where bears and sheep can be found. Pilots often hang a rag or two in nearby saplings to help with the wind the next time in—which can often be shifty and bumpy in the mountains.

In the lower forty-eight states, flying close to the ground was always dangerous because of unexpected towers or wires strung here and there, but during my earlier years in Alaska, I took great pleasure in flying along at about tree height *(Always downstream!)* watching animals and enjoying the challenge of following a river or a stream's course. Back then, there simply were no towers or wires beyond the edges of a community.

It is said that Alaska has more airplanes per capita than any other state, and the report seems correct. If you hunger to be a light plane pilot, go to Alaska. The restricted zones are few, and the flying is exciting. If you intend to become a hunting or fishing guide, learn to fly and fly well.

A final thought is that a hunting guide does not have to be an instrument-rated pilot (although that is not a bad idea), but he should be able to execute a one hundred and eighty degree turn in the thickest soup. He should practice that maneuver often and stay razor sharp on it. That getaway maneuver can save your life when—as it surely will sooner or later—a whiteout or something similar drops in. Which encourages a final flying story.

My buddy and I had flown some trophies into Fairbanks and were attempting to get back to Fort Greely by flying under overcast that eventually forced us down into the riverbed of the Delta River. Not to worry, we knew the area and would recognize the exact spot to turn left, pop up into the soup with one eye on the ground, cross the Richardson Highway and sit down on the immense Fort Greely runway. (Fort Greely had been a Lend Lease airstrip during WWII where Russian pilots took over the airplanes the USA was giving them. The runways were so large that anything flying could land and take off without difficulty.)

Unfortunately, weather closed in ahead of us, and I could only roll into a very tight turn and head back out—back to Fairbanks. Only, the ceiling had dropped behind us, and we were flying in an increasingly small bowl of clear air. Instant deciding was essential. No time for discussion or reconsideration. I picked a likely-looking gravel flat and stalled the Cessna in as short as I could manage. Made it. Bald-assed luck, mostly.

When the overcast lifted a little, I backed off as far as I could get, full flaps, stood on the brakes, and revved the engine until rivets strained. I got the back wheel up and let off the brakes. We staggered aloft and made it into Greely. Hardly worth talking about—we claimed.

Master guide, Ray Atkins, Cantwell, Alaska—a bush pilot with more than thirty years experience.

Landing on a snow field and setting up camp almost under a wing. The wise thing is to immediately tie down the airplane by screwing anchors into the snow, one for each wing and another for the tail. Winds can come from nowhere in the mountains. If the temperature is going to get really low and the plane will not be used, the oil must be drained so that it does not freeze or get too thick in the engine. You warm the oil over a stove or a fire before you put it back in the engine. If the engine does not immediately crank, you drain the oil and do it over again—before you run down your battery. If you fail to restart, someone has to fly in a generator and a Herman Nelson air blower to heat up the engine. Have a good radio and file an excellent flight plan—just in case.

This is a reduced-in-size copy of the Hunters' Flight Plan that was introduced more than forty years ago. The idea is that if a pilot runs into difficulty and cannot fly out, the Alaska State Police will have his whereabouts on record and can initiate a rescue.

```
─────────CLIP AND MAIL─────────
HUNTERS' "FLIGHT PLAN"  Date..............., 19......
Name................... Age....... Address............... Phone..........
Number of Party.......... Names of Others..................
.................................................................
Date of Departure............... Date of Return..............
Area of Hunt................................................
.................................................................
Alternate Area of Hunt....................................
.................................................................
Type of Transportation (Describe)........................
.................................................................
Check Return with (Name, Phone, Address)............
.................................................................
Emergency Equipment......................................
Mail To:
  ALASKA STATE POLICE
  Anchorage, Alaska or
  Fairbanks, Alaska        Signature......................
```

It can go badly. An undetected hollow, perhaps disguised by loose powder snow, or a bump that catches a ski tip. Now what?

It can go REALLY bad. When landing, a gust of wind can cause a ground loop by going under a wing and swiveling the airplane so that the opposite wing tip touches, and over she goes. (Or, maybe this pilot was slow tying down his aircraft?)

Chapter

14

The Mountain Goat

My Favorite

Because I prefer to hunt goats before all other Alaskan animals, I am especially concerned that readers gain a genuine feel for the unique conditions of mountain goat hunting. In many Alaskan publications, the mountain goat is not even listed as a prominent game animal. Some list the Alaskan **Big Four**, and do not include the goat. On the other hand, if you decide to hunt goats with a guide, you discover that the cost is as great as hunting a Dall sheep. Properly hunted, goats come hard!

Only one thing derogatory can be said about the Rocky Mountain goat. IT WOULD BE NICE IF HE HAD LARGER HORNS. Otherwise, the goat provides the finest hunting there is. His climate is delicious, his scenery breathtaking, the climbing and stalking unsurpassed, the shooting long and challenging.

Goats live above the Dall sheep. They look down on all other furred game. Their lands are a fortress primeval. From their battlements they can sneer at the great bear, the skulking wolf, and most of the time, at the panting, laboring hunter.

The mountain goat is one of only two game animals in the western hemisphere that remain white year-round. The other is the Dall sheep.

(The Polar bear which also remains white is considered an ice living animal that comes ashore only irregularly.)

A mountain goat often appears to be disdainful and almost disinterested in the approach of a toiling hunter. While seated comfortably on some rocky prominence, he is prone to gaze down his long nose with only casual interest in a hunter's upward struggles. Just as the stalker decides to risk a long and imaginative shot, the goat rises, surveys distant vistas, and with a step or two disappears from view.

Most goat hunters have experienced such mountain goat arrogance. The goat is accustomed to being master of all he surveys, and until the shot, you are not likely to worry him unduly.

While we have pretty well worked out the number of game animals in other species of the northwest, I have heard and read little concerning authoritative estimates of the number of goats. The lack of mountain goat data seems strange in these times of cataloging and labeling everything else. While dedicated naturalists tag and spot-paint "dangerous" grizzly bear, and while worthy organizations produce a million miles of "Life among the moose, jackals, eagles—you name it," we don't see much on mountain goats.

The Dall sheep with his magnificent curl of horn has lured trophy hunters to about every sheep-occupied mountain meadow in southeastern Alaska and the Brooks Range to the north.

Fascination with sheep hunting has probably been to the goats' advantage. In most of their remote areas the goats have been allowed to flourish without heavy hunting pressure.

Goat hunting can take you all the way to the top of the mountains, but is there a goat on your mountain? You glass to find out.

As mentioned before, the problem with goats is that their horns are too small. Few trophy room viewers get excited about seeing a mountain goat mount. So, the-run-of-the-mine trophy hunter—who may be more concerned with trophy exhibition than challenges of the hunt—tends not to go after the high ranging goats.

Goat hunting is more physically difficult than sheep hunting and provides more challenging shooting. This appeals to me, but it is peculiar how hunter/writers differ even in basic mountain goat appreciation. A few have found goats easy and knocked them off with little effort. That can occasionally happen with any game animal, but most writers claim to have worked hard for their goat trophies.

The most respected Dean of shooting editors, Jack O'Connor, found nothing good to say about eating mountain goat meat. He thought it tough, stringy, tasteless, and virtually inedible.

Russell Annabel, author of **Hunting and Fishing in Alaska**, agrees with this writer that the flesh of the goat is among the best tasting of any in the arctic, and that is going some. So, we disagree on more than a little.

I believe that goat hunting in Alaska might best be introduced by including the stories of three hunts that I enjoyed. Thereafter, we can discuss mountain goat hunting in a more technical manner.

Goat Country

This handsome goat, moose, and bear country is in the Chugach Mountains—as the crow flies, not fifty miles out of Valdez. Yet, almost no one goes there. If the photographer had turned around after taking this picture he would have gazed across a mile-wide rocky bowl where we have taken brown bears and many goats.

In the valley below, our hunting parties have taken black bear and moose, as well as an occasional brownie.

The Richardson Highway, the road to civilization, lies at least seven hours of hard hiking down this valley with some difficult fording of the stream seen in the photo.

There is a glacier out of the picture right behind me. This is a nice hunting ground that we never tired of—and we never met another human or saw anyone's sign.

Chapter

15

Goats are Tough

Going and Coming

Talon-like, my aching fingers clutched at the ragged stone. My boots dug for purchase on a narrow ledge. I pressed my body tightly to the cliff face. Still, I knew I was not going to make it. Thirty feet below my straining body roared a deep glacial stream. I was in trouble.

The seventy-pound pack bulging with hunting gear and crudely boned-out mountain goat tugged me away from the rock face, and my .300 Weatherby rifle had flopped from my shoulder and dangled clumsily near my elbow. I had to act quickly, or I would topple backward into the stream. I had to shuck the load and hope that, without the pack, I could work my way back off the ledge.

Awkwardly, I freed my left shoulder from the pack harness. Immediately, the weight of the load and rifle on my right arm became unbearable. I gripped the rifle sling in my teeth, pulled my arm free of the sling, and gave the pack a clumsy heavy into space. The sudden release was almost my undoing, and I fought frantically for balance as my right hand clawed for a new grip on the crumbly rock.

Carefully, dripping sweat and shaky with tension fatigue, I eased my way back out of the gorge and onto safer ground. I had relearned that the shortest route to camp is not always the best.

Three weary hours later, I recovered the soggy but little injured pack from where it had grounded on a gravel bar a mile below the gorge.

That is mountain goat hunting as I know it—a rough, rugged, and occasionally dangerous adventure.

This is a goat meadow. Somehow the animals find sustenance from these barren slopes. There is safety up here, and goats like it. A goat can speed across any of the mountain you see in this picture. They might choose to go up the slanting meadow, but if desired, they will stride across the rocks as if the route were a highway. No other animal can follow them.

Unlike most goat hunting experiences that we read about, I have found that "coming home" with the trophy should sometimes be the story told. Anyone who has climbed a cliff has discovered that going up is easier than coming back down, and in hunting the wily mountain goat the adventure does not always end with the killing shot. Mountain terrain, weariness, and heavy loads can produce difficulties and dangers quite as confounding as the hunt itself.

The mountain goat is big, fast, and tough. He is proud, rugged, and to my thinking altogether handsome. His area is remote and all stood on end. The old hunters' adage, "You can walk where a sheep walks, but never try to follow a goat," effectively describes the ruggedness of hunting old Billy.

Personally, I would pass up two sheep hunts for one go at goats. I like their clean lonesome country. I like their arrogant down the nose appraisal of the toiling hunter, and although it sometimes makes me want to cry in frustration, I glory in their ability to trot fearlessly across an apparently impassable cliff face. Of the more than two hundred head of big game that I have taken, my fondest memories concern goat hunting.

While all goat hunts do not include cliff-hanging experiences, the goat hunter exposes himself to an almost incredible variety of hazards.

Of course, there are the expected (and accepted) rigors of thin air and steep slopes, but when one is after the really grand trophy, there may also be glaciers to cross, treacherous rockslides to negotiate, and icy streams to ford.

I have, while returning to camp from goat hunts, taken bad falls, been temporarily lost, trapped by fog so dense that I could not always see my own feet, and once while wrapped in our sleeping bags, my hunting partner and I were nuzzled by a yearling brown bear who, with its mother, was passing by.

Perhaps typical of the rigors of bringing home a goat trophy was a hunt for goats near Valdez.

Our day's hunt had been arduous and unsuccessful. On the way back to camp we decided to delay the final one-mile plunge down the mountain and take a last look across the summit of the ridges surrounding our base camp.

Although evening dusk was beginning to thicken in the valley, We muscled our way up the lichen covered ledges and across the rocky slides until, gasping and wheezing, we topped out a few hundred feet above a small snow field.

Without the mountains to block it, the breeze was sharp and cutting. We sought shelter from the wind below a crest where the sunlight was still warm and where our legs and lungs could resume normal functioning. We half-dozed, as hunters often do, just soaking up the comfort of warmth and enjoying good companionship.

Suddenly we heard rocks falling, and after a moment, we again caught the rattle of dislodged stones. We were quickly on our feet and moving, rifles at ready. Our single packboard was left neglected in the sunny hollow, and in my haste I unwittingly stepped on an already battered sandwich just removed from a jacket pocket.

Jerry in the lead, we darted along a spiny ridge to where we could see more country. A shallow, bowl-like depression came into view. Climbing the opposite slope, slowly working his way across the rubble, was what appeared to me to be the granddaddy of all mountain goats.

Recognition was mutual. Grandpa took one, apparently all encompassing look, shifted into high gear, and really began laying tracks up the rock pile.

Beside me, Jerry's .270 began to boom. I was dimly aware that he was standing up, and I thought, "He'll never hit him shooting off hand."

I do not remember estimating range, judging wind, or making any other significant calculations. I jacked a round into the chamber, sat down, and caught the goat in my crosshairs. I saw rock shatter where one of Jerry's quick shots splattered itself. I held on the back of the goat's neck and touched off the .300 Weatherby.

My position was not exactly Camp Perry, and by the time I got out of recoil and back on the target the action was over. Old Billy Goat Gruff was tumbling limply and slowly, end-past-end back into the grassy bowl.

I kept the Weaver 4X glued to the seemingly immense expanse of white fur until the goat came to rest, limp and sprawling, near the bottom of the meadow. I became aware of Jerry thumping me on the back and calling it a great shot. Not until then did I realize that the range approached three hundred yards. My heart began to thud mightily as the old adrenalin belatedly went to work. I felt so shaky that I wondered if I could get over to where the trophy lay without a decent rest.

It is often said that the fun is over once the shot is fired. However, a one-mile downhill clamber did not appear overly difficult, and as I skinned out the goat I gave little thought to the trip back to camp.

Possessing only one packboard between us, we quickly reduced the goat into a very heavy single pack that Jerry willingly shouldered. As the victorious hunter, without a pack, I was elected to drape the head and goat hide around my neck for the journey down.

Only the mountaintops still held dim light, and our return trip suddenly presented more than an awkwardly loaded downhill hike. There were now the added problems of avoiding stepping off a cliff edge, misjudging the stability of a rockslide, or even ending up in the wrong hollow.

In the deepening dusk we were casually negotiating a steeply slanting patch of grass when Jerry's feet shot out from under him. Feet first, he skidded down the slope, his heels and hands scratching for holds but still sliding. Only a few feet from an ominous looking black edge he came to a jolting stop. Burdened by his huge pack, Jerry sat unmoving, gathering himself before calmly asking for a hand up. I complied without much thought, chuckling to myself over the way he had looked skidding and bouncing along.

When we were past the meadow and on solid rock, Jerry dropped the big pack with a sigh of relief. He unslung his .270 and examined the scope. It was battered and the rear lens was packed with dirt. The only way he had kept from going over the cliff edge had been by digging the ocular end of his scope into the ground to act as a brake. (Try that with an iron receiver sight!) As a lover of fine arms my senses cringed, but the idea of being weighed down by a heavy pack on the lip of a precipice, and held there by only a few 6 x 48 screws far overshadowed the possibility of scope damage.

The way down the mountain seemed endless. We repeatedly backtracked when a route proved too difficult. We discussed just sweating it out on the mountain all night. Each time camp seemed so close that we went on.

As true dark settled in we practically felt our way downward. We smashed and clawed through thickets of brush and torturously worried ourselves across rockslides and icy freshets.

The raw goat hide about my neck proved to be the world's most efficient insulation, and I itched and sweated buckets of brine into old Bill's thick fur. I began to feel like the Ancient Mariner—in my case condemned to forever wear the defunct goat as a necklace. I fervently vowed never again to set foot outside camp without every man carrying a backboard.

After another eternity of stumbling blindly down talus slopes we reached the creek edge with the friendly campfire crackling on the other side.

Our companions had long before become aware of our painful approach, warned no doubt by the clatter of tons of loosened rubble and the accompanying groans and un-muffled curses.

So, that goat came home. When I sit in my trophy room and gaze at his mounted head I seldom dwell on the shot itself. But, I can again feel the cutting wind on the mountain, the strain of packing down the slopes, and I picture Jerry bouncing toward the cliff edge. My heart raises the beat a little, and I live again that good hunt with a grand trophy, shared by a close and valued friend.

Goat camp! The author reads. A pulp novel is always along. It is nice to get into sneakers (Does anyone use that term anymore?) after long hours on the mountain.

The rifle? Usually close by. There are brownies around.

So, I didn't shave (that week). I occasionally bathed in the glacial stream that ran just beyond my feet, but those dips were quickies—more sloshes off than real bathing. No one else in any of my hunting parties got into the stream, voluntarily. Man, it was cold. Shaving was hard and almost murderous in cold water. Heating shaving water over a twig fire or a camp stove rarely seemed worth the effort in the high country. So, I was grubby, but so was everyone else.

Hey, living primitive has been one of the great attractions of big game hunting, and I suspect it always will be.

Chapter

16

Learning About Goats

Take a look at a goat mount and you see a spike-horned little old head that might make a man wonder why any hunter would hunger enough for such a trophy to flounder his way across the moose pastures, claw past the sheep meadows, and struggle up into the tortured crags of Alaskan mountain goat country.

I had a friend like that. He kept telling me that goats just did not interest him. His gaze fell unappreciatively on my favorite Billy mounts, and my tales of pursuit among the high pastures brought more yawns than gasps.

So, we went into the high country for goats. He went because he is a good hunting partner. I went, as I always do, with churning anticipation.

We gasped our way into likely country and rested in an alpine meadow, letting a gentle breeze dry the sweat that dampened us. My friend condescended that it was mighty fine country, which it was, with lesser peaks falling away before us and higher elevations raising forbiddingly shadowed monoliths above and around. Still, I knew he wished a curl-plus Dall ram was our quarry.

A little later we began to see goats. Unlike rams that keep their heavy-horned heads out in the open, goats curl into tight balls, resting with their heads tucked in. My buddy did a little cussing because he could not easily judge the half-hidden horns.

A nice Billy scampered an improbable passage along a cliff face that would have given any sheep a severe case of vertigo, and my friend could not shoot because the trophy would have dropped hundreds of feet to impractical recovery and almost certain destruction.

We watched big, long-horned fellows ogle us with interested arrogance from well out of sensible shooting range, and the unexpected appearance and hasty flight of a pair of average nannies almost underfoot nearly precipitated a similar panic in my startled companion.

When his shot finally came it was a long one, more than two hundred yards and across a small canyon. A strong wind blew, and the goat had to be anchored in his tracks lest he step off into space, as they often do when hard hit.

My buddy crawled into a nest of rocks that matched a benchrest for steadiness. Using both our hats to cushion his rifle, he cranked his Bausch and Lomb variable up to 8X and proceeded to plant a .338 Winchester Magnum, 250 grain bullet solidly into old Bill's spine and shoulder area. The goat simply slumped.

Per our shooting system, he had another bullet on its way without waiting to examine response to the first shot. The second bullet bit just as solidly, and watching through our spotting scope, I called the shooting off while my buddy was rattling his bolt on a third round.

The scramble down and the climb back up to the trophy took a while. We found that either bullet would have turned the trick, but we never regret extra shots fired the way we would rounds that we should have touched off and did not.

It was a long carry down the mountain. We talked a lot going downhill, reliving the hunt and the shot the way big game hunters do. The horns went just ten inches, and that makes a mighty good goat.

My friend allowed that the head would make a nice mount. I agreed. He talked no more about spike-horned, barnyard animals, and I noticed that he moved a pretty fair Stone sheep aside to place his Billy in a prominent spot on his den wall.

The dessert for this story is that he and I went again for goats—more than once. That pal is dead now. Gone to a great reward, I hope.

I wonder if they will have good goat hunting up there.

Chapter

17

The Doc's Hunt

Back in the 1950s, the old guide got a yen to hunt goats, so we loaded the Bombardier tractor onto the Ford flatbed truck, hooked on the trailer with all our camping gear in it, and struck out for Ernestine Creek.

In those days, Mac MaGill had a cabin at mile 62 out of Valdez, and we stopped there overnight to renew acquaintance with Mac and to organize for the seven-mile crawl into our favorite camp a mile or two below Ernestine glacier.

Mac and his bunch were moose hunters who never hiked higher on a hill than they had to, and goat hunting left them unimpressed. There was, however, one wild-eyed young fellow with Mac's party who thought goat hunting might be worth trying. The next morning he threw his gear on the trailer with ours and expectantly mounted the back of the tractor. Art sort of rolled his eyes around, but made no objections, and seeing he didn't, we didn't. But, three guys bumping together back there was about as comfortable as the same three guys sharing a sleeping bag. Jerry and I didn't like it much. We were also a sort of closed company and did not prefer more bodies going along.

The new guy had remarkable equipment. His tent was exotic for the time with then rarely seen outside aluminum poles. He had two Weatherby rifles, one a .270 magnum, and the other the old .375 Weatherby Magnum. He also packed enough expensive camera equipment to man a small studio, and his personal gear was by Eddie Bauer, which we all admired but could rarely afford.

It turned out that this fella was the doctor at Valdez and was on some kind of contract where everyone in town paid a certain fee and got their doctoring free thereafter. As Valdez placed her city limits some twenty-three miles from the center of town (big claim for a village of 2000 souls), Doc had a large parish going for him.

The hunt went as usual on Ernestine. Jerry and I climbed and looked at goats. We took one, and Art plunked another on a high shelf that Jerry and I had the privilege of climbing for and packing down.

While we were after Art's goat, the Doc did me the favor of removing my goat's skull from its skin. Actually, I had been saving the delicate job for an evening task around the fire. It stays light late in the early part of goat season, and I enjoy having something to keep my hands busy.

It was nice of the Doc to tackle the task for me, and I was not displeased until I discovered that the fathead had split the hide under the chin (the way you would a bear or something you lay out for a rug) instead of down the back of the neck, the way head mounts should be. Thereafter, I found it a little hard to warm up to the Doc, and as it turned out, it got even tougher.

That evening the Doc informed us that he was a diabetic. He heated up a little something in a spoon, and shot himself a big charge of it. He assured us there was nothing to worry about as long as he took his medicine. Looking at my savaged goat trophy, I was not too worried about him anyway.

Whatever was in the medicine he took, it did wonders for the Doc's creative instincts. He broke out a camera with multiple lenses and a shockingly bright strobe light and started shooting pictures all over the camp. Fond of candid close-ups, he must have then and there accumulated an unmatchable photographic collection of inner ears, flaring nostrils, and rolled eyeballs. Rolls of film fled through that camera without the Doc showing the slightest tendency toward slowing down. I feared to answer a call of nature lest I be forever recorded on film, and Jerry finally sacked out with a blanket over his head as the mighty strobe readily penetrated common eyelid protection.

In this more enlightened era, I would have suspected the Doc's medication as being imported from Columbia. It certainly provided ebullient spirits for an interminable period.

The Doc did not emerge from his glorious text until about noon the next day, but one of Maw Rausch's meals then raised his spirits, and the old guide took him out to shoot a goat.

An hour or so later a horrendous firefight broke out up toward the glacier. Rifle fire echoed and reechoed from the cliffs in an unceasing roll that was unfathomably out of place within a company where good shooting resulted in little shooting. We in camp could only surmise that a brown bear had been wounded and that the hunters were firing desperately at it as the bear headed downhill toward our camp. Nothing less dangerous could seem to account for such a barrage.

Seizing our rifles, Jerry and I moved into position to intercept anything moving down canyon, but no slavering bruin appeared. Disturbed and intrigued, we moved with some caution upstream toward the high ground.

A short way along, we met the Doc and Art. The Doc looked pleased. Art was clearly discomfited. It seemed the Doc had spied a goat hanging on a cliff a couple of hundred feet above the stream. Art looked it over and declared the goat too small and in a bad spot. He had just turned away when the Doc opened fire with his .270 Weatherby.

At two hundred yards the Doc was bringing down a lot of rock, and the little goat decided to move around some. Emptying his rifle, the Doc shook out a full box of cartridges and really got down to business.

Finally, he stung the small Billy. Leaving a wounded animal is, of course, out of the question, and Art knew they had to take the goat.

The Doc shot up all of his ammunition, mainly blasting where the wounded goat had just been, but sometimes turning the animal when a bullet struck ahead. When the Doc's ammo dump ran dry, Art handed over his trusty rifle and let him pound away with it. While flinging a magazine full of 150 grain Hornaday 30/06s skyward, the goat was hit again and plunged off the cliff and into the stream far below. Art swore the Doc was still shooting after the goat had disappeared into the gorge. Anyway, they hustled down the mountain to where Ernestine comes swishing out of the canyon, hoping the goat would float out to them. Of course it did not.

After silently listening to the tale, Jerry offered to accompany the Doc up the thigh deep creek and help get the trophy out. We found out then that the Doc had a bad knee that would not allow him to pack heavy loads. We gathered that the quarter mile scramble through icy water would not do the Doc's knee any good either, and we were right.

Resignedly, Jerry and I waded in, and bucking the too fast current, plowed and skidded up through Ernestine gorge. The rock walls tower forbiddingly in there with monstrous loose slabs hanging menacingly overhead. It is not a place for idle conversation, and we shared none.

We found the goat, a pathetic little thing with about six inch horns wedged into a rocky corner. To lighten the load and protect the meat we gutted the animal, and Jerry began to pack him out. Built like his Dad with short, powerful legs, Jerry had sensitive parts in the icy water most of the way, and if the treacherous overhangs had allowed it, his curses would have resounded far down the valley.

Between us we packed the Doc's goat to camp, and on the way got the head-jerk from Art that said, "Out!" The speed with which we folded camp would have startled the quickest. The Doc's magnificent equipment received insensitive treatment, but the Doc did not notice; it was medicine time.

Art had the tractor running when the final lashing was in place, and we gratefully accepted the Doc's decision to ride sitting in the cab of the tractor with Maw and Art. Art did not think too much of the Doc's riding choice, but we were transparently unsympathetic.

The old guide took the Bombardier down Ernestine Creek in record time. We roared to a halt at Mac's cabin, tossed the Doc's gear into a pile, ran the tractor onto the truck, latched the trailer to the truck, and rumbled away while the Doc was still fumbling around trying to remember where Mac cached the cabin key. I never saw the Doc again.

It was a number of years before I got back to that particular spot on Ernestine Creek, and somehow all of the good hunts there get shaded in my memory by that crazy one with the Doc.

One year I found a great pile of empty cartridge cases overlooking the gorge, and even before I read the caliber on the tarnished case heads I knew it had to be the Doc's old shooting stand. I looked at the cliff face across the way and marveled how a rifleman could have repeatedly missed a goat at that range.

The goats are still there on Ernestine. Now and then I stop at Mac's old cabin. Someone else owns the place now. I pack in the tough seven miles to the old hunting camp. Nothing has changed. The hike is still murderously rough, but someone, perhaps a trapper, has kept a trace partly open, and that helps.

Everything is still the same at the creek head. The glacier is slowly drawing back, and it varies a little each year depending on the winter's severity. The creek still boils out of the dangerous canyon.

In 1974 the old Alaskan guide, Slim Moore, and I were reminiscing about Ernestine. He fondly remembered the goats there and good hunts for them with good companions. Slim noted that it was past for him. He had grown too old for those kind of hunts.

Now, it is my turn. I have reached my eightieth year, and I shall not go back up Ernestine again. It is all right. Many memories were made there, and at this late date I choose not to disturb them or unfeelingly pile on others. They are too precious.

In 1990, I had an adventure novel published in which most of the action took place at the Ernestine headwaters. **The Book Cache**, whose outlets determined much of what was read in Alaska, would only buy the novel six copies at a time, so my publisher did not bother to sell the book in the Great State. I was truly sorry about that. The title of the novel was *Chugger's Hunt*. It is out of print now, of course, but copies are often offered on E-bay. If you can find a copy, you can enjoy a fine read—I guarantee it.

In 1993 I ended another novel titled *Old Dog* with the action near Mac's old cabins on Ernestine. I guess I love that place so much I cannot let it go.

Arthur Rausch and a buddy, whose name has escaped me, with a pair of good goats. Notice that there is no blood around the mouths. Blood is hell to remove from white fur. I could not say that we always avoid heavy bleeding, but we try hard. We like hump shots, not lung hits—which often cause copious bleeding at the mouth.

Chapter

18

Goat Hunting Details

Mountain goats are not found all over Alaska. In fact, goats are hunted only in southeastern Alaska, including the panhandle and Kodiak Island. Most goats are taken on the southeast Mainland. The next hottest spot is the Kenai Peninsula, just a comfortable drive from Anchorage. I prefer to hunt goats in the Valdez area.

An unseemly number of goats are taken from cliffs by shooters that approach by boat. Goats on the cliffs can be seen from afar, motored to, the engine is shut down, a bit of rowing ensues, and the animals potted. There is no hunt, no fair chase, and no sport. The system stinks! It should be abolished.

However, a hunter who goes in and climbs to locate and take his goat can have a memorable hunt.

Checking my records of goat hunting in Alaska, it appears that I hunted an average of six hours per goat. I spent a typical seven hours getting in, exclusive of the hunt, and a comparable time getting back out. I succeeded on all except two hunts.

Shots that took goats varied from 150 yards to 300 yards. Much of my recorded data on shooting distances refers to shooting done by other goat hunters, and there is a lot of it. Admittedly, most of those ranges are estimates that were impractical to step off. However, the people with whom I hunt are not deliberate range stretchers, and they mostly limit their ranges to three hundred yards. I can accept that our median goat was taken at 185 yards.

Hunter: Joe Rhyshek, *Boone & Crocket* listed, .30-378 Weatherby, Kodiak Island

Goats are big animals. Judge the size of this monster—while realizing that he could run at full speed across rocks and slopes and along cliff faces that would wilt the heart of a mountain climber. Those odd looking feet can grip anything they touch.

Even in black and white it can be seen that a mountain goat is not the color of snow. A goat usually looks yellow against snow, and because they keep their heads tucked in, goats at a distance often look like yellow lumps on the mountain. They can be hard to see.

Many of my hunting companions were .270 Winchester and .30/06 fanciers. Belatedly, many moved into various magnums. Part of their delay in changing to bigger guns has been due to their ages. Some have now passed away. Most surviving are now crowding their Golden Years (Yeah!) and began hunting many years before the popularization of more powerful rifles. Most admit their current .300 or .338 Winchesters are just the ticket, but they gave up their old muskets reluctantly.

Few hunters have enough opportunities to see mountain goats taken to be able to objectively and knowledgeably compare the effectiveness of various cartridges. In earlier, less powerful cartridge years, I saw too many goats flounder and struggle mortally hit but not killed outright. That kind of thing was not necessary and patently undesirable.

A goat is not a small animal. His head is small, and he carries it low, but he is big bodied. A mature goat may weigh close to 300 pounds. A goat is, of course, steel muscled and can take a lot of punishment. A hunter should choose a powerful rifle. To plink at a mountain goat with a .25/06 is not sporting; it should be morally repugnant.

A goat can also be a deceptive target. His shaggy fur is four inches or so long, and careless aiming can merely wound and not anchor.

Because of the goat's proclivity for high lookouts, the goat hunter must be careful to make his first shot the only one needed. Unlike most wounded game that take the easiest way, a wounded goat will often seek safety by heading for the most inaccessible cliff he can find.

Hunter: Johnny Rhyshek, .270 Weatherby, Kodiak Island

Goat horns are difficult to judge. This excellent goat's horns are probably about nine inches long—which is a fine goat, but can you appreciate how hard an inch longer (a great goat) or an inch shorter (a so-so goat) would be to judge at two hundred yards?

Sometimes, a wounded mountain goat appears to commit suicide by stepping off into space. Whether such falls are deliberate or not I have been unable to determine. No one seems to know, but such acts are frequent. My own opinion is that wounded goats fall to their deaths by mistake and accident. Hurt, confused, balance lost, they err. To misstep in their country is to come down the too short, hard way.

A hunter should attempt to anchor his goat by killing or immobilizing it with his first shot. When practical, I have always aimed to hit the junction of spine and front shoulder. If made, the shot is a certain paralyzer. On a goat standing broadside, the aiming point is straight up the front leg to eye height. I refer to this shot as a "hump shot," as the aiming point is below the goat's prominent hump. On all game, the hump shot is a sure "right now" anchor.

Goats do not normally perch on the highest peak around. They prefer grassy, steep slanting meadows or small nooks on cliff sides that afford them safety, protection from wind, and escape routes both up and down. Therefore, it is often possible to get above goats.

Making a high approach and taking a goat from above is the ideal way. Goats generally face downhill and rely on ears and scent for warning from above.

A goat is believed to have natural vision about equal to a 2-1/2X scope. This may not be true. An animal living its life on familiar terrain becomes aware of anything out of the ordinary. Human shapes floundering about and smelling peculiar can be unusual.

Despite their arrogant appearance, goats tend toward the cautious and can walk away faster than a hunter can approach. Conversely, I have seen goats, apparently curious, come to a hunter. They look with interest, then glide away over rocks that we have difficulty negotiating at all.

The Rocky Mountain goat is not really a goat. He is related to the European Chamois and our plains Antelope. His feet are soft in their centers so that they sort of wrap around rock. I do not think their feet actually create suction, although it is often written that they do. Suction or not, a goat's feet cling in improbable places.

Goats do not roam widely and generally remain within their three or four miles of territory. During hunting seasons the big Billies are often found alone. The nannies and kids hang together in bands up to thirty or more.

Obviously, the mountain goat has little fear of height, but he does respect it. Goats move with a careful precision. They rarely run wildly or scurry. They are not remarkably swift, but with their stopping, starting, and direction changes due to terrain they can be difficult to hit.

A common shooting error is to hold the shot until a goat stops. Usually, the bullet then strikes where the goat had been. As with a bounding deer or dodging coyote, the hunter should figure his lead and get at it.

Unless a goat is unsuspecting, a sitting position is more practical than a prone for most goat shooting. The sitting position raises the shooter a little higher with less chance of a jutting rock obscuring the target. More important, sitting is steady yet allows the shooter to follow and adjust on a moving target far better than does prone.

Offhand shooting is always a last choice, and despite popular calendar artistry, taking shots standing is rarely necessary while goat hunting.

A view of a goat hunting camp along a creek. From there we climbed for the goats wearing packboards with sleeping bags attached. This camp is high enough that there are no trees. A trio of sticks was cut to keep our rifles off the ground. The rifles appear to be more or less flung at the tripod, but the important secret is to hang them muzzle down so that moisture will not leak into the actions. When viewing this photo, I am always reminded to note that the stripes on the canvas fly are not telephone pole shadows. What we are looking at are tape repairs. No poles in there.

A Pack for One Week Hunting Goats

- Air mattress*—for aging bones
- Backpack
- Binoculars
- Boot laces, extra
- Candle*
- Cup, tin*
- Gloves, cotton
- Handkerchief, Red
- Insect repellent
- Jacket, w/hood
- Knife & stone
- Matchbox, with matches
- Mosquito bar*
- Nylon line
- Pants, extra pair
- Pistol*
- Poncho w/hood
- Rifle
- Rifle ammo
- Salt (for trophy)
- Sleeping bag (hat on top)
- Sneakers*
- Socks, two pair
- Stuff bag w/mess kit
- Sweatshirt, sleeved
- Toilet articles*
- Toilet paper
- T-Shirt, extra
- Windbreaker, lightweight*
- FOOD, freeze dried

*=Optional

What a hunt! The year was 1956 (or maybe it was 1957—it gets hard to remember). We had been up Ernestine Creek about sixty miles north of Valdez hunting goats and bear. In this ancient photo you can see the tractor that got us in and the trailer that carried the gear that made the trip a luxurious safari—until it became time to hunt. Then, the cliffs were as steep and high as ever. My 300 Weatherby took the bear at less than one hundred yards (running) and the goat was dropped by Jerry's .270 Winchester at about 150 yards.

Chapter

19

The Great Bears

In Alaska, there are three kinds of bears. They are the brown, the polar, and the black.

Little will be said about polar bears. Those mighty ice bears have quite wisely been removed from the common hunting list. A group called The World Conservation Union claims there are only about 25,000 polar bears across the arctic. The count sounds about right, but I view most organizations using Conservation in their titles with suspicion. Too many such clubs are anti-hunting and are fanatically (and militantly) wed to the "catastrophic collapses" about to occur due to human-induced global warming. A recent pitch has been that loss of arctic ice will force the polar bears ashore and separate them from seals, their primary food source. Perhaps they are right, but even forty years ago, polar bears were too few and too endangered to be hunted except under rigidly controlled conditions.

We have never hunted polar bears in part because the hunting was rarely fair chase. Of course, the chase (the hunt) is never absolutely fair. We humans do not strip naked and attempt to do in animals with rocks and clubs. By fair chase, we mean that we pit our hunting and basic abilities against our quarry's natural skill, caution, and rage. Too much technology reduces fair chase. Adoption of breech-loading firearms began the most serious erosion of fair chase principles, flat trajectory cartridges further unbalanced the scale, and telescopic sights really wounded the fair chase concept. Yet, we believe in the idea of fair chase. We do not hunt from airplanes or helicopters, and we do not deliberately bait game. We do our best to actually hunt the animals, and unless a hunter goes for polar bear in a dog sled, there is zero fair chase involved.

The usual technique for polar bear hunting is to take two light aircraft from Nome or Kotzebue out over the ice and search until a satisfactory bear is found. The bruin is then herded by one aircraft while the second lands. The shooter dismounts, walks as far as necessary to get his shot, executes the bear, and loads the hide with head intact onto his plane while the other aircraft circles. The sport in that kind of hunting has escaped me. I do not do it.

Something will be said about black bears, but they are so common throughout our continental states and Canada that there is little significant or different in hunting them in Alaska.

The mighty brown bear will be our main bear topic.

The most desired North American hunting trophy is a brown bear. No other game animal so captures a hunter's imagination as does the great brown bear. The sheer size of a big brownie excites any serious trophy hunter, and the idea of a wall-to-wall bear rug is certainly appealing.

Hunter: Leo Neuls, 200 yards, .375 H&H Magnum, 10'2" Brownie

A big brown bear shot in open country.

However, it is the hint of danger attached to brown bear hunting that primarily intrigues big game hunters. On the North American continent only the polar and the brown bears can honestly be considered dangerous game. Only those big bears genuinely add the spice of personal risk to a hunt.

There are a few facts to be gotten in order before brown bears can be intelligently discussed.

1. A **brown bear** can be any color. Brown refers to the bear's species, not his coloration. There are black colored **brown bears** and yellow **brown bears**. Most **brown bears** are brown.

It is unfortunate if that all sounds a little like the old, *Blackberries are red when they are green,* but that is the way it is.

2. A **black bear** also refers to species and not to color. **Black bears** can be almost any color from blond, through cinnamon, to jet black.

Unfortunately, there is one further breakdown that demands clarification.

3. Trophy hunters divide **brown bears** into two types. Those types are the **brown bear** and the **grizzly bear**.

The differences between a **brown bear** and a **grizzly** are NOT biologically justifiable.

4. Trophy hunters have peremptorily ruled that any brown bear taken within 75 miles of the sea is a **brown bear**.

5. A **grizzly bear** has been determined to be any **brown bear** taken more than 75 miles from the sea.

The only justifications for the existence of the name grizzly are that it has been around a long time, and trophy hunters refuse to let the name go.

The brown bear lives close to the sea. Because he eats a lot of salmon, he grows immensely large. The brown is the biggest of the bears.

A brown bear killed on Kodiak Island is traditionally called a Kodiak bear, but it is simply another brown bear.

The so-called grizzly lives in the interior of Alaska and has a hardier existence. The grizzly does not eat as well. So, he does not grow as large as the brown bear.

Maintaining a grizzly class for trophy hunters allows the inland bear to be judged separately from his monstrous salmon-eating relative. A big brownie can square ten feet. A comparable grizzly will square eight feet.

Square means to measure a laid flat bear hide from front paw to front paw, then from nose tip to tail root. The two measurements are added together. Then divided by two. That result is the square of a bear.

Incidentally, a bear is never judged by his square. I have seen hides stretched until the bear's legs looked as long as a deer's, just to make an impressive square. Bears are judged by skull measurements which cannot be altered.

A big brownie can weigh 1200 pounds. A big grizzly will run about 800 pounds. Obviously, the two bears should not be grouped for trophy judging.

Hunter Ray Dillman, who has taken everything in the world that there is to take, with a nice brownie. As I look at Ray, hunting attire comes to mind. In Alaska, the real hunters seem to simply wear old clothing. When I see Dillman on the street today, he is dressed about the same. Only the new guys coming to Alaska have the latest "Hunter Garb" from the out-of-doors catalogs. The rest of us just go out wearing what we own.

Unfortunately, the 75 mile rule encourages cheating. It is not difficult to load a big brownie hide into a camper or onto an airplane strut and haul it quickly into the Alaskan heartland where the bear is instantly transformed into a record book grizzly. Do such things happen? Yep, and let me include a horrific example of trophy cheating.

Back in the fifties an army test pilot (helicopter) stationed at Fort Greely was transferred outside Alaska. I happened by as his household goods were being loaded. Out came some of the grandest trophy mounts I had ever seen. I was stunned. I thought I knew every successful hunter in the area, and this unrecognized pilot had game mounts and rugs that put ours to shame. As I watched, superb examples of every Alaskan animal native to that area emerged.

I had never realized the pilot hunted at all. Well, to make it short, he didn't. He and his crew chief flew the Tanana flats and the various mountains looking for animals. When they found what they wanted, the pilot herded the animal to a good spot, landed the copter, and shot the beast. They flew to Fairbanks and popped the trophy into a taxidermy shop. I got the whole story from the crew chief who thought it was all pretty funny.

Hunter Arthur Rausch with a huge grizzly taken in the big burn between the Richardson Highway and the Alaskan Highway near Big Delta. Art's rifle was always a Winchester Model 70 in 30/06.

Because of easy fakery, the grizzly class will always be a bit problematical. We might also recognize that it is not improbable that occasionally a world class brownie wanders upstream past the 75 mile limit and gets nailed as a Boone and Crockett-worthy grizzly bear.

Despite any such classification problems hunters claim, with some justification, that there is more than just a size difference between the brown and grizzly bears.

Fifty years ago there was a continuing battle between ranchers on Kodiak Island and the big brown bears. The ranchers held the bears in disdain and shot them as cattle killers. The ranchers shot them with about any rifle handy and showed little respect for the vaunted brownie charge or deliberate brownie vengeance. Familiarity can bred contempt, I guess.

Ninety-nine times out of one hundred a brown or grizzly will do its best to avoid humans. Often, a bear will flee when encountering one of us. Bears do not like us. To them, we smell bad. After a week or so in the bush I suppose any hunter is pretty strong, but that probability aside, the scent of a human is repugnant to most bears. Catching our scent, the big bears act much as we do when we get downwind of a skunk. There can be a snort of disgust, a shake of the head as though to clear nostrils of stench, and immediate departure toward clearer air.

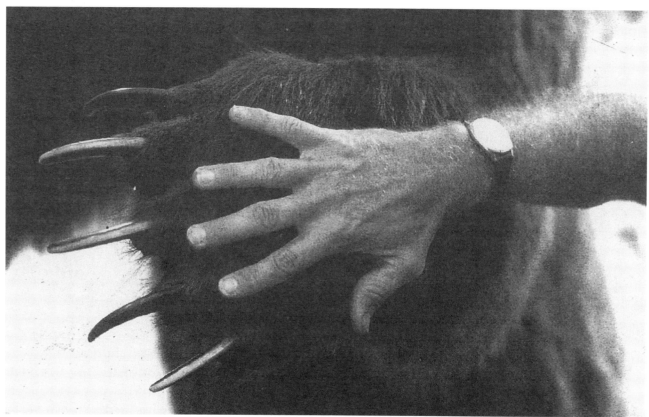

I took this big guy wrist wrestling—NOT! This was a large brown bear, and seeing the size of his claws gives one pause. (A Jonas Brothers mount)

Of all the bears, I like most to hunt the griz. No one should hold a grizzly less because he does not weigh quite as much as a brownie. An ancient Alaskan once told me that a grizzly was born with a stomach ulcer, and that accounted for its alleged ill-nature.

A doubtful conclusion, but grizzly bears can be unpredictable, and an angry grizzly is an unnerving vision of rampaging power.

My first close and personal experience with an irritable bear occurred while pike fishing in Quartz Lake. (This was long before they killed off the pike and put in trout and opened a road to the lake and let in cabins and just about ruined the place.)

A pair of good pike were laid out on a flat rock when a large, black colored grizzly stepped soundlessly from the brush and stood snuffling at the fish.

Some fifty feet away, I saw the bear appear almost magically beside our fish, and it took me a moment to accept what my eyes claimed they saw. Ordinary bear noise would have helped, but that seven hundred or more pound grizzly turned not a pebble.

By the time I got myself unwound, the bear had one pike dangling from his jaws and was turning to leave the scene. I encouraged him with an angry bellow that I expected would frighten him a little while I salvaged the remaining fish. Instead of tucking his hindquarters and moving off smartly, the big bruiser came to a halt, faced me, and snarled with all the hair on his neck seeming to stand straight out in an instant bouffant styling.

How a bear can snarl around a face full of fish I do not know, but he did, and my own furious rush in his direction jerked to a precipitous halt.

The bruin flipped the pike aside, lowered his head, and I saw muscles stand out as he came straight at me.

He came, and I went! Straight into the lake! Never has ice water felt so good. I plowed for deep water and distance as hard as I could go.

When I could no longer resist looking back I trod water, as best I could with a big pistol pulling me down and hunting boots getting heavier each instant. The grizzly was on the bank, crouched low, almost tigerish, with his hump high and neck still bouffant with hair on end.

Then the big bear roared, and a grizzly's roar will put an African lion to shame. I am sure that my own wet hair stood out as straight as the bear's.

A grizzly can swim, and I had no wish for that irritable brute to join me in the lake. So, I did no shouting back and disturbed the water as little as possible.

The bear calmed himself by pacing along the shore, and finally sat down like a great shaggy dog and watched me still valiantly treading water.

The scent of the fish must have overpowered the grizzly's anger, and he stalked majestically to the undisturbed pike, and getting a good grip on its middle he started toward the woods. At the timber edge he stopped and fixed me with a hard look. I said nothing, and he stepped from sight.

I crept ashore cautiously, shaking water from my .44 Magnum pistol. I did not shout belated insults after the bear. I knew who was boss around there, and it was not me.

Roy Lindsley's 1952 world record brown bear mount. The Karluk Lake, Kodiak Island bear was taken at thirty feet, three shots with a 30/06. The bear squared ten feet, four inches.

Big bear mounts are usually doctored a little by placing the trophy on a natural looking mound or on a platform—as is this one. Makes the trophy look even bigger. A convenient 10-foot height measurement is a . . .
Basketball basket

Assault by a brown or grizzly bear must be a horrendous experience. I have never been reached by a bear, but I have known a number of people who have been. I have never had an acquaintance killed by a bear. My friends survived but, in every case, they felt their survival was a result of their surrender to the bear and their successful attempt to appear dead.

A grizzly attack is usually a combination of savage, almost maniacal bites, coupled with fierce shakings of the victim in the bear's jaws, and a number of powerful cuffs in the form of left and right hooks with the front paws.

I have seen a grizzly in the throes of death bite through half-inch thick alders, so a grizzly bite can be a serious matter. Their front teeth and powerful jaws can apply a merciless hold while their saber-like claws rake and tear. The immense power of a grizzly can effortlessly rend a human body. An unarmed man cannot defend himself against a grizzly bear.

Every survivor of a grizzly attack is seriously scarred. While the mighty jaws create deep and dangerous puncture wounds and some chewing damage, it is usually the raking by claw that does the most injury.

The inherent strength of a grizzly bear's arm that allows casual brushing aside of huge boulders while searching for marmots, or that can propel an 800 pound bear into full speed quicker than a horse can start, or that can smash the skull or spine of a moose with a single swipe is capable of dismembering a human at will.

Hunter: Brent Ebling   .416 Lazzeroni Meteor

Happy hunter, contented guide, and a superb bear trophy. Note the iron-sighted rifle leaning against the brush. Wow.

A human survives a grizzly attack only if the animal loses interest. Survivors have regained consciousness to find themselves covered with leaves, twigs, and tundra apparently stored for future meals. Most survivors, however, "played dead" until the bear went away.

There is strong evidence, demonstrated in part by the high survival rate among bear victims, that a human is distasteful to a wild grizzly. Even humans killed by the bears are rarely eaten (by the bear). Grizzly bear attacks appear to be the result of bear rage rather than interest in something to eat. There are the usual exceptions where bears lay in wait for passersby, and in a very few cases bears have eaten some of a victim.

If attacked by a grizzly, an unarmed man's only hope is to lie on his stomach to avoid those great claws getting into his vitals and wait for the bear to go away. Attempting to fight off a grizzly is hopeless and will usually prolong the attack.

There is no reliable record of an unarmed man defeating or driving off a serious bear attack. There are a great many windy tales of such feats, but they do not withstand close examination.

A typical grizzly attack is initially ferocious, as though the bear had "blown his cool," gone berserk, or run amok. He is not fooling! He lunges, snarls, bites, and claws. He shakes his victim as a dog shakes a rag doll. He pummels his victim with one or more front paws.

An attacking bear's rage seems to cool quickly. Following his initial assault he is apt to sniff about his victim and poke at him with a paw. The slightest show of life by the victim can initiate another attack as furious as the first.

Assuming the human victim is unconscious or has the courage to lie "doggo," the bear is most likely to wander off. However, grizzlies are also known to withdraw and lie watching a victim for signs of life. At the first movement, the bear again attacks and again mauls the helpless human.

I once encountered a young survivor of a grizzly attack. The man had been hiking along a trail through dense willow growth. He saw a bear cub close by and attempted to withdraw by retracing his steps. The sow attacked and removed his backpack with a single swipe knocking the hiker to the ground.

The sow grizzly attacked the pack tearing it into bunting. Anger apparently dying, the sow sniffed at the prone man, and in parting took two swipes at him with a front paw. The first blow badly tore the side of the man's head. The second ripped his thigh to the bone.

In agony, but fearful of the bear's return, the hiker lay in a drizzling rain for three hours. He then dared to move and made his way to help. He nearly died from pneumonia.

The victim was one of those sensitive environmentalist souls who would never hunt and did not like those of us who did. Yet, he told me that during the mauling and the long hours of playing dead he would have traded all he had or hoped to have for a loaded .44 magnum pistol. To that I say, *"Amen!"*

Following is a story of grizzly bear attack that I included in a book titled, *The Sweet Taste*. This description encompasses both bear and victim's actions during such an incident.

. . . A quarter of a mile along we broke into a clearing. Twenty yards across it a yearling cub stood up to look at us. I stopped short and stuck out an arm to hold back the senator. Just in case, I began unslinging my rifle—looking hard for the sow that could have been close by, perhaps with another cub.

Gill walked right through my restraining arm, brushing it uncaringly aside. He headed for the yearling and said right out loud, "By God, Gene, there is one!"

One hell! The cub squeaked in fright, and mama came out of closer cover like a freight train.

The senator froze between me and the sow grizzly. I took a step to the side, jacking a round into the chamber of my .458. Then Gill hit the panic button. For all of his hunting, he had never faced a five hundred pound charging grizzly bear at forty feet, and he didn't this time.

The senator made an instant one hundred and eighty degree turn and started for camp. Concentrating on the bear, I leaned to let him go by. I saw his eyes like silver dollars just before he knocked me ass over teakettle. I held onto the rifle, but that was about all. Gill let out a fear-filled squall—probably because the collision slowed him down—and kept going.

The sow was in my face before I could begin to reorganize. She plowed into me the way Gill had, and I landed on my back—which isn't good with a bear on top of you.

I shoved my rifle stock into the bear's mouth, too scared to even gag on her foul breath. The sow shook the rifle out of my hands with a single twist of her head. A forepaw cuffed me in the ribs and about tore me half. In case the first one failed, another ripping kind of smash to the same area made certain. The sow turned away to savage my rifle—leaving me for later, probably. I went for my pistol.

Not one man in a hundred carries a pistol hunting, but I do. A .44 magnum is only about as powerful as a common 30/30. That is not enough for a grizzly, but it beats the hell out of trying judo. When the sow remembered me, I was grateful for the handgun.

I shot fast and as straight as I could. I saw a chunk blow out of the bear's head, but she still got to me. Her jaws closed on my leg, and she swung me into the air before a willow thicket stopped my progress. I put a second bullet somewhere into her, but she just got wilder, jerking me around and clawing with a front paw.

The sow had me, and a piece of my mind knew I was already hurt awful bad. I stuffed the pistol's muzzle against her head and double-actioned a third and a fourth Keith flat-nosed slug into her. This time I got nerves, and the bear's weight collapsed on me. She didn't even twitch, but I placed my last round carefully to make sure.

I couldn't get a decent breath, sweat blotted my vision, and my hands shook so badly I could hardly hold the pistol, but where was the cub—and there could be a pair. A yearling grizzly would weigh one hundred and fifty pounds. That much bear was more than I needed. I got the revolver open and thumbed the ejection rod. Fumbling extra cartridges into the chambers took forever, but I got it done and felt a lot safer with the Smith and Wesson reloaded.

Still no cubs. I pushed my unchewed leg against the sow's weight and got out from under. A lot of red meat showed through my ruined pant leg, but my ribs hurt too much to look further.

I heard Dave, the cook, coming, banging pans together and whooping like a Comanche. I hung on until he and the senator got there. Then I faded out and stayed gone for an hour or so.

The trip out was about what you would expect. Morphined up, I hadn't a care in the world, and Alaskan hospitals know what to do with bear maulings...

There is rarely any sense in seeking revenge on Alaskan bears that have attacked a human. While elimination of such "man-killers" might be advisable in a lower forty-eight National Park, there is no indication that brown or grizzly bears in Alaska develop a taste for humans or support aggressive anti-human attitudes.

The big bears seem above such petulant practices and appear to be merely enforcing their determination to be left alone, especially by the ill smelling creatures that move about on two legs.

In 1930, author John M. Holzworth wrote a beautiful book titled, *The Wild Grizzlies of Alaska*. Holzworth's lifelong love affair with grizzlies permitted him to record the life style of Alaskan grizzlies with an accuracy that has withstood a generation of high-tech research. Holtzworth's is an admirable study and essential reading for anyone striving to understand the wild bears of Alaska.

The observations recorded by Holzworth more than fifty years ago are accurate today. Nature, undisturbed by human fumblings is slow to change, and the bears live today much as they have since before man escaped his tree. I have found Holzworth's book useful in supporting my own grizzly observations, some of which follow.

Grizzlies are engaging creatures. I often experience an intense desire to approach a grizzly and let him know that I am his friend and that I admire and respect him immensely. I would like to hug a grizzly.

Such inclinations are controllable. Otherwise, I would not be available to write these words. Grizzlies are never your friends! The inexperienced can need that warning for grizzly bears can be handsome, humorous, lovable, and always interesting. But, friendly, they are not. They do not even socialize much among themselves, and if aroused they are ferocious fighters.

My old hunting companion with a pair of remembrances our taxidermists used to offer. Right hand holds a moose foot. The left a grizzly paw made into an ashtray

I remember this paw. The weather turned sultry, and it came from a bear that we could not get tanned or refrigerated quickly enough. The hide "slipped," and all we could save was a skull and two front paws.

Grizzlies are loners. Far from gregarious, bears meeting on a trail or at a fishing spot tend to ignore one another. They act like human strangers on a beach. Eye contact is avoided, and if close proximity occurs, recognition is in the form of a grunt or a bobbed head. Still strangers, each bear continues on its way.

A sow grizzly stays devoted to her cubs (usually two) for two years. During that period she does not mate and nurses the cubs for most of that time. A bear cub can gain an incredible five pounds of body weight in a single day.

The boar (old daddy bear) is gone, and if he showed up he would be absolutely unwelcome. In fact, if the sow did not protect her cubs, mature boars would probably maul and perhaps kill them. A sow with cubs will fight so savagely to protect her young that huge dominant boars turn away, apparently feeling the game not worthwhile.

A sow grizzly will feed away from her cubs. In open country she may stray as far as a quarter of a mile, but the slightest yip from an endangered cub will bring her back in an attack so sudden and savage that it would cause any animal to turn aside.

In time past, grizzly bears have been matched in pit battles with animals foreign to their experience. California grizzlies were matched against fighting bulls. Occasionally, a bull got a fatal horn into a bear, but he rarely got it out again; the bears killed the bulls.

No doubt, rhino, Cape buffalo, or elephant would be too much for any bear, but that short listing about covers animals capable of defeating a mature grizzly bear.

Grizzlies are not necessarily cruel, however. An example that comes to mind occurred in a dump outside Black Rapids where we used to park during the evening to watch bears and other animals.

The dump was a big one created by the nearby intermittently used, military installation. We often saw caribou, buffalo (bison), and black bear sharing the dump with an occasional moose. As long as we stayed within the vehicles, animals ignored us.

One evening the animals began casually departing one after another until the last to unobtrusively leave was a sow black bear with her two yearling cubs. A few moments later, silent as ghosts, a large yellow grizzly with two small cubs appeared. The sow began scrounging in cans while the small cubs explored close to hand.

One of the yearling blacks appeared at the dump edge and, unable to resist the good smells, he slipped into the dump and began sampling goodies.

The mother grizzly appeared not to notice—until the black cub's head was deep in a can. Then, she crossed the dump with lightning-like speed and fetched the black cub a stiff swat on its chubby behind. The cub departed just as hard as it could run, uninjured, but sternly warned. Obviously, the big grizzly could have eliminated the black cub, but she chose just the correct amount of disciplining to teach without hurting.

Unfortunately, there is an awful amount of silly bear information floating around. The foolish stuff clouds facts, and most people do not genuinely understand a bear's merits and failings. Study of any decent volume about bears would destroy many of the bear myths that have been developed by scores of irresponsible writers seeking to sell their work. But few within the general populace will ever read that kind of book.

Mama, Papa, and Baby Bear with their bowls of porridge often initiate a child's silly bear information. Joel Chandler Harris, with his enjoyable but equally ludicrous "Brar Bear" perpetuates the folly of endowing bears with human attributes. Bears do not wear pants, cohabitate with foxes, or speak English with a folksy, southern accent.

While such tales appear harmless—and are among children—they encourage delusions within our supposedly mature societies that bears should not be hunted because they too are just folks. Obviously, the same poor reasoning applies to the "Bambi Set" that sees deer as un-huntable and all of the overgrazing or upset natural balance arguments as only poor excuses to go out and slaughter the cuddly bears and darling little deer.

The other side of the coin is equally distressing. Countless stories of ferocious bear attacks, hacked out by imaginative writers have so convinced people that bears of any species are mean devils that mere passage of an old, black honey bear causes consternation and fear among observers.

Too many artists have portrayed attacks on trappers and hunters by huge bears that fight on their hind legs in modified John L. Sullivan stances. Created from whole cloth, the artists' imaginings are inaccurate and misleading.

Fear of the great grizzly is not new, of course. Primitive people feared the bears. Armed only with simple weapons, primitive hunters had little chance against such adversaries.

American Indians of many tribes thought of the bear as a distant relative and called him uncle or cousin, but until fairly recently science has understood little about grizzlies. During the last sixty years or so scholars and researchers have looked deeper. Now they know a lot more.

Perhaps, not surprisingly, old and seasoned hunters already recognized much of what the scientists have cataloged and labeled, but for every fact the hunters thought they knew, a dozen fallacies also existed. Scientific method has been able to interest the people of our lands in the bears where hunters could not. Science has brushed aside many of the silly bear fables and is helping everyone to understand the grizzly.

It might be pointed out here that the National Park Service's warnings to hikers to beware of bears, and their efforts to discourage hiking within grizzly country, is almost as much for the bears' benefit as it is for the hikers'. Grizzlies and people do not mix well, and if the bears are to exist, they must be granted solitude.

Hunter: Jerry Watson, dropped at 6 paces, .375 H&H Magnum, Alaska Peninsula
A mighty brown bear dropped just free of the water. Can you imagine attempting to haul this large an animal out of a pond for gutting and skinning?

Here are a few details that will probably broaden most hunters' grizzly bear knowledge. Apply this information to the brown bear as well.

Grizzlies roam mostly at night. During daylight, they sleep and forage. During the heat of a day a grizzly may be found resting atop or alongside a recent kill. Or, they may doze in the shade of deep woods.

It is accidentally stumbling across and inadvertently startling a grizzly (especially a sow with cubs) that causes most bear attacks.

A grizzly ranges over some twenty square miles. The old guide gave me that figure back in 1957. Scientific studies show it to be correct.

Female grizzlies adopt stray young.

Sows are tender and loving toward their cubs.

Cubs typically gain 100 pounds a year.

Grizzlies do not genuinely hibernate. They do den up during cold weather, but the grizzly may come out if there is a warm spell. A den is usually dug under a bank. It is lined with moss and needles.

A grizzly has great self-respect which he defends.

In his book, *The Wild Grizzlies of Alaska,* John Holzworth lists nineteen grizzly subspecies.

Bears fresh out of winter sleep are ravenously hungry. They scratch for the roots of the snow lily and eat early grasses that grow below melting snow. They search snow banks for animals that died during winter and were preserved by the cold. The hungry grizzly smashes open logs to eat ants and grubs. He chases marmots fiercely.

The first known literary reference to the grizzly in America is recorded in *The Present State of Hudson Bays,* by Edward Umfreyville in 1790.

In 1795, Sir Alexander MacKenzie, the explorer reported nine inch tracks on the banks of the Peace River and commented that the Indians feared the great bear.

During 1805–1806, Lewis and Clark on their expedition to the Pacific Ocean encountered numerous grizzly bears and reported many actions by the bears as well as the taking of grizzlies by members of their party.

Different opinions on the meaning of grizzly as used in regard to bears are recorded. Some believe the word to come from "grizzle," which is an adaptation of the French word "grisel," and before that from the German "gris," meaning hoary or gray in color. Others, primarily the naturalist George Orr, who provided the scientific designation, seem to prefer the word derivation from the old English "grisan," which meant to shudder in terror or horror. He named the grizzly "Ursus Horriblis."

Brackenridge, who wrote at length about grizzly bears, alleged that he used the journals of Lewis and Clark as his source. He seemed to have originated the belief that the grizzly was more fierce than a Bengal tiger or African lion and, as the enemy of man, actually thirsted for human blood. Such statements are not supported by the journals; although there were encounters with grizzlies, the few bear charges were provoked and humans won the encounters.

When we talk about an eight hundred pound bear, many find it difficult to visualize just how large that is. I once measured a bear of about (estimated) eight hundred pounds and attempted to reduce the bear's size to some generalities that might mean something to those who do not see grizzlies very often.

For example, I found that my hands stretched to their fullest would just barely reach around the bear's wrist. I found that measurement highly impressive.

Next, I measured the bear at the bicep. Those are some of the powerful muscles that toss one hundred pound boulders about like beanbags when the bear is digging out marmots. The bear's arm measured the same as my waist. That is a lot of arm! The same bear's front claws were about as long as my fingers.

The print of a big grizzly left in the sand. This print measured 12 1/2 inches long. The arrow points to the claw marks. A grizzly's claws are far out in front of his pad marks. A black bear's claws are very close to the pad.

The head measured ten inches between its ears.

Yet, the cleaned skull was only seven inches wide. The grizzly's long incisor teeth measured an inch and a half long. I put my arm inside the bear's mouth, and it fit quite easily. That bear's rear foot measured just shy of thirteen inches long. His front paw was six and one half inches wide.

That bear squared eight feet.

A grizzly has surprisingly small bones. A number of times I have returned to the scene of a grizzly kill and examined the bones left after the wolves, coyotes, and wolverines had finished cleaning them. The bone pile was always so small that I stopped to look closely. It seemed strange that such small bones could support such a large body.

The author with his shortened 12 gauge shotgun. His bear-in-the-brush gun.

Bear color is startling. Although I have never seen a spotted grizzly, such a bear would not surprise me. While most grizzlies are some shade of brown, Jarvis Creek bears are often yellow. Grizzlies in the McKinley area are often a grizzled gray that fits the "grizzly" description, and a bleached blonde coloration is regularly found on the north slope of the Brooks Range.

I have mistaken small grizzlies for large black bears, especially where dark brown fur is common. Of course, a big, mature grizzly bear is unmistakable, but that it because of his shape, not his coloration.

Bear populations vary dramatically across Alaska, and that is of direct interest to the grizzly hunter. An aerial survey of the North Slope sighted an average of only two bears per square mile. That is in North Slope bear country and does not include improbable terrain. The opposite extreme disclosed 129 brown bears within one square mile along the Gulf of Alaska.

If I were reincarnated and had a choice, I might return to earth as a brown or grizzly bear. I would enjoy the gourmandizing in blueberry patches, munching on salmon, and pulling down an occasional animal. The long winter's sleep would be pleasant with bear dreams, and having no natural enemies, there would be few tensions or worries.

I think I might choose to live in Denali Park where the rangers would watch but not interfere. Life would be good, with one exception. Old age in the animal kingdom is never pleasant, and death is usually a time of pain and misery. But, being a bear, I would not know the fate in store for me, and so I would not brood about it. Ah, that we humans could be so fortunate.

If fate decreed that my bear's mind did know the severity and agony of death in the wild, rather than succumb to slow starvation or the wolf pack, I might, when the going got too tough, just cross the park boundaries, growl at a hunter, and have my hide live a generation more on a den wall or floor.

Or, I might return as a mountain goat...but that chapter has already been done.

Black bears can be read about in a thousand journals. There is little to add except to take notice of a truly interesting variation that occurs in Alaska.

We have mentioned that black bears appear in many colors. Cinnamon is seen, and brown in various shades is commonly encountered.

However, in Alaska there is a coloration called **Blue Glacier** that is fascinating.

There used to be serious disagreement as to the glacier bear's proper species. Some thought him a grizzly offshoot, and others believed he was a separate species altogether. Now, authorities have pretty well lined up behind the decision that the Blue Glacier Bear is a color variation of the black bear.

When a black bear changes color enough to become a glacier bear is still shrouded in disagreement. I have seen bears identified as glacier bears that I felt did not approach the proper coloration.

A classic glacier bear has an azure blue fur color. Whether he gets that way through heredity or from his environment is still argued. Having watched a blue sow with a pair of matching blue cubs poking within glacial moraine in the Chugak Mountains leaves me a believer in hereditary coloring. But, such observations hardly provide proof.

The blue glacier bear is perhaps the most rare of bear trophies. Hunters have searched lifetimes without encountering a blue bear. This hunter feels fortunate to have observed a number of the rare bears at length. I have never taken one.

Chapter
20

Grizzly Hunting

"If you wish to harvest a grizzly, go sheep hunting." That is a popular old saying in Alaska, and there is truth to it. Grizzlies do roam the sheep country, and with all the glassing and spotting a hunter does on sheep, he may sight a grizzly.

The only grizzly I ever wounded and lost was shot while hunting Dall rams in the 1950s. My hunting partner and I had run into foul weather while hunting in the Granite Mountains above the Johnson River. We bedded down on a rocky flat spot in a drizzling rain and encroaching fog. We heard rocks rolling and looked back the way we had come to see a really fine grizzly following our path across a long rock slide.

The weather was so poor, and my sleeping bag was so snuggly warm that I almost hated to consider taking the bear. We were primarily after sheep, but the grizzly was really prime. So, what could a young and hungry hunter do? I just rolled over in the sleeping bag, got a really good rest among the rocks and bag, and placed the crosshairs on the bear. When he stopped and sort of turned sideward at about two hundred yards, I thought the conditions perfect. I held right on the top of his right shoulder blade and drove the bullet at the joint of his spine and shoulder. The position was granite steady, and a hunter knows when he has made a good shot. The bear collapsed with a squall and tumbled into a tiny hollow and out of my sight. I held on the spot for a few moments just in case, but there was no movement.

With Jerry watching the hollow, I got my boots on, and we clambered over the slide to skin out the bear. Only, there was no bear!

To say that we were astounded would be gross understatement. There was blood and some hair with a lot of dry stones turned over, but no big lump of a bruin. Suddenly, things got really tight, and we became intense about what we were doing.

The turned-over stones led off from the hollow through a low swale that I could not see from my shooting place. We moved very carefully because there were enough large boulders around to allow an ambush. Our only way to track the bear was to follow the dry stones, which would not be dry very long in the rainy drizzle. We hustled along, but the trail led away and out of sight. To make it short, we hunted for that bear for three hours. It then became too dark. We were not sure how vengeful that grizzly might be, so we sat up all night, back to back.

Of course, we discussed why the shot had gone wrong, and I denied the possibility of having pulled off the target. The bear's squall bothered me, and I should have immediately realized that an animal with a shattered spine would be unable to make any cries. So, what had happened? We favored a bad bullet, but doubts lingered because we hand loaded and prided ourselves on good ammunition. With first light we began searching again, but we never saw any more of that big bear.

For that hunt I had a new gun. It was the latest thing, a lever action Winchester model 88 in .308 caliber. I had zeroed the rifle with great care and had taken a couple of caribou with it. There had been no falls or other abuse, and the gun should have held its zero. We tried it out anyway. At 200 yards the rifle had moved its zero four feet to the right and down a foot. I probably hit that grizzly in the hind leg!

Examining the rifle we could see that the rain had gotten to the walnut stock and warped it hard to one side. Because the barrel was secured to the stock at the forearm, there was no way to free float the barrel. I put the rifle away and never used it again.

In retrospect, I never had good luck with that model rifle, anyway. Every model 88 I ever examined had a creepy trigger, and who needs that? When I carried the 88 on my packboard, the magazine release used to hit a packing ring and drop out. I ended up taping the magazine in and loading from the top like a bolt-action. I could never recommend the 88 to anyone. I am glad Winchester stopped making it.

Then there was the .308 Winchester cartridge. I have never preferred the .308 for anything. When the military dropped the 30/06 and picked up the .308 (7.62, NATO) they lost a couple of hundred feet per second of muzzle velocity. (See the following chart.) The military sacrificed velocity for the .308's lesser shipping volume, and they probably saved a million tons over the various wars, but for a hunter? The swap was ridiculous with less wallop down range.

So, what was I, a committed high velocity and big bore advocate, doing in the mountains with a pipsqueak like the Winchester .308 cartridge? My only explanation is that I was a gun buff and always wished to try out something new. Compare the .308 with the better 30/06 (which most can agree is marginal in Alaska) and the 300 Weatherby or the .338 Winchester—that I should have been carrying.

Cartridge	Bullet Weight	Velocity 200 yards	**KO 200**
.308	180	2259	**17.8**
30/06	180	2500	**19.8**
300 Wthrby	180	2620	**20.7**
.338	200	2500	**21.1**

Anyone who decides that he wants a grizzly and can then go out and locate one (without spotting from the air) is a mighty fine hunter. A coastal hunter may do that with some regularity when hunting brown bear down along the panhandle, but the grizzly is not found that easily. Grizzly locating can be long and frustrating.

To hunt a grizzly, you should at least know that a bear has been about. To simply choose a piece of terrain and start hunting will not be rewarding. If hunters have taken other game in an area, a grizzly is likely to move in and store the leavings for his own use. The big bears pull grass and brush over their kills and sometimes lie on top of them guarding until they are hungry.

More likely, a grizzly will bed down close by and come to his cache for a meal. So, old kills are good places to watch. Hunting in that manner is legal, but the result is little different from using bait—which is illegal in Alaska.

Grizzlies fish when salmon are running, but the fish are not around most of the time. If a hunter knows of a bear fishing place, however, he can wait until one he likes arrives.

Perhaps I should mention now that few bears are passed once they are seen by hunters. It is an unusual grizzly bear hunter who will refuse a shot on a decent bear in the hope of getting a bigger one later on. While this is not as true of brownie hunters along the coasts who see many bear, the grizzly hunter sees far fewer animals and finds it difficult to turn away from any legal trophy.

A good many grizzlies are taken by hunters primarily after other game. Where hunting seasons overlap, hunters glassing other game sight bear and go after them. The open sheep country is especially good for that. A bear working on marmots can be seen from a long way, and the bear is often so preoccupied that he can be readily approached.

Take a bear from downwind. A bear's eyes are poor, but his nose is sharp. Get upwind and the odds are great that he will scent you. Look him over carefully. A rubbed trophy is not much, and as most hunters see few bears, they all look big until given calm and objective scrutiny. Few hunters want an oversize cub for their wall.

When you do shoot, try to break major bones. Your intent should be to kill the bear if possible, but anchor him for sure. The author's favored shot is the juncture of the front shoulder and spine.

This is a bear trail. Because it is heavily used it has become one track. Often seen are bear trails with two adjoining parallel paths (made by left and right legs) with undisturbed growth between them.

Hit there and your bear will be down and paralyzed. If the hunter shoots low he will still get a shoulder and, with a proper gun, deep and killing penetration. If his bullet strays too far he may hit spine or upper lungs or heart. If he is too high, the bullet will not seriously injure the animal. A hit too far forward has a good chance of breaking the bear's neck.

At least as important as the good places to hit are the good places to avoid. The worst place to hit a bear is in the paunch. That is true with any big game animal. The wound is a slow killer amid much pain and suffering. The hump shot keeps your bullets about as far from the paunch as any aiming point can.

Most hunters seem to choose a heart/lung shot for all game. Most hunting writers recommend that shot. My experience is that too often the bullet strikes too far back—*gut hit. An absolute bummer!*

Some professional hunters recommend what they call "a high/heart shot." The idea is to strike the lower shoulder blade, and in so doing rake the lungs and the top of the heart. By breaking the shoulder, the shot drops the animal in place, and that is always desirable. If anyone is considering the above shot, for heaven's sake have a powerhouse of a rifle—not your run of the mine 30/06 and the like. Heavy bones or thick muscle can reduce bullet effectiveness and allow a solidly hit animal to walk away.

Grizzly or brown bear spoor. Spoor? That is what professional African hunters call it. Bears gulp, much as dogs do, and indigestible debris is swallowed along with the edible stuff. During blueberry season, bear manure is mostly undigested trash sticks and leaves that one would expect to pierce intestines—but somehow do not.

Never shoot at a bear over two hundred and fifty yards away. It takes wallop to keep a bear down. Bullets have lost a lot of their initial steam beyond 250 yards, and a grizzly that gets up and runs at that range can be difficult to hit, particularly as the shooting distance lengthens.

A heavy caliber is needed for a bear in the brush. The author has two preferences. My "bear in brush" favorite is my old Ithaca 12 gauge shotgun with its barrel cut short (shown earlier). At close range I use the Ithaca loaded with Brenneke rifled slugs, which expand tremendously and are loaded hotter than most domestic shells. With the Ithaca, I can pump four or five heavy slugs into a bear well before I could fire a second round from a bolt-action rifle. With the Ithaca, one simply holds the trigger back following the first shot and operates the pump. Each time the slide goes forward, the gun fires. A rifled slug in 12 gauge has tremendous impact at close range, far more than a rifle of less than huge caliber.

When shooting is a matter of a few feet it is important to keep the bear down. Fire hosing rifled slugs into the bear, and into the right spot, of course, is hard to beat.

Once, along Banner Creek, I had the less than enjoyable duty of going in after a bear wounded by another hunter for whom I felt responsible.

I did not see the grizzly until it was almost under my feet. We had given him nearly a half hour to stiffen up from the earlier wound, but how far that bear might have been able to move I never discovered. At the first glimpse, I turned the Ithaca on him and emptied it into his right front shoulder. The bear seemed almost battered back by the five heavy slugs driving into him at about ten-foot range. He never wiggled after that.

My other choice for brush shooting is the .458 Winchester Magnum. That cartridge hits with such terrible power that a single bullet, reasonably placed, ends the battle instantly. The .458 is a marvelous cartridge, and I highly recommend it.

When you get a grizzly down, never wait to see if it is going to get up again. Keep shooting him. With a little bit of reservation, my companions and I have adopted this system for all Alaskan game. We do not sit around bragging about one shot kills. We make certain for both our own and the game's sake that the animal is down and dead. That means following shots until you are certain.

It is important to recognize that a bear is very easy to knock down. They seem to fall over at any excuse. I suspect a bear does not have the world's best balance. They surely roll around a lot. The problem is that they also often get up again.

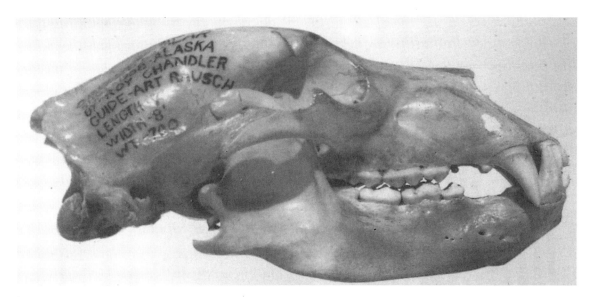

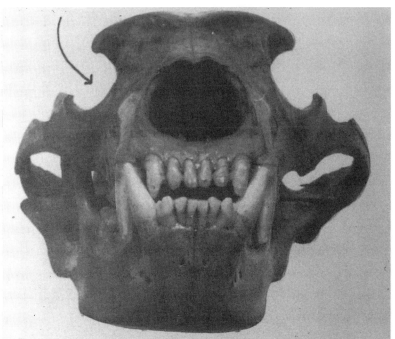

Two views of a grizzly or brown bear skull. In profile (top photo), the bear's nose hole is just above the front teeth. Nose on (lower photo), the nose hole appears as a black cavern just above the teeth. The bear's brain lies behind the writing on the profile view. Note that if a bear is charging, his head may be in the lower photo position with his nose pointing directly at you. A bullet driven straight into the nose will be guided by the skull cavities directly into the brain. Instant death! But, a shot striking a hair high can glance from the sloping skull. Bears find that irritating.

A bear's eyes are outside his skull and are inside the holes shown by the arrow. Do not shoot a bear in the eye. You could anger him. You will not kill him. In this position, the best shot is straight in the nose. Unless the bear's nose is down, avoid that sloping skull.

Remember that at point-blank range, your bullet will be traveling an inch or so below your crosshair and will not be dead on until the bullet has traveled about twenty-five yards. Allow for that in your aiming.

A hunter can be fooled into thinking the hunt is over because his bear falls. Approaching the fallen animal he is astounded to see it up and running. Usually, the direction is away, but not always. It is very wise to put following shots into a grizzly bear.

A bear has relatively small vitals. For its weight, its bones are small. Its heart and lungs are also small. Much of a bear's apparent size is in its legs. Legs are not vital areas and are not legitimate aiming points. A bear's fur is long and thick and makes its body appear much deeper that it really is. A shot a bit close to any "edge" of a bear is likely to merely cut through long hair and a bit of skin. A hunter must never aim for the "mass" of a bear. He must place his shot with precision just where he wants it.

Defense against bear attack is a consideration present in any bear hunt. Improbable as it may be, anyone hunting bear should not ignore the possibility of a charge. These are points to remember:

First, a grizzly may false charge just like an elephant will. He will come smashing, roaring, and quivering. His hair will stand out on his head and neck. His little eyes will glare, and he will shudder all over as he comes to a stop, probably too close for comfort.

Such a false charge is fearsome. I have experienced them on a number of occasions. I know of no way to tell a false charge from a real charge except by holding fire until the last possible instant. Waiting that long can leave a hunter in cold sweat, believe me. However, if a hunter does not wish to take the bear, and if he is a cool shot with a proper rifle, it can be done.

A standing bear is never attacking. A bear charges on all four legs. If attacked by dogs, or fighting another bear, a grizzly often gets up on its hind legs. It does this to protect its hind quarters from the dogs (or wolves). In the case of another bear, they let it all hang out and battle ferociously in every conceivable position. Incidentally, bears usually break off the fight with each other before either is seriously injured. A bear standing on two legs is just looking around. It can see further by being higher, that's all.

An unwounded grizzly whose nose is toward the ground and whose head is swinging left to right as it runs is <u>probably</u> NOT charging. It is just running away no matter what direction it is headed.

If a bear drives at you on all fours with its nose pointing straight at you, it may be charging. That is the way a grizzly attacks. (Of course, it may also simply be departing post-haste.)

A shot at a charging grizzly should go straight in the bear's nose. We have just shown photos of a bear's skull that demonstrate clearly why this is so. In one photo the skull is positioned "nose on," the way a hunter would see it. A bullet directly into the nose cavity is guided by the skull itself, straight into the bear's brain. The profile shows the slanting skull and why a bullet can ricochet without putting a bear down.

If the hunter is not that certain a shot and doubts that he can hit the bear dead on the nose, he must shoot into the charging bear's breast. If the hunter has a powerful rifle that will shoot through a bear side to side, his frontal shot will deliver immense impact, but if he is shooting with a pipsqueak cartridge . . . ? He had better put in his follow up bullets fast!

The Marlin lever action with the new Garrett cartridges in .45/70 may be top notch against a charging bear. A fast handling rifle that is hard hitting with fast follow up shots . . . sounds pretty good, although I have not tried it.

A little bit more should be said about proper rifle actions for use on dangerous animals—like the great bears. I choose to mention one facet of rifle selection that is being ignored by most Americans but is strongly advised in Africa where more than a few animal species are truly dangerous.

Here, in Alaska, we have only the great bears to worry about, but the rifle feature I am about to mention should be recommended here as well. No one wants to lose an animal because of an avoidable malfunction, and no one wishes to be overrun by a disagreeable bear.

A bolt-action, dangerous game rifle should have controlled feed!

What that means is, that when the bolt pushes a cartridge into the chamber of a rifle, the cartridge rim is gripped at the extraction groove throughout the process. If for any reason the bolt is not fully closed or the cartridge is partly withdrawn and then re-pushed, the case is held securely and moves with the bolt until the empty is ejected following the shot.

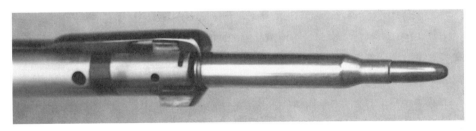

This is *control feed*. The long, strap-like extractor grips the extraction groove at the cartridge head and holds it securely throughout feeding, firing, and removal. The cartridge will not fall out or get out of line if stressed while loading, and it is not possible to double feed and have two cartridges wedged into the mouth of the chamber—as can happen with *push feed*.

The other type of bolt-action is called a **push feed**. That means that when the bolt pushes the cartridge forward from the magazine, the cartridge is guided toward and into the chamber, but is not held securely. The cartridge simply rests on the follower. Not until the cartridge is being seated in the chamber, does the extractor snap over the rim and grip the case ready for extraction and ejection.

"Ho hum," you might say.

Suppose, with your **push feed** rifle, you are momentarily distracted while feeding a new round, and you recycle the action. You could stumble, or suppose that you are rolling wildly to avoid being run over by a charge—won't happen? Maybe or maybe not.

What can happen is that the partly chambered round you were pushing is jammed part way into the chamber by the nose of the next bullet as you recycle the bolt. Your rifle is then out of action and may take a ramrod to clear. Or, your round can simply fall out of the rifle, and you close your bolt on an empty chamber.

Never encountered it? We have, hundreds of times, and by some of the world's best shooters. Military and law enforcement sniper rifles are almost always Remington push feed actions. Should they be? No, but that is another discussion.

We teach those super-fighters at various training centers including the justly famous Blackwater Center in North Carolina. Even there, among those master shooters, we observe and encounter push feed malfunctions. If you have a push feed rifle, or are not sure which type of action you have, partly feed a round into your chamber, then withdraw the bolt and see if the cartridge comes with it. If it does not, you have a push feed. Push the bolt forward again. You may get a jam with a push feed. Another simple test is to watch your cartridge being fed into the chamber from the magazine. When it is partly in, grab the cartridge and see if it is held in place. With **controlled feed,** the extractor will tightly grip the cartridge. With a push feed you will remove the cartridge.

Which rifles have controlled feed is a legitimate question. Most Mauser actions—old or new, all Springfield 1903 actions, all Enfield 1917 actions, all pre-1964 Winchesters and their latest models have controlled feed as do many others—such as Ruger, Dakota Arms, and Kimber (manufacturers I mention because I particularly like their products).

Finally, imagine yourself facing a charge and in your nervousness fumbling and repeat chambering a cartridge. Believe me, having **controlled feed** will seem important, and it can be life saving.

I have neglected writing enough about the mighty brown bears, particularly those on Kodiak Island. Kodiak bears are hunted quite differently than mountain grizzlies. Kodiak Island is brushy, and even average-range shots are rare. Most bears taken on Kodiak are shot at less than fifty yards. A big, heavy bullet is strongly recommended! Cartridges that are **best** for grizzlies are also right for brown bears.

Kodiak hunters mostly move around in boats, and that includes those hunting on lakes. When ashore, it is difficult to see bears, and few hunters have mastered quiet approaches, which can turn out to be very dangerous if the bear spots you first. A favored technique is to float around glassing mountainsides as you pass them. If a good bear is sighted, the party goes ashore and stalks the animal. Even after seeing a brownie from your boat, a bear can be extremely hard to locate once you are ashore. There is also a strong possibility of running onto a bear that you do not want before you reach your chosen trophy. At point-blank range that can prove interesting.

A guide is required for a non-resident hunter going after Kodak bear, and even a resident hunter who is not familiar with the island would profit from having an experienced local guide showing the way. Most bears look huge to the inexperienced eye, and a good guide will not only keep you safe and locate animals, he will hold you back from shooting something you will later discover is too small.

If the grizzly's head is somewhere inside that fur pile, this is a heavy load. If the head is boned out, the weight is a little better. The hunter is using an ancient US Army packboard, and for carrying heavy and awkward loads, they were the best—perhaps they still are. The author's only complaint about these boards (with a large canvas sack attached) was that they do not have an upright over which to hook a rifle sling. Within the hour, this hunter will be sick of gripping his rifle and would pay a handsome sum to be able to hang it from the pack.

Patience is not a novice bear hunter's strongest attribute, and even the experienced can choke more than a little when a brownie is the target. Patience to wait for just the right animal and just the right shot often make the hunt.

Yes, that is a grizzly hide lashed to the rear of the tractor. Hey, after the boredom of taking a huge bear one always pauses to shoot a few birds for the pot.

Dall Sheep

Chapter
21

Dall Sheep

The greatest thrill of my Alaskan hunting was the taking of my first Dall ram. For a hunter who prefers goat hunting and who has killed a lot of bear, moose, and caribou that is a powerful statement. But, I can still remember the thrill of that hunt. This is how it went.

Jerry and I had camped along Morning Star Creek in the Granite Mountains and with the early dawn climbed the steep ridge that forms one side of the canyon. The climbing was steady, and the packs dragged heavily on our shoulders. We were bound for three or four continuous days of hunting, planning to hike into July Creek and perhaps scout the Gerstle River. That meant extra rations and decent sleeping gear.

The morning started bitterly cold but warmed swiftly until we were hiking in short sleeved sweat shirts. About noon we saw a sheep far ahead and planned to swing over and take a look. It seemed a bit soon to see rams, but who could be sure about Dall sheep?

We reached a good lookout perhaps seven hundred yards from the lone sheep and set up our spotting scope. A quick look showed us a really fine ram, and closer examination disclosed his buddy dozing close by.

Both were good rams, but it was a little far to tell just how good. A ram can move its head a little up or down and appear to change from an almost full curl into a curl and a quarter. We decided it was worth turning aside to find out exactly what we were looking at.

I can remember the hope mixing with a certain hesitation because our hunt could be so swiftly over. But, we made our way over the slides until we found another good glassing spot perhaps four hundred yards from our quarry.

This look was very cautious because we were already within a range that many hunters consider close enough. Sheep have fine eyesight, and a human head jutting above a ridge or rock could not be expected to go unnoticed.

This second look ended our hesitation. Both sheep were beauties. One was a big old ram with thick horns that were not broomed away. His friend had longer, beautifully pointed but thinner horns. Both were full curl rams. Back in those days, a three quarter curl ram was legal, but even then, everyone wanted full curl rams. We decided to go after them.

A handsome pair of full curl Dall rams

We surveyed the ground between them and us. A route through a small feeder stream looked as if it would bring us close to the drowsing sheep. We retreated behind an intervening ridge and made our way downhill and up a small feeder stream that again moved us uphill and much closer to the sheep. The rushing water of the mountain run should help mask our approach, and scent was most likely to travel up or down the stream, not to the side and toward the rams. We grounded our packs where the climb steepened, and taking only rifles, we began an approach up the narrowing streambed.

The mountains were high enough to make our lungs pull, and we rested a little now and then so that we would get into shooting positions in good physical shape.

A waterfall blocked our way, and Jerry stood solid while I climbed onto his shoulders and slid both rifles above the falls. Then, I got a good toe and hand hold, and Jerry used me for a ladder. We rested again, now quite close to the sheep.

Carefully, and very slowly we crept to the lip of the stream and saw the sheep still lying down about two hundred yards distant. The sheep on my side lay with his head down between his front feet—just like a dog might. My only shot would be directly between his horns and into his spine. Even the slightest error could bounce my bullet off a heavy horn, and the ram would be off and running.

Jerry's shot was less critical, and he agreed to let me get my bullet underway before he touched trigger. If my sheep moved his head even a little, I could be out of luck.

I had a .270 Winchester in model 70 on this hunt. Jerry was using the same. We were both zeroed two inches high at 200 yards, and things looked really good.

We sprawled among the boulders until we were both ready. With my Balvar 8 scope on 4X, I laid the B & L tapered crosshairs just above the junction of the ram's horns and squeezed as carefully as I ever have. The recoil rocked me a little, but I felt very good about the shot. I tried to again find the ram in my sights, but he had slumped out of view.

Jerry's rifle went off in my ear, and I looked up in time to see his ram catch its stride as a bullet struck him. Jerry fired again, and the ram once more staggered a little. Still, he ran away down the mountain.

As the range lengthened, rocks rose between the sheep and Jerry. He rose to his feet and sent one final shot after the ram. Down went the sheep as if struck by lightning.

I took time to slap Jerry's back; his last shot had been long and a tough one. Then, I became concerned with my own sheep. Suppose he had been only stunned and had leaped up and run off while I was enjoying

Jerry's efforts? I hastened across the broken rock and came rather suddenly on the great ram. Even sprawled in death his presence took my breath away. All of my hunting life I had wanted to take a full curl Dall ram. My heart pounded and flooded with gratification. I was content to slump against a rock and just look.

The ram was truly heavy in the horn. The tops of his horns were cracked and broken from fighting. He had a huge lump of gristle in the middle of his nose where he had caught a hard butt. He reminded me of an old prizefighter, scarred and aging, but still tough and hard. I sat a long time admiring that ram. He was all I had ever hoped, and in a way, the culmination of my dream of becoming a serious Alaskan hunter.

My bullet had gone true. It had slid between the horns and struck the sheep directly in the spine. It was as good a hump shot as I had ever made. The sheep died almost instantly. He felt the shock, but died without pain. You cannot have it much better than that.

I met Jerry at our packs. We agreed to do up our own sheep and meet again to begin the hard hike out. I returned to the ram with my packboard and got out my Case knife to begin skinning and butchering.

I suppose that sheep went about 180 pounds. He was big bodied as well as heavy horned. I got his skin off and boned out most of the meat. I dumped the meat into a big plastic bag that nearly filled the carrying sack on my packboard. I lashed the head, horns, and hide to the top of the load and tried to stand up with the whole works. Lordy, how my muscles popped. By getting onto my knees first, I was able to rise, but I feared my ankles would buckle with each graceless step.

Jerry met me at our agreed point, and he was in just as bad shape. We wondered how we would ever make the long hours back down the mountain. There was no other way than to begin, so we did. We staggered and struggled. At first we giggled, joked, and groaned over it but, as the agony increased, the humor disappeared, and the whole thing became a grim matter of wills.

The law said that edible meat had to be brought out and used. Those I hunted with prided themselves on doing just that, but both Jerry and I wondered what we would have done had our sheep been killed a couple of miles further in, perhaps on the wrong side of the mountain we were now descending. Our conclusion was that we would be far less exacting as to what was edible.

We fell increasingly often, and rather than risk a twisted ankle, we rolled with the load, sometimes skinning a spot and having to again fight to our painfully weary feet.

We made it, of course. How else could it end? The hike out, exhausting that it was, remains a fond memory that touches my emotions every time I pause to look at that fine ram's head hanging proudly among others on my walls.

He is not the best, but he deepens my breathing and I remember.

When I look at that sheep I am younger again. I hear the wind whistling off the mountains, and I feel the strain of packing and climbing in my now aging body. The scramble up the waterfall comes to mind, and I see flashes of mostly forgotten things, like Jerry's huffing at the climb or his concentration when shooting at long range. I wonder often if memories are not the important spices of hunting. I find I savor them more each year.

Suppose that we had taken our shots at 400 yards as we could have? Many hunters would not have hesitated. Lost would have been the rigors and memories of the stalk and the practicability of my shooting directly between the ram's horns.

My First Sheep

Suppose Jerry's or my ram had run at four hundred yard range? Could he, or I, have still collected him? Pretty doubtful in the real world. Getting close is always the right choice.

Dall sheep inhabit many of the mountains in Alaska. Occasionally, sheep and goats share the same mountain. I found that to be true more on the Kenai Peninsula than elsewhere.

Sheep are gregarious and are rarely alone. The exceptions to this rule are a few ancient rams that become loners and can be found living isolated on rocky crests.

Ewes and lambs form flocks that can number fifty or more animals. The rams, however, live separate from the ewes and lambs. Even those lordly creatures prefer the company of their own kind, and bands of rams numbering a dozen are not unknown.

More commonly, the hunter will find a pair of rams staying together, or a small group numbering five or so animals that graze and sleep in close proximity.

As horns grow, they sometimes interfere with a ram's peripheral vision, and he rubs them away on rock outcroppings. We call this "brooming," and there is little more frustrating to the hunter than to find a huge ram that has broomed away one or both of his horn tips.

Just backpacked in from the mountain, Jerry and I are removing the heads and hides from our Yukon boards. The big sack below the white sheep hide is packed with sheep meat.

Then, we got to pose for the camera. The old guide, in the center, had shot his ram the day before. Please note the shape of a case jackknife in my left hand shirt pocket. That tool is mentioned in the chapter on knives.

Jack O'Connor stated that a heavy set of horns that has been broomed, but still measures 35 inches around the curl is a good trophy. I am in agreement. Admittedly, the pointed sweep of un-broomed horn is preferable, but some of the finest of mature rams have scraped away a horn tip. They should not be ignored.

The biggest horned Dall rams come from the more southern Alaskan mountains, and the Brooks Range in the north produces a lot of tight curled rams. The middle ground—the Alaskan Range—has been less noted as a sheep hunting area. So, that makes it better for those of us who hunt there.

There are a vast number of sheep in the Alaskan Range, and their very numbers legitimize consideration of this thought:

A mature ram, the kind that has trophy horns, must be at least eleven years old. It takes that long to add not only the annual growth rings that give length, but also the lateral growth that provides thickness of horn. So, although an area may have been hunted heavily a decade or even five years earlier, means not that the place is hunted out, but that some really superb trophies will probably have matured in there since the hunting eased.

A wise hunter can hunt back hollows, minor stream sources, and some of the smaller nooks in the big mountains to great advantage. World record trophies will come, as they have in the past, from these kinds of places.

For decades, my friends and I have concentrated on just such obscure spots. We go into the Chugachs or up into the Brooks Range for the fun of something different, not to get a better ram.

The Alaskan Department of Fish and Game has a marvelous volume available that geographically points out every known body of sheep in Alaska. It is an extremely useful book for a hunter seeking greener pastures. The Fairbanks Fire Department has a copy and will allow its use.

Years ago, Cliff and I were rehashing our thoughts concerning the Jarvis Creek glacier and why the whole line of Granite Mountains past Fort Greely was so "sheepy." We turned to the Fire Department's copy of the above-mentioned volume. Clearly pointed out were not the **two** mineral licks we knew of, but **five** mineral licks. No wonder sheep like it in there.

Since, I first came to Alaska, I have hunted goats and brownies in the Ernestine Creek area, north out of Valdez. Until I saw the Game Department's study, I did not suspect that a band of Dall sheep lived only a couple of miles distance. Since then, we occasionally combined moose, bear, goat, and sheep into magnificent hunts. There are few areas in which a hunter can conveniently do that. Thank you, Game Department.

Where a goat has a small head, a Dall ram has a large one. But, there is not much difference in typical overall animal size. A sheep might be favorably compared in weight to a White-tail deer. Obviously, his configuration is different. Because of their relative size, some hunters assume it is therefore proper to use a deer rifle on a ram. I do not concur in this thinking. In my opinion, the ram is a much tougher hombre than a deer and is usually shot at greater range.

In the east, whitetails are mostly shot at 100 yards or under. Out west, the ranges can vary greatly. Although a 30/06 will absolutely kill a properly struck sheep, it does not usually smack them down to stay the way a heavier and more powerful bullet will. I have seen too many rams run around (or away) after being hit by one or more .270, 30/06 class cartridges. Jerry Rausch's ram mentioned in early pages was hit with a .270 Winchester solidly in the body twice before a third body hit flattened it. The great Jack O'Connor who popularized sheep hunting for my generation often reported having to shoot his sheep more than once. Jack used and loved the .270 Winchester above all other cartridges, but I often wondered why he would not use a more powerful gun.

My favored sheep rifle has been my .300 Weatherby. I have almost always used a 180 grain Nosler Partition bullet. I have never had a failure because of the choice, but I think the .338 Winchester Magnum is even better. That bullet really hits! The .338 bullet is heavier, and it keeps on going and going.

If we accept Energy figures as they appear in common ballistic tables, the Weatherby looks superior to the .338, *but* if you can, as I do, put faith in **KO** values, the .338 squeaks ahead. Note: Ballistic tables vary, and the figures used below may not match those on other pages, but none will be seriously different, and all will provide practical comparative guidance.

		\multicolumn{6}{c}{Yards}
Cartridge	Bullet Weight	100 En	KO	200 En	KO	300 En	KO
.270	130	2340	13.4	1920	12.9	1550	9.7
.300	180	3501	22.8	2925	20.8	2448	20.5
.338	200	3210	25.9	2580	23.2	2090	20.8

I table only to 300 yards. If you feel it is correct to shoot longer, work out your figures. You might be surprised to discover that the .338 Winchester remains a cartridge of choice even as the ranges increase.

While some will sneer at the author's insistence on heavy calibers for almost all of our Alaskan game, my thoughts are a result of a lot of hunting up here. I think, before rejecting them, a hunter should decide who is claiming otherwise. Most of our light bullet claims and recommendations come from lower forty-eight plains hunters (who may live in California). I think they are wrong.

A truly controversial subject is where to shoot a sheep. I cling to my favored hump shot. I like to break bones and paralyze the animal whatever its species. Never has a shot seemed right to me if the animal travels even four steps. He should go down and out on the spot.

Most hunters and writers advocate a lung shot on most big game. That includes Dall sheep. It is true that nearly all sheep are taken in open areas where there is a reduced chance of a final run carrying them beyond recovery—although I have known that to happen when wounded rams fell into canyons. A lung hit usually kills more quickly than a heart shot. Lungs are also a bigger target than a heart. Lungs are a good shot, but next I must ask, just where are the lungs on say a ram, and a moose, and a bear? All in the same spot? Not so. Not being sure is the reason most hunters hope to hit close behind the shoulder.

If they manage that, they expect to hit something important. Unfortunately shoulders move a lot.

Examine this photo of the Dall ram running along the ridge. Shoot him behind his shoulder and you have a paunch shot. Look at the hump shot. That point does not change position.

Unless it is the only shot offered, the head shot should be ignored. A bullet in the skull can really mess up a trophy, and if the horns are to undergo Boone and Crockett measurement, a shattered skull can void the count because broken head bones can allow horns to be spread or tipped resulting in false measurements.

The neck is considered an excellent shot by many hunters. I dislike it. The neck shot in a big animal is sudden only if the spine is hit. I have seen animals run off with their throats torn away and great gouges taken from their heavy upper muscles. I recall a moose taking three .375 magnums through the throat and still having to be finished off. Whitetail deer hunters often take neck shots and that may be all that can be seen of a deer in brush, but my advice to sheep hunters is to forget it.

I have spoken some in these pages of continuing shooting although the animal is hit once. I have taken this philosophy to heart. Using big bullets moving slower, we do not bloodshot much meat, and we do not hesitate to put another bullet into an animal.

Our thinking is that there is no better time to shoot than when an animal is still. Get him then and look later. If he needs more shooting, we wish to get the bullet in before adrenalin starts flowing in the wounded beast and he gets twice or thrice as hard to keep down.

To allow an animal to suffer so that a hunter can claim a one shot kill is not, in our minds, exemplary sportsmanship. On bear, of course, a hunter is foolish not to continue to shoot until certain. On other game, there is no personal danger only sportsmanship, but we consider that important as well.

Too often I hear men claiming to have held off on a second or third shot because it would ruin good meat. I think that on game animals such as Dall rams we hunters should be quick to admit that the trophy— not the meat—is the point of the hunt.

My feeling is: Make the shot as perfect as you can, and if a second bullet still does not do the trick, shoot another time. Let no animal suffer longer than you absolutely must.

I have been uncertain of where to place this photograph. We were ram hunting, so it will go here, but that trailer is packed with three sheep, four caribou, and one moose (all dressed out, of course). Cliff glasses (note his .357 Magnum revolver. He could not hit a bull in butt with it). The old guide stands between the vehicles, and I am perched (smiling) atop the load. The ladies are Maw Rauch and her friend Mimi, who often went with us. We were out a week on this hunt and had just returned to where the truck was cached. We hooked the trailer to the truck, and Jerry (who took the picture) and I delivered the game to the freezers. We were the first successful hunters back from the field that season, and to say the least, we were made much of—as we should have been. That was one hell of successful hunting trip.

Sheep mountains are often very steep and the higher elevations can pull on the lungs of hunters not yet acclimatized. Assuming a hunter uses common sense, climbing those mountains is rarely dangerous, but the footing can be rugged with boots moving from rockslides and mossy meadows to ankle-tripping vine tundra.

Although we read of dramatic long distance shooting on sheep, the overwhelming majority of these shots need not be. I think that physical weariness accounts for many too long shots on rams. Hunters see the animal, think they can make the shot and cringe at the thought of laboriously creeping and crawling closer.

An example of that situation often returns to haunt me. Three of us chanced crossing an extremely treacherous rock slide near the Yanert glacier. We were already pretty well bushed but kept going in the hope of coming onto some rams we had seen earlier.

That old rock slide shifted and grumbled under our boots, and by the time I got to the far side I swore never again to attempt such a foolish act. My pal made it across about the same time I did. We slumped to the firm ground and looked back to see our companion squatting in the middle of that shifting rock slide, just sort of looking around.

Things were so shaky we feared hardly to speak. Finally, we urged him off the slide with gentle comments like, *"Get off there, you stupid bastard."* He looked surprised at our vehemence and vowed he was tired and could shoot a sheep from there as well as a mile further.

That scared me half to death. I looked around praying that no ram would appear. Eventually, the guy got some strength back and clambered to safety. We discussed his actions in loud tones. All he could say was, *"I was too tired to care."*

As well as pooped-out hunters, those with limited time that have paid a fat fee or that are inexperienced find it hard to wait or work for better shots. They are prone to let go at extreme ranges. I have never had to shoot a ram (or anything else in Alaska) at over three hundred yards. I know I've said that before. I wish to spike down the point. You do not have to shoot at extreme ranges, and you should not.

Two hundred yard shooting seems far more common on sheep than two hundred and fifty yards. My records show me that we took an average ram at just about 200 yards. It might at first seem strange that we shoot our sheep at a little longer range than we do the high climbing goats. (They averaged 185 yards.)

The primary difference seems to be in the possibility of other sheep being around. Often, an otherwise easily approachable ram is sort of guarded by a lesser trophy between the one you want and your rifle muzzle. So, you take a little longer shot. Sheep also live in lower country than the goats do, and the winds do not blow as true and cleanly. Vagrant breezes whipping around can reverse on themselves, and you have had it. So, you end up a bit further away from your quarry.

One of the great moments in a big game hunter's life. The hunter's pleasure shows.

A ram smells to high heaven most of the year. With the wind right, I have smelled sheep that were over a quarter mile away. I assume that a ram has at least as good a nose as I have. So, he smells us as readily. You have to watch the wind, and that can mean taking a longer shot than you might prefer.

Mountain sheep do not pay much attention to sounds that are natural to their environment. For example, a hunter can often kick stones loose without disturbing sheep. Metallic noises such as a gun barrel striking rocks are not good. However, I have never known a sheep to be scared off by ordinary hunter noises. I wonder if a sheep has hearing that is any way exceptional? I think not. Sometimes, strange noises will cause them to get up and look around, but unless you are right underfoot or let out a bellow, even huge rams are likely to wait around for a long look. A hunter should not need more.

When sheep do panic it can be amusing. Unlike goats that tend to move with deliberate speed, sheep may run in all directions. They bump and swerve, dodge and leap about. Their actions can be unnerving for the hunter, and moving they can be very tough to hit.

If you can, try to take a ram from above. Not only is he more watchful of things happening below him, but shots taken from below are more difficult to make than those from above.

If you are below, a ram lying down may expose only his back and head. You may find you have to risk a standing shot. If the ram moves after your uphill shot, obstructions can loom out of nowhere and stop or delay your following shots. Other sheep are prone to intrude between you and your quarry as well.

From above, all those difficulties are lessened, and if you blow your shot, the ram's chances of running from view are smaller.

It is practical to get above sheep. If a hunter gets on top in the Granite Mountains, he will find ridges running in many directions on which he can stroll with relative ease. The sheep will be found below him. Cross canyon shots are not long in many of these kinds of mountains but can usually be avoided by a little extra legwork on the hunter's part.

These "on top" conditions exist throughout the Alaskan Range. A wise hunter will study a good contour map of the area he intends to hunt. He may find that a single climb to high ground and judicious use of high passes will keep him above the rams he is hunting.

One summer, Jerry and I flew many hours in my Cessna 170 dropping supplies into selected spots high in the mountains. We put canned goods, sheets of plastic, even firewood in surplus army sandbags. I brought the plane in low and slow over a chosen spot, and Jerry dropped a pair of bags on target. Occasionally, we flew back over the drops to see if bears might be disturbing our supply points. They seemed OK, and in the fall we were able to hike into the mountains and stay a long time without lugging immense packs.

Using an airplane in support of any hunt is open to rational disagreement. My position these days is that the airplane should not be allowed in any capacity. I would like to see them removed from the hunting picture completely. I am aware of the hardship such legislation would place on registered guides and hunters with limited time, but things are getting tighter all over. There are way too many of us (including wolf packs) hunting for trophies, and we are becoming ever more conscious of the need for fair chase hunting.

Hunter, Ed. Piabola, 360 yards with an 8mm, Talkeetna Mountains

I have never seen a ram as blood soaked as this one. Examine the huge exit hole. The bullet angled in from further front and came out near the paunch. Incredible penetration and expansion. The sheep apparently fell on the bloody side and bled out in one spot. The hunter rolled him up for the photo. Notice that the [excited?] hunter, perhaps jubilant is a better word choice, still has his bipod extended.

Fair chase hunting is, I fear, determined in the mind of the hunter, but shooting over bait is frowned on, using aircraft the same day as the hunt is out, and helicopters should be completely and permanently barred—except for life saving medical services.

How about harvesting wolves via fixed wing aircraft? We used to do that a lot, and it is discussed elsewhere, but fair chase, such hunting is not.

Some years back a group of field grade officers stationed in Alaska gathered a magnificent collection of US Army camping equipment from their various units and placed it all within specially prepared 55 gallon drums. These drums were flown by military test pilots using helicopters into the sheep lick on Granite Creek. The pilots set the barrels on a convenient gravel bar as near to the lick as they could manage. One chopper, in fact, ruined a set of blades touching a cliff face getting back out.

When hunting season arrived, these special people were motored in army track vehicles to within walking distance of the lick. The officers camped and hunted there for a long and completely fruitless hunt. **Because:** The use of helicopters was so blatantly illegal we decided to do something about it, and we did.

Each day, *before the season began,* I flew the mountains driving every sheep in the area back across St. Anthony's Pass and out of the officers' reach.

In the past there was much misuse of military equipment in Alaska, but the military itself has taken hold and reduced the problems a hundred fold.

I suppose the mountain sheep have been the most affected by illegal aircraft hunting. Airplanes place hunters into areas nearly inaccessible by foot or even by horse. I used to land my Cessna on a flat plot up on the spine of the Granites. It was less than a half mile walk to an excellent mineral lick. Piper Super Cubs could do better than that, and I doubt I am the only pilot to discover the improvised strip. As handy as it was, I would prefer to see an end to it all.

I personally credit the before mentioned remarkable hunter/writer Jack O'Connor with popularizing sheep hunting in our country. His appreciation of the mountain rams, his stories of grand hunts in **Outdoor Life** magazine, and his numerous books brought home to all of us the potential adventure in hunting North American sheep.

As O'Connor so long ago described, ram hunting is not for the fragile or the puny. The ridges are too steep and the bumps and bruises too numerous. But, for a vigorous hunter with sound wind and enduring enthusiasm, searching the high country for trophy rams is an experience difficult to match.

Sheep hunting is usually hefty work, and a young fellow I met in a restaurant at Glennallen in the fall of 1974, who was fresh off a sheep hunt in the Wrangells, typifies how a hunt can go.

He and his partner had climbed for nine hours when the partner settled for the first legal ram they could approach. He made his shot and quit. (That ram worried me. It looked so close to the legal minimum that I would have been nervous about showing it. I was glad it was his and not mine to have measured—which game protectors often do at the various taxidermy shops.)

The remaining hunter then climbed alone for another four hours before he took a nice full curl ram going over 38 inches. By the time he had his load ready to start down it was dark, and he wisely sat out the night, but he shivered and shook the night away on the cold mountainside.

Of course, there are times when sheep walk through the camp. I remember one such incident in area 20D. A pair of full curl rams nervously crossed the canyon within 75 yards of us. We were resting in camp, and no one raised more than a groan or a chuckle. To us, the hunt counts as much as the trophy. Potting a ram under camp conditions would have ruined the adventure—at least on that occasion. Some days a hunter is more hungry than at other times.

In all of Alaska, there are only about 35,000 Dall rams. The Wrangell Mountains produce the most ram trophies, but we who mostly hunt the interior have nothing to be envious about. Annual Dall ram harvests run about 1,200 rams. Our Alaskan Range might typically account for 300 of those trophies. Or, if you prefer, hunting the interior of the great state provides a fourth of all rams taken in Alaska each year.

For most Alaskan hunters, a Dall trophy ranks second only to a grizzly or brown bear. Many hunters would go further and rate a Dall equal to a good bear.

I have noticed that visitors to my Alaskan trophies first admire the bear rugs. Then they examine the rams. Perhaps that indicates something.

Sheep hunting is certainly more demanding than bear hunting, the country is prettier, and the shooting is usually longer range. I guess that shows I rate sheep pretty high on the old totem pole.

I show this picture more for the Yukon packboard than the sheep. These packs could carry anything, and look at the upright over which a rifle can be slung. *Importante!*

Another marvelous ram and hunter photo, but take note of the country where this sheep was taken. Rock slides—everywhere. These slides can be very dangerous. This one appears old and steady, but I have walked across too many that shifted and grumbled under my feet. Care should be taken on all slides, and most seem to end in steep cliffs.

Handsome, alert, and . . . well, just *beautiful*.

Hunter: John Waike, 7mm STW, 400+ yards, Guide: John Rhyshek

One good shot that went in at the right shoulder and exited a bit further back. These sucking exit wounds reinforce my belief in the importance of an exit pumping out blood and leaking in air. This hunter has the most effective camouflaged clothing I have ever seen.

Dall Sheep

You don't like my broomed horn? Too bad. Shoot somebody else.

The Lordly MOOSE

Note: The Lordly Moose shown on the preceding page is the 1962 Boone and Crockett world record shot by Bert Klineburger.

Chapter

22

Moose

First times are usually remembered as something special. They have ways of burning deep into the memory. First love, first car, and first hunt all have special places in the human heart.

My first moose hunt was like that.

There was some prestige to getting the first moose in our area. Art Rausch, Jerry, and I located a cow accompanied by a bull whose antlers were in their first year of palmation. We wanted meat, so the young bull was just right. My experienced friends gave me, the novice moose hunter, the opportunity to take the bull.

The range was about a hundred yards over flat ground with some low brush that prevented assuming a rest position. I remember how disturbed Art became when I chose to shoot offhand. Never having seen me shoot on game, he was perhaps justifiably nervous about my performance. He was all for quartering around until we found a spot from which I could shoot sitting.

In those days, I shot constantly. My arms were unusually muscled and hard (I have been a weightlifter since before it was popular), and I held a rifle rock steady. I am naturally left handed but have learned to shoot a rifle right handed. That puts my strongest arm out forward under the gun. I have always believed that strong left arm holding up my rifle helped me to be an unusually effective offhand field shot.

I held on the bull's spine just at his shoulder and touched off the .300 Weatherby Magnum. Getting out of recoil, I peered about and saw four moose feet sticking up in the air. We walked to the downed animal and had to shout and wave to drive the cow away. My shot had hit just where aimed and had smashed the bull's spine. He lay utterly paralyzed, but possibly still alive, and I quickly drove another bullet through his head.

That simple hunt demonstrated a number of never to be forgotten points. It was, for instance, nice to arrive back in civilization with the first moose. Everybody gathered around to admire and comment on the kill.

More important from a hunter's standpoint, I relearned the devastating effect of a hit at the juncture of spine and front shoulders. Even on a huge animal, the shot is a complete paralyzer. There is no following of blood spoor or waiting until a wounded animal stiffens. There is certainly no charge! In my opinion, it is the most effective spot to put a bullet on any animal in North America.

Another point I immediately absorbed was that Alaskan game is god-awful BIG. Standing next to that smaller than average moose I began to realize the importance of having a way to pack out such a thing. You do not hitch an old clothesline around an antler base and man-drag a moose out of the fields—the way you might a whitetail deer. That moose carcass looked like a dead horse and just about as movable.

Finally, I began to think more about the practicality of getting shots from a rest when hunting flatland game in Alaska. I looked at the terrain with a more critical eye and noted that a lot of it has brush or a roll to the ground that leaves the hunter shooting from his hind legs.

A moose hunter should expect to support his rifle with only his arms. There are not many convenient trees, fallen logs, or grass hummocks to rest over. Of course, there are exceptions, but I have been sufficiently impressed by the amount of offhand shooting required to continue to recommend special practice to develop and maintain a strong standing position.

I add the thought that if a hunter develops a powerful offhand he has also perfected trigger control and cool nerves so that he need practice other positions very very little. Except for zeroing, my friends and I rarely practice shooting at positions other than standing and occasionally kneeling, which is also a shaky position at best.

Generally speaking, hunters (from any state) are poor shots. Oh, off the benchrest they make nice tight groups. Impressive! But all that kind of shooting demonstrates is the rifle's inherent accuracy.

In the 1949 *Gun Digest,* Claude Parmalee wrote, *"Not one out of one hundred deer hunters* (a moose is a deer, remember) *could take a standard* *hunting rifle as is and hit a buck twice out of ten shots at 200 yards in the offhand position. Not even with the deer standing **broadside**."*

Benchrest shooting does not show a hunter's ability to hit game animals from offhand or even when braced against a tree trunk.

A hunter should practice the type of shots he will normally encounter. Most hunters ignore that logic and are therefore rotten field shots. Many do nothing more than fire a few preseason rounds into any convenient target. Those may be the jazzbos who shoot poor groups into road signs. Some hunters fail to do anything more preparatory than to make sure the bore is clear and that the action works. Many do go to a benchrest, check their zero, and believe themselves prepared. Appalling! They are not ready.

Here are three easy ways to improve your ability to **hit** wild game animals.

After zeroing at the bench:

Shoot offhand in ALL practice. If you can hit standing (unsupported), you will be all the better if a rest does materialize.

Shoot at various ranges using irregular hunks of cardboard for targets. No bulls eyes allowed; moose to not have them. Decide on where you wish to hit the cardboard, and shoot a three shot group (standing, of course). If the hits are close together in the right spot you are doing something.

Guide: John Rhyshek (L), Hunter: Jeff Rahn (R), .338 Winchester

Shoot swiftly in practice. From seeing to shot must not exceed a count of three. Moose may not wait around for you. A simple way to practice speed is to stand before your TV set, choose a target, and dry fire at it. You will find the scenes shift so quickly you will learn to be swift.

Dyton Gilliland with his 1953 world's record moose. A change in measuring rules gave this mighty rack 1st place after it lay in Dyton's yard for nearly six years.

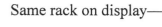 Same rack on display——————

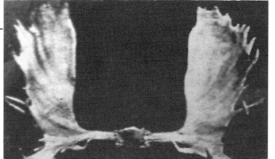

The Alaskan moose is a browser. He feeds on the leaves and twigs of nearly any kind of tree. The moose pulls food into its mouth using its long tongue. In addition to goodies from the trees, the moose is inordinately fond of grasses that grow on the bottoms of shallow Alaskan ponds. The great animals are regularly seen wading in water to their necks and dipping their heads out of sight to reach the long grass growing beneath the surface. A moose grazes from pond bottoms for about half a minute before surfacing to munch and gaze around.

Willows—moose food

Because of its long legs, a moose does little grazing other than in ponds. I have seen moose kneel to munch tender shoots from clump grass, but that is not his custom. Moose do not appear to be frantic food searchers—like domestic cows for example. They seem to eat a little and loaf a lot, but anyone cleaning a moose finds a full belly waiting for him. How the moose is able to fill his immense stomach each day remains a mystery to me.

Moose country is meadowland dotted with shady groves of both deciduous and evergreen trees. The animals feed from both. They enjoy shifting from sunny glens to shaded hollows as the mood strikes them. Nearby shallow ponds add to a good moose country, and recent burns where young trees are growing over the ravages of fire are bonuses.

The Granite Mountains east of Big Delta, where for many years I preferred to do my hunting, has all of those things. It is a decently dry area, so the hunting can be comfortable without the necessity of rubber boots and slogs through marshland. There are marshes, but these can be skirted. There are numerous shallow ponds and a dozen or more significant streams, one of which (Granite Creek) disappears underground to surface again as a feeder of Clearwater Creek many miles away.

This is a moose meadow, and passing moose made the tracks. Now, if you could catch your giant bull wandering across here . . . Wow.

The slopes beneath the Granites are perfect moose country and run all the way to the Delta River and in the other direction to the Tanana River. (See included map of Hunting Area 20D.)

Across the Delta River lies a large game preserve that helps seed the hunting country when herds grow thin. Moose, caribou, and bison withdraw to the preserve, and the buffalo regularly calve there.

Since the 1970s, the Game Department has clamped down hunting in the Big Delta/Delta Junction area. These days, too many people live close by. Still, even obeying the current regulations a great hunt is possible. Moose are still there although not as numerous as they were thirty or forty years ago.

A moose is an immense animal. By far the largest of the deer family, he is also bigger than almost anything else around. Mature bulls of the Alaskan Peninsula are said to go up to 1800 pounds on the hoof and can stand seven feet tall at the shoulder. Their magnificent sweep of palmated antlers is inspiring to gaze upon, and the thought that the moose grow those giant appendages each year overwhelms the imagination.

During the first part of the moose season in Alaska the bulls may be in velvet. The antler covering called velvet is actually a blood supply and protective layer over the growing antlers. As the velvet dies it dries and decays. The bulls are irritated by its itchiness and rub it from their racks by polishing on tree trunks and scrubbing their antlers in the earth. A hunter that shoots a moose still in velvet and desires keeping the trophy should strip the soft velvet material away from the antlers immediately, or it will become hard and arduous to remove.

While there are four distinct types of sub-species of moose in our hemisphere, by far the largest is the Alaskan moose. And, of the moose in Alaska, the largest seem to inhabit the Kenai and Alaskan Peninsulas. But, good moose live all over Alaska, even in the far and barren North Country.

The native Alaskans claim a human can live well and healthy on nothing but moose. Conversely, it is claimed that the caribou has weak meat and man cannot subsist on it alone. To me, the difference in animals seemed small, and I wrote here and there requesting opinions.

Response was vigorous, but evidence supporting those opinions was thin. The consensus seems to be that to live entirely on moose, one had to eat **ALL** of the moose, and that included, fat, brains, and other even less enticing portions of moose anatomy. There were no satisfactory explanations for the caribou meat weakness concept.

Whether moose is the dietitian's dream may still be in doubt, but anyone who faults moose as a tasty dish has let his imagination overrun his palate.

Art Rausch used to feed visitors moose steaks wrapped in Super Market wrappers. The visitor picked his cut of "beef" from Art's freezer, and after he enjoyed the tender and tasty "beef" he was informed he had just eaten moose. Art did this both for chuckles and to end unfounded grimacing and whining about "wild taste."

It is not be denied that any meat can be ruined by improper handling after an animal is shot, and unknowing souls have been permanently turned off wild meat due to exposure to some vile slab that was hung in the hide, fender draped, or gut shot and run for half a day. The most prime and marbled beef would be equally bad tasting if it received such treatment.

There was a time when I was intent on entering the archival records of Boone and Crockett and other such listers. Therefore, I headed for "Big Moose" country when I trophy hunted.

In more recent years, I have reasoned that the biggest moose in my area is as much of an accomplishment as is going to a neighbor's territory and shooting the biggest one there.

Really, what is the difference, other than ego expansion, whether you hunt diligently and take a grand specimen of what is available in your part of the world or travel great distances and do the same thing?

In the Granite Mountain area, a moose that goes over fifty inches is a big fellow, and sixty inches is a giant moose. I would estimate that typical bull moose in Alaska would **average** about a 45 inch spread. Despite the lack of really huge bulls, our Alaskan Range moose probably still average about 45 inches.

This is moose manure. The spoor looks like over-size "bunny bullets" (rabbit manure). People actually dry this stuff, varnish it, and sell it to tourists as souvenirs called Alaskan Jewelry.

A bull grows only short stubs of antlers during his first year of life. The second season he is a fork horn. The third, he can boast palms and might go 28 inches in spread. Thereafter he will wear a full antlered head of at least 40 inches and possibly move into the mighty moose class of 60 plus

This is moose country, and the photograph demonstrates the improbability of shooting other than offhand. Arthur B. Troup is the hunter.

I have never encountered one of the "Old moose" that hunters describe—the ones that have begun to wither and have seriously lost antler size. Maybe there is a moose graveyard, such as legend claimed for the African Elephant, and as they are about to die the old moose go there to expire. It is more likely that, although I have seen a hellacious number of moose over the years, I just haven't learned to identify an old and shrunken-down bull.

Alaska has in the neighborhood of 140,000 moose. The numbers vary significantly with how many wolves are harvested because if wolves are numerous, they will kill nearly all of the second moose calves. A cow moose typically has two calves but can usually protect only one. If you want a lot of moose, keep the wolves down.

Annual hunting harvests run about 25,000 to 30,000 moose.

The Game Department recognizes both the moose's problems and value. They keep a close eye on the moose herds. Department closures to hunting and other restrictive rulings make us groan, but I suspect they are more often right than wrong.

Moose possess the innate curiosity of the deer family. While you cannot lure a bull by waving a rag, as you might a caribou, moose demonstrate their curiosity in other ways.

I recall a spike camp on the Tanana River flats where I woke from a nap in the warm fall sun to find a band of moose, including two bulls, ranged in an arc examining me. We watched each other for some moments until they tired of the game and wandered away.

Perhaps a classic example of moose curiosity lies in the observation of moose droppings on the very summit of Donnelly Dome. The dome is a prominent landmark overlooking the Richardson Highway and rears some hundreds of feet above the surrounding land. I have twice been to the highest point of the dome. It is not an easy climb, the sides are steep all the way around, and the top of the dome is barren—except for the moose droppings, more than a few piles, some ancient, others quite recent.

What reason other than curiosity (to just look around) could a moose have for laboring to the summit of such a mound?

A logical question would be, what was I doing up there? The answer is, curiosity, of course—just like the moose. Hey, I left a bottle with my name and date in it on top. One seeks fame where one can, I suppose.

There is an ancient Japanese saying that everyone should climb Mount Fuji once, but only a fool climbs it twice. I climbed it twice.

Donnelly Dome

As interesting as the dome is the lengthy beaver dam in the foreground of the photograph. The dam is very old and has become a permanent feature of the terrain. The beavers were gone when I arrived, and I have never noted their return. The dam is about a quarter of a mile long.

Curiosity can get a moose into trouble. On a hunt along the Salcha River, Art Troup and I heard the grunting and struggling of a nearby moose. We eased into shooting positions but withheld our fire when we saw a mature bull tangled and bound in the remnants of an old military double apron barbed wire fence. The bull was down on his side, so entangled he could no longer rise. His side was ripped in a hundred places, but still he fought the ever-tightening wire.

All thoughts of hunting left us, of course. How could we execute an animal with a heart obviously as big as a house? Conferring, we agreed the moose should live, providing we could get him loose. As I had once before tried to release a cow moose from a similar predicament on a military rifle range, I expected the bull would fight us as hard as he did the wire. In fact, we finally had been forced to put the cow out of her misery.

We drew lots, and Art headed for our truck a mile or so back to collect our rope and our only tool—a pair of side cutting pliers. I sat down to evaluate the situation.

Art drove the truck a lot closer, and with his return we decided to lash the bull securely to a heavy pole so that he would be immobilized while we worked at the tough wire.

We tied the bull's head and legs to a log using an array of slip knots. Then we began cutting wire. It was necessary to roll the eight or so hundred pound animal over several times as we wrestled the rusted but still strong wire. The bull's struggles had imbedded barbs deeply into his hide, but his soft underbelly was free of serious tears.

Our hands blistered as we took turns on the rapidly dulling pliers and belatedly realized that we should have cleared away a considerable area of wire around the bull lest he blunder into it again.

It took over an hour to remove all the barbed wire. Bushed, we sat on the bull's ribs and contemplated freeing him from our own lashings. The bull's eyes rolled at us, and his snorting and panting was anything but reassuring. I have never seen a bull moose charge and have serious reservations about the frequency of such attacks, but this did not seem the time to test any passive moose theories.

We rigged four release ropes that would jerk all knots free at once—we hoped. The bull's head was freed ahead of time, and we stayed clear of it thereafter.

With all ready, we hauled mightily on the ropes. The knots fell free as planned, and…the bull simply laid there looking at us. Maybe he could not believe it.

We took advantage of his relaxed attitude and hauled all the lines we could away from him.

Suddenly, he gave a snorting heave and was on his feet almost instantly. His hide rippled the way a horse's does when irritated by flies. Then he slowly strode away. His flayed body trailed bloody rivulets, but he walked strong and sure. We feel he made it.

Even with our hunt delayed, our ropes cut into pieces, and our hands in about the same shape as the moose's body, we felt really good and glad we did it; even if the bull did not say, *"Thanks."*

Alaskan moose have been hunted during two seasons—we will assume that remains the case. We commonly refer to them as the early moose season and the post-rut or late season. (October is the serious rutting period.) My experience indicates the early season to be the most enjoyable moose hunting time. The weather is much milder then.

The late season can be harsh—some years with too bitter cold for top hunting enjoyment. I do find post-rutting season moose more drawn and less tasty than early moose. The rut, with all glands working, leaves the bulls leaned down. Their meat seems spicier to my taste, but admittedly, any properly cared for moose meat is fine eating.

There are advantages to the late season. Leaves are gone. Undergrowth and bushes are thinned, and polished antlers show more clearly. Meat is easier to care for in the sharper cold, and flies are gone. When it is cold, moose are less often in the ponds or near the water. After about the middle of September the moose move around more. They can often be called (bugled) after about mid-September.

No doubt, there are more moose available in the first season. It could be that most of the best racks are picked off then. Still, the wise old bulls that have outfoxed hunters over a number of seasons will be out there for the late season hunter.

Chapter

23

Moose Shooting

More than once I have said, *"Shooting a moose is like executing someone's milk cow."* Now, that is not exactly a fair comparison, and it puts down one of Alaska's great game animals.

It is true that most moose hunts involve a lot less huffing and puffing to find the game than do sheep or goat hunts, but moose also do not often stroll up and pose for the shot. A lot of us that get used to high country hunting with hard climbing and fairly long shots at smaller targets get to bad mouthing flat country game animals; much as fly fishermen sneer at salmon snaggers.

The facts are that a moose on a quiet stroll through the willows can leave a hurrying man far behind, and a moose can walk away with a mighty load of lead in him, although that is not common.

A moose is a big target, and a hunter should not miss, but I have seen more shots blown on moose than on either goats or sheep. Admittedly, a lot of "non-hunters" who would never consider climbing for the white animals are out blasting at moose, but there is more to it than that.

Part of the difficulty may be that, unlike goats or sheep, a moose is likely to be blundering around behind brush and trees. A shooter that is not careful can spoil a good opportunity by ricocheting bullets off branches.

A note suitable for inclusion here is that over the years the poorest trained hunters that are most likely to rain bullets into brush piles have been armed with high velocity, small bore rifles that are least able to bore through the tangles.

And that entry demands inclusion of more on the subject of brush bucking.

As long as I have been hunting (and I am sure long before that) it has been gospel that a heavy, slow moving bullet penetrates brush better than a light fast bullet.

More recently there have been controlled experiments that attempted to determine exactly what kind of bullets at what velocities **DO** buck brush most effectively.

All researchers are quick to point out that no bullet tosses aside big stuff, but in exact opposition to all of our many years of field observation, some of the experiments show a light, skinny bullet getting through brush better than a fat, heavy bullet.

Hunter: Karl Feisl, .338 BAR, Iditarod River

A huge bull moose. You can bet that the shooting was short in these woody conditions. Incidentally, a way to make a trophy look extra impressive is to have the camera up close and place the hunter well back at the rear end of the animal. Antlers look bigger, and the hunter is small in relation to the game. Bear hunters always do that.

To every brush hunter I know, such results are inexplicable. I cannot accept the figures, nor do any of the "big name" hunters.

My (our) advice is to stick to large caliber, heavy bullets for big animals in and around brush. They will work for you, as they have for us through all of the decades we know about.

It seems that the very size of a moose induces sloppy shooting. It is sort of like banging away at a barn side, and it takes a little special attention to place the bullet in a proper location.

As mentioned earlier, I saw a moose hit in the throat three times with a .375 magnum and begin to walk away. I could see a spray of material as bullets exited, yet the moose appeared uninjured. When the animal was taken, there were six holes in his neck, three in and three out. The bullets had not expanded in the soft tissue, and the exit holes looked little larger than those going in. That is not a condemnation of the most excellent .375; it is a commentary on not hitting a vital spot.

Thinking of threes, I recall a hunter up from Washington shooting a bull three times in the head with his damnable .243 Winchester woodchuck rifle. The moose shook his head at every hit like a punch-drunk fighter and started away. The old guide slid a 180-grain Nosler into his spine, and the bull collapsed as if his legs had been scythed off.

Hunter: Gary Herriman, .338 BAR, 58" bull on Bonanza Creek

It is generally conceded that a moose is not a difficult animal to bring down. Even the biggest bulls seem to lack the vitality to fight bullets the way a bear, sheep, or goat might. Often, when hit in the body, a bull moose will merely hump his back and stand immobile until he falls over. In other cases, when hard hit a moose will wander away almost casually, acting as if untouched until he suddenly crumples.

If a moose is caught in the open, any cartridge .308 Winchester or above will take him. But, it is a rare hunter who can resist taking a shot at the rump of a fine trophy disappearing into heavy cover. Then, the light .30 calibers are not adequate, and 7mms, regardless of their initial velocity, may lack the penetration to slug their way through muscle and wet guts into the boiler room of such a hulking animal.

A moose seeing a hunter will often turn his rump to the hunter and observe back along his body. The only shots then offered are his rump or his head. Most headshots are avoided because the big bony thing is often moving a little. A hit forward of the eyes will only wound, and, of course, a headshot moose is not a taxidermist's delight.

Shooting a moose in the rump, unless the bullet is placed exactly under the tail, will require a bullet to range forward through many inches of hard muscle and perhaps through some really solid bone. Nothing like a heavy bullet for that job.

It can be rare to **have** to take a moose at long range. A browsing moose is easily stalked to within two hundred yards in most open country.

It is not improbable, however, that a moose moving away from a hunter might be encountered. Then, only a novice tries to catch up. A longer shot will have to be taken, again into the animal's rear. You cannot expect a skinny little bullet to expand beautifully or to break big, heavy bones way out there. And, I assure you, moose bones are very heavy!

Too often, we get all wrapped up in theoretical ballistics and become overly concerned with flat trajectory. If we expended the same effort practicing range estimation that we do reading factory ballistic tables we would be little concerned about two foot more drop that a big bore might have at four hundreds yards. First, we should wisely restrict our shooting to three hundred yards, but if the extreme shot came, we would simply hold properly and let that big pumpkin drop right in.

Most hunters hold close behind or on the shoulder when shooting moose. Both are fine shots if the animal is considerate enough to pose broadside for the shot. Often he does not, and angled shots are necessary.

As noted, I have never been fond of neck shots, although when executed properly they may produce remarkable results. I have seen too many animals taken that had a hole through their neck or part of their throat shot away. Hydrostatic shock reads nicely, but unless bones are broken in the neck, a large animal like a moose may run away.

The author with an average moose on our meat rack along Granite Creek. Even average means big when talking about moose. Judge the size of those bones—real big, and strong and heavy. Now, how do you get all of that meat out of the wilderness and into your freezer? Backpack? I don't think so. Horses? I'd rather stay home and shoot the horses. Horses are . . . no need to go into that. Try a tractor like our Bombardier.

I have written of my favorite, the hump shot, which means striking the juncture of the spine and front shoulder. I rarely use any other shot on moose. I do, of course, use a powerful rifle, and I have hunted enough seasons to be able to locate the right spot from about any angle.

My .300 Weatherby or .338 Winchester Magnum does the job, but my .375 H&H Magnum really slams them, and the .458 Winchester Magnum is probably a maximum and most effective moose cartridge. When that big 510 grain soft point sledges into a bull, all of his lights go out, and that is the way shooting moose should be. These days, I usually have another round heading down the tube before the first one really takes hold anyway. I do my looking after I know the bull is kaput.

With the big, slow moving .458 the meat is not bloodshot for a foot all around, but it is extremely rare not to have a very large exit hole, and I approve of bullets that go all the way through.

The .458 is more than you need, however. It kicks hard and most shooters should use a recoil reducer. I would select the .338 as the more practical moose cartridge.

This is how you transport dead moose. A side view follows on the next page. If you look closely, you can see a cable crossing the cab of the tractor. That is the hand-operated winch cable from the front of the tractor. We just cranked the travois and moose into position, secured it with a chain come-along, and drove off. The poles only slowly wore down and were not a problem. This photograph was taken on an army tank trail in the big burn on the Delta River flats just north of the Granite Mountains. See the map on page 7. Since the army Test Center left Fort Greely a few years ago, these old trails have begun to fade away, but it will take a hundred years to lose them completely—maybe more.

Will moose charge? My old guide always said, "No," but a lot of people tell me moose charging stories, and I saw a cow moose on television that wandered into a town kick to death a human that insisted on crowding her. Tales are hard to investigate. I suppose the consensus is that a moose will attack very, very rarely, and then for sometimes unrecognizable reasons.

My own rationalization on moose attacks is that there are probably nutty moose, just as there are goofy people, and occasionally there is a charge. Additionally, a cow moose will almost always defend a calf—an instinct present in all living creatures it seems.

I have seen cow moose fake and bluff a charge many times. If a hunter panicked and let fly before the animal backed off, he could believe he had been charged. I suspect this happens regularly. A cow moose may stomp and snort and make short rushes toward a human. Shouting and waving will turn her.

Bulls in rut are claimed to charge. One year I watched a herd of 23 moose nearly every day from a position on higher ground. At the heart of the rutting season, when I figured the bulls would be most aggressive, I rode into the herd and also tried to walk into it. As they usually do, each moose took a long and studied look at me (usually over a shoulder before heading away) and walked into the brush on which they had been browsing. The bulls were most timid of all. They left first.

Although I tried to initiate a moose charge, I never succeeded. However, a moose is a wild animal and should be treated with great caution. Observe a pair of bull moose fighting during the rut and visualize how much chance a human would stand in such a melee. An enraged moose would be a devastating fighter.

When moose hunting, I usually take a location with a great range of land before me. Assuming a comfortable position, I begin glassing with my 7 x 35 binoculars.

Propped comfortably against his pack, Jack McMillin studies an entire world of moose country. There are lakes and woods, and meadows. You do not see what is out there in a few minutes of looking. If you locate a possible trophy, wouldn't it be nice to drive a few miles closer by tractor?

For long periods of glassing, I prefer seven power binoculars. I can get away with eight power, but higher than that seems to tire my eyes more quickly. If an animal requires a closer look, I turn to my old B & L spotting scope. I have found 20X magnification to be the best.

First, I check out all the likeliest spots. This is perhaps not the most efficient procedure. It might be better to scan the entire area methodically from start to finish, but I have never been able to resist that first checking out, in case a big fellow is standing out in the open waiting for me. He rarely is! Thereafter, I begin covering the area left to right and closest to farthest with the greatest patience and care of which I am capable.

I remember being camped under three large tents in a favored moose pasture when a friend came looking for us. He later claimed he glassed the area thoroughly and never saw our camp. I believe he tried, and I have kept that memory clear in my mind. If a hunter could miss big tents and a tractor with an attached trailer, how easy would it be to pass over a moose lying in the shade of a spruce?

Glassing an area is a matter of hours, not minutes. It is not a matter of looking, it is a matter of seeing, and there is a great difference.

A binocular moving slowly can cover a hundred yards of land at a clip when the range is only 500 yards or so. Unless that passing ground is studied with care and patience a moose ear can be easily missed. A bull can raise his head, a cow can take a step that puts her in view, yet unless you are really working you will see nothing. Each area examined must be studied long enough to allow animals to move a little. It is movement that best catches the eye.

When glassing further distances, such as a mile or two away, even greater care must be exercised. It is in no way unreasonable to spend half a day glassing a large moose pasture. Often, moose are located but are not of the size desired. The glasser continues keeping the located animals in mind and returning to them occasionally. Sometimes, a big fellow, previously hidden, steps into view or one band joins another group until then unnoticed.

There are hunters who have eyes particularly capable of locating game. These are the fellows who walk along and see rabbits sitting in their beds. They can spot a mountain goat curled into a yellow ball on a distant hillside. They are the ones who spot the mule-like ears of an otherwise hidden moose.

Jerry Rausch has those kind of eyes. When we share binoculars, he cranks the eye pieces tight together, but boy can he see! I have never located an animal before he did. He has pointed out many moose and caribou that he located with his naked eyes that I still had trouble finding with my binoculars. Seeing in that manner is a wonderful ability. I envy those who have it.

I have to labor over my spotting. Most will have to do as I do, using all of the tools available and still struggling to see. It is noteworthy, however, that Jerry and the others with super-eyes that I know still sit and glass and glass and glass. There is no other way to regularly find moose.

On our hunts, we gut our game as soon as we are sure it is dead. The old guide always said, *"You should have the skin off the animal before it hits the ground."* Maybe that was a bit extreme, but it emphasized that the quicker a game animal is dressed out, the better the meat will taste.

It is mighty rare to take a moose convenient to a tree strong enough to haul him off the ground. That assumes you even have a method of raising an animal weighing over 800 pounds. Moose are regularly cleaned where they fall.

As we hunt only bulls, the deceased moose's head can be propped nose up on his antlers. That keeps his big old head from flopping around and getting in the way.

We open the moose from anus to chin (assuming no intention of mounting the head), split open the sternum, cut loose the cords and tubes in the neck, and pull all the innards out between the animal's hind legs.

Viscera is held in place by easily parted tissue, and with one man pulling while the other cuts, everything comes loose and is removed without tainting the meat.

In actuality, it is not much harder to do than to explain, once you have done it a few times. But, you must act while the kill is fresh. If the animal is cooled out, the tissue hardens and the difficulty level leaps. If you do not follow this procedure, gutting a moose can be one of the messiest and clumsiest tasks undertaken by a hunter. An accompanying photo shows a pair of young fellows too deep into it.

Next, the animal's head is cut off, the carcass skinned as it lays, the legs clipped off at the knees, and the shoulders separated from the body at the natural joints. Each shoulder is a man-sized load.

The body is then halved by *cutting* across the spine, and finally quartered by *sawing* down the backbone.

Jerry, Cliff, or Art Troup and I can pair up and reduce a moose to eight parts in well less than an hour. Antlers and hide increase a moose from eight carrying loads to ten loads.

Our meat is thoroughly peppered if the weather is at all warm. Blood is left on the meat to form a hard glaze that helps protect and seal it.

Although we experimented some with aging our moose, we never found improvement by hanging the meat any longer than a hunt required.

There is no question that a moose, or any animal, should be cleaned and cooled as quickly as possible. After cooling, meat firms and tastes as tender and delicious as it ever will.

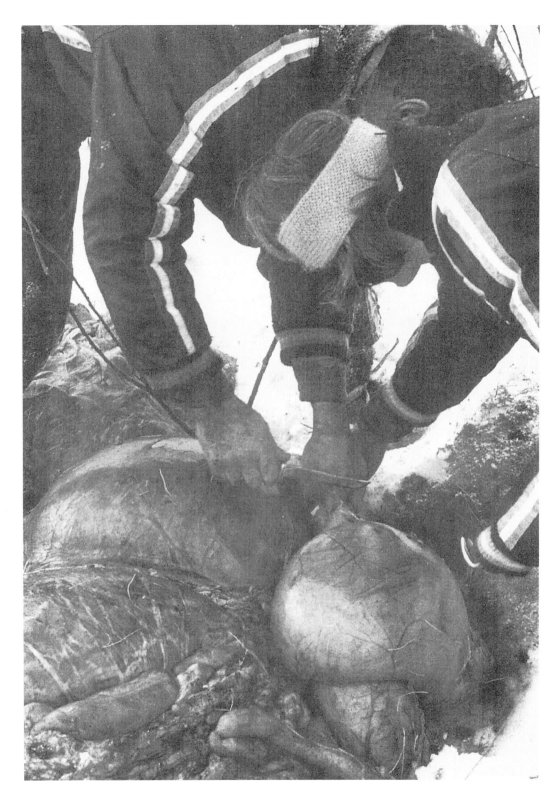

Moose guts are immense. If you find yourself as deeply involved as these two young men, you are doing it wrong. The knife isn't much either.

Until there got to be too many hunters around, our favorite moose camp was along Jarvis and Riley Creeks where they widen after leaving the Granite Mountains.

After preliminary glassing, we set up camp on a grassy island that lay well out on the half-mile wide gravel bars. For a dozen years we used that spot as a base camp. It had many advantages. For one thing, we were off the tundra and out of the bush. That meant fewer mosquitoes.

We could set up spotting scopes at tent door and study the rising ground around us for many miles.

There is some value in looking slightly upward into *distant* woods. Animals that might be hidden from higher spotters can be picked out and examined as they browse or rest under trees. The old Jarvis Creek camp was especially well situated in that respect.

While the tents were going up, perishable foods were placed in the cold creek water, and the Bombardier tractor dragged in old logs to use on nightly bonfires. Most of our cooking in moose camp was done on Coleman stoves, but the crisp evenings were warmed by comforting flames that never failed to induce storytelling and a sense of close companionship.

Camping on gravel bars, we could build large fires without possibility of their spreading, and after successful hunting the flames often rose high in celebration.

A meat rack is important in moose camp as it is expected to hold many hundreds of pounds of meat. Ours on Jarvis Creek was made of eight-inch thick logs and placed a little to one side where the wind off the glacier blew across it. At night, the Bombardier tractor was parked so that its highlights bore on the hanging meat. If a prowling grizzly approached, it could be quickly exposed and probably driven away.

The old guide took no part in our camp preparations. He established his spotting scope and began examining the area in detail. If a spectacular bull was sighted we went hunting, but more often the camp went up with little interruption.

When we were ready to hunt, Art would show us the various moose he had located. Often there would be a dozen or more. Most were cows, and many were quite distant. We would talk it over and lay out the hunt.

Our hunting system from that camp was simple. A pair of hunters moved toward the moose. Periodically, the hunters turned and observed the camp through their binoculars. In camp the old guide watched both moose and hunters. By arm signals he would tell the hunters which way to go. The normal folds of earth and intrusions of woods and brush usually kept the hunters from sighting the moose until quite close. Without guidance from afar, the animals would not often have been located.

Two arms held straight overhead was the signal to keep going directly away. Two arms held low (similar to the military position of Attention) meant, you had passed the animals, come straight back. An arm pointing in a direction meant, go there. A circular arm swing said, "Look around, you should see them."

Using this system, most moose were shot at less than 100 yards. Many were unsuspecting. Rarely, was a second shot needed, but it was usually taken. A second bullet quickly and accurately delivered is excellent insurance.

Finished with Dall sheep hunting, we moved down to our Jarvis Creek camp. With rising ground all around, we began glassing for eligible moose. Note the second spotting scope on top of the tractor.

A lot of hunters take cow moose these days. At this time, the Game Department permits it. There is certainly nothing immoral about shooting cows. However, it has always seemed to me that cows should not be taken unless it is intended to reduce the moose population.

While that may be desirable in some areas, it seems inapplicable for most of Alaska. I admit to being only a hunter and do not profess to understand all that game management people know.

Time will tell if we are wise in allowing antlerless moose hunting. Those of us who have gone after and taken the big bulls sometimes fail to adjust to new ways. Some whitetail buck shooters in the lower forty-eight states still resist doe hunting, and for the most part they are wrong.

Since I shot my first moose, that little 28-inch meat moose, I have never touched trigger on anything under the magic 45-inch measurement. After all, could you imagine a hunter mounting a cow moose head?

Ok, a nice moose, and great way to get him out. My first question is: Where is the meat? A moose of the size indicated by the rack would half fill this johnboat.

There have been various changes in the laws, and a decade or two back some trophy hunters alibied their failure to bring out what they shot by challenging the law requiring a hunter to save and make use of what he killed.

Their pitch was that they had a right to hunt only trophies—period. And, they won. I have never understood that decision, and I think it an unforgivable waste to leave entire carcasses of great animals to wolves and bears. The policy smacks of the old days of shooting buffalo from moving trains or for their hides and leaving the rest to rot.

We should have learned better, and I hope that the hunter who took this moose was even then bringing in the meat for loading into his boat.

This is my hunting pal, Stan Thomas. Stan shot the moose he is shown with when he was nine years old using a cut-down Swedish military rifle. The smaller photo shows the mighty hunter lying within the moose rack only moments after his successful hunt. In the larger picture, Stan is twelve years old, but the moose rack still looks big. It is. The rack measures 63 inches in span, it is well balanced, and it has a lot of points. A trophy and a memory to be savored for a lifetime.

Chapter
24

CARIBOU

When compiling a list of Alaskan game animals that have fallen to my gun, I find that caribou lead the rest—combined. That surprises me, as I have never hunted caribou particularly hard.

There are about 600,000 caribou in Alaska, although in some decades that count has fluctuated wildly. I suspect their vast numbers explain in part why a hunter like me would shoot quite a few. The facts seem to be that many caribou are taken while out hunting other game. To paraphrase an old tritism, "They are taken because they are there."

One might expect that a caribou would be found sharing pastures with moose because they are both deer. Although this may occur, it is not the usual way of things.

The caribou has an unbelievably effective fur that keeps him warm in the bitterest cold. It also keeps him too hot in the warmer hunting seasons. So, we are likely to find caribou in cool spots. Where a moose might settle for the shade of a spruce, the caribou is more apt to stand on a snow bank. Where moose are found in the tall tundra or browsing on young willow growth, the caribou is probably out in a cooling breeze, down along a damp creek, up in a sheep meadow, or munching on the green things growing below a glacier.

Caribou

The caribou is the most curious animal in Alaska. I have enticed them into short range by waving my handkerchief and I have simply sat while they maneuver on their own, getting closer and closer.

Stan Thomas and I were photographing grizzlies in the fall of 1974 when the best double shovel caribou I have ever seen appeared on a skyline. He eventually saw us and came down to determine what we were. He kept coming until he stood in a typically awkward caribou stance (which means splay-legged and sort of twisted) only about forty yards from us. I shot a bunch of pictures until the wind shifted. He got a scent of us that acted on his system like a hot poker. He went straight up in the air, bucked like a stallion, and took off. Those are typical caribou actions.

I could believe that caribou suffer some sort of short circuit between their ears. They may dash about, perform blatantly idiotic gyrations, stand looking really dumb, yet prance with the most handsome stride in the Alaskan kingdom, all within the space of a few minutes.

In summer heat a caribou, like this weary looking young bull, can seem a sad and dispirited creature. They sort of sag in the middle, they stand around a lot, and their fur appears to be molting. We do not hunt them then. Caribou like it cold.

The caribou is the only deer that I know of that both male and female wear big antlers. The cows' antlers are smaller and very spindly, but they are still large if compared to those of other animals.

A big, white necked bull caribou is a magnificent sight to behold. Not only is a bull caribou the size of an elk, his spread of antlers is at least comparable, and he can move with a grace that is stunning to watch.

The caribou runs with a high knee action and lays his vast antlers back along his neck, adopting a stride that track coaches should point out to their middle distance runners. Whew, he is beautiful. His run is poetry—high knees, long springy stride, everything flowing in harmony.

Even ordinary caribou boast very impressive racks of antlers, and their size takes some getting used to. Hunters from outside are often overwhelmed by their first sight of a caribou bull. They shoot an animal they believe is monumental but, later as they encounter a lot of caribou, they find their trophy to be only average.

A caribou rack is judged by its spread, heaviness of beam, number of points, and whether it has two shovels. A shovel is the palmated section of antler that runs down over a caribou's nose. A typical caribou has only one shovel and a long point on the other antler. The width of the palmation on a bull's shovel is also important. A sixteen inch wide shovel is very good, but the double shovel is what we all look for.

I would say that unless your bull has around thirty points and very heavy antlers with wide palms and two shovels you do not have a truly super rack. Then, I have to add, with caribou you do not need a super rack to have an impressive trophy. Even a typical set of caribou antlers is attention getting—outside Alaska.

Our barren ground caribou bull (which is the kind we have in Alaska) may weigh as much as 600 pounds. I would guess that 500 pounds is a more likely figure.

A typical annual caribou harvest in Alaska will number around 35,000 animals. A great many of those taken are killed during the migrations. Many others are shot by hunters out for other game, or, perhaps out for any game would be a more honest way of putting it.

Migrating caribou near the Denali Highway in the Alaskan Range

Our parties have not hunted caribou for many a year. When we encounter caribou we do take them for meat, however. A quota of caribou can fill a man's larder for most of a year. With the price of domestic meat in Alaska, a freezer full of wild game is not a small thing.

Years ago, nearly every home took a couple of caribou. The limit was three caribou per license back then. The quarters were often tossed onto the roof or hung in an unheated shed where they froze rock hard. The weather provided a free deep freeze, and one used a bow saw or whacked off a desired chunk with a hatchet. Certainly, there were less crude methods of storing winter meat, but the old way proved pretty effective.

Caribou meat is tender and tasty. Not having a discriminatory palate, I think it tastes as good as any meat I have ever eaten. Some tell me that to them the meat tastes weak. I gather that means a bit tasteless. I believe it is all in their heads. There is no evidence that I know of to support such a contention, and most people like caribou meat.

I have rich memories of caribou shoots. I recall sitting on a rock over Dry Creek watching a bunch of caribou loafing near the stream banks. A big, white chested bull saw me as something different and decided to investigate. He high-stepped his way closer in widening loops until he was within a hundred or so yards. Then he stood looking at me awhile. When a caribou looks, he is likely to get himself twisted into genuinely grotesque positions. His back may get all out of line, and his legs will probably end up splayed as though he was wind-broken.

This inquisitive bull moved closer with his nose high trying to wind me. He closed within seventy-five yards as I sat still with only my scope following his movements. The bull was so close that I could clearly see his eyeballs through the 4X glass. Eventually, a breeze drifted my scent down to him. He nearly shook his antlers off trying to rid his nostrils of such a foul smell. Then, he sun-fished a bit and took off, tail up. Horns laid back, with his high knee action trying to hit his chin. He was so beautiful in stride that I let him go a long way before I plunked him. That was a long time ago. I guess now I would not shoot him at all.

Either sex of caribou can be legally taken. Either is fine meat. The best meat caribou is not your mighty bull. Young animals are the best eating. So, most of the racks we have taken over the years have been of less than trophy size. After all, how many big caribou racks should a hunter hang in his home? Too many can weaken the display.

The photograph above is of Mimi, Andy J. Mefford, and the old guide posing with their caribou on a hunt into the Granites. Unfortunately, the picture is old and has become poor, but in the background you may be able to make out two tents and a track vehicle with a trailer. The old guide leans on two sets of small antlers. Those were his meat caribou. Andy is standing in front of a truly fine set of antlers. As I recall, Andy J. rose early and stalked the bull alone. Took him with a .270 Winchester, I think. Mimi shot hers from over a clump of grass at about 100 yards with another .270. A funny part is—we were on a sheep hunting trip. We did fine on caribou but lousy on the rams.

All three friends have now gone to their great reward. I hope there is good hunting up there for them.

One other point in the old photo is worthy of interest. A close look may show that Mimi's trophy is still in perfect velvet while Andy's is polished clean. Both bulls came from the non-migrating herd at the foot of the Granites. Now, how do you account for that?

The caribou may be the easiest of all Alaskan big game to shoot. It is not that they are so weak that they cannot take a bullet. A big part of it is that they are out in the open and, in most cases, offer good shots. That caribou are so incredibly curious and often pose for the hunter helps as well.

A caribou's eyes are not the best and make rather open stalking practical. I doubt caribou vision is much better than a grizzly's. Caribou rely mostly on sense of smell and use of their great speed to get away. If caribou hearing amounts to anything special I have never detected it.

Hunter: Skip Hoecher, .300 Winchester Magnum

This trophy is an outstanding white-neck bull. A classic caribou in antler size and in coloration.

Of course, there are so many of the animals! When they migrate they are blind to most other things, and many hunters just line up along a march route and pot them going by. More about that later.

If a .30/06 or .270 is ever a right cartridge for Alaska it would be for use on caribou. There are fewer hurried shots on caribou. There is time for follow up shots, and usually there is a chance to shoot from prone or sitting.

But, I am in no way convinced that .30/06 class cartridges are the *best* even for caribou. Nearly always (unless the shot is perfect) a caribou will run around with a .30/06 in him. He will fall down eventually, but that should not be considered good enough. Down and out should still be the rule.

If you read critically the writings of O'Connor, Annabell, or any of the prolific hunting writers, you will note how often those using .30/06 class rifles have had to use two or more shots. Jack O'Connor, I found to be an honest writer. Jack was a .270 Winchester man and made no bones about it. He also admitted to using two shots or more on about everything. Not extra shots to be safe, but extras to get his animal down. While I like his honest reporting, I fail to grasp his reluctance to use more gun. If O'Connor had used a .300 Weatherby or better yet a .338 Winchester Magnum, he would have saved a lot of ammunition over the years.

One year, Art Troup and I were out along Shaw Creek. We saw a group of caribou that included a very nice bull. I sat down perhaps 600 yards from the animals. Art went out 200 yards or so in front of me. Our plan was for me to entice the caribou in close enough for Art to shoot.

I began waving a red bandana over my head, and after a while the caribou began edging closer. Pretty soon they came at a trot, apparently looking only at me. They passed Art upwind and never turned a hair. He let them get by and swiveled around to watch them coming up to me.

The caribou milled to a stop about 150 yards from me and shifted around with their noses sniffing in my direction and their rumps pointing at Art only fifty yards behind them. The bunch of them circled downwind a little and finally got my scent. They whirled, bumped each other, started in a couple of directions, and settled into a sort of stampede—right at Art. Seeing them coming, he jumped up and waved everything he had. The dopey animals stopped short, milled some more, and trotted off a little to one side, apparently to think it over. Finally, they trotted away, except the bull that casually began feeding. The range from Art's big gun was about 75 yards, and I saw him raise and lower the rifle repeatedly.

I knew the feeling. You are hunting for the trophy, the meat, and the challenge of the shot. There he is, but it is so easy you hate to take him.

The bull again got wind of one of us and after frantic snorting and jumping he took off as hard as he could run. Art laid one into his butt under his tail, and he tumbled head over heels with the heavy .338 bullet plowing nearly the length of him.

Oh, it is not always that easy. Still, I have never *had* to take a really long shot at caribou, and there have been many times when I *could* have shot long. All who hunt encounter long shots. The difference seems to be whether or not the hunter decides to chance the imaginative ones. I get closer. Over the years, I have lost caribou by trying to get in tight, but I also wonder how many I have taken cleanly that might have been missed or at least made a mess of by shooting at long range?

The most shameful caribou hunting I know of is the slaughter along the infamous Denali Firing Line. Hunters in throngs gathered on or near the Denali Highway to meet the migrating caribou herd determined to cross. In the old days, men stood right on the road and shot up, down, and across it. That was illegal even then, but they did it, and the road was not a safe place to be during migration.

Years ago, some people in the Game Department set up a metal silhouette of a caribou and attached an old pair of antlers to it. They placed the rig illegally close to the highway. When a hunter shot it, the thing rang like a bell—gave off a hell of a clang. Still, within a week the device was shot into a sieve and even most of the antlers were shot away. Hunters continued to screech to a halt and blast away at the remains.

As sad a demonstration of slob hunting as that was, I must point out that such rotten sportsmanship is not unique to Alaskan hunting. I can recall an almost identical incident occurring in Pennsylvania whitetail deer hunting.

Things are better now, but I find it hard to accept standing in the path of a migration as fair chase hunting. Many explain their conduct by stating flat out that they are not sport hunting. They are taking their winter meat. It is food they are after, they say, not sport. It is legal hunting, and it is not a game for them.

They have a point. As a consumer of overly expensive domestic meat, I can comprehend their wish to kill in the most certain way, and if such shooting was too tough on the herds, the Game Department would outlaw it. Still…I would be less dissatisfied if all those "meat hunters" did not take so many mighty bulls and did not display their magnificent antlers so proudly. As meat hunters they must know the younger animals are the most tender.

Caribou

Guide: Johnny Rhyshek (L) w/.375 H&H Magnum. Hunter: Brian Roth, .300 Weatherby

After you shoot 'em you have to move 'em. The tractor does it best. Here a guide and his hunter (with the trophy) do it the hard way.

Caribou are found all over Alaska, except along the southern panhandle, on the Kenai Peninsula, and on Kodiak and Afognak islands.

Alaskan caribou have been divided into 13 distinct herds. Most migrate, but some small groups do not.

The scientific name applied to these more than half a million animals is "Rangifer Arcticus." Most hunters know them as Barren Ground Caribou.

The caribou is really a reindeer, but as far as I know, none have shiny noses or are named Rudolph, much less Dancer and Prancer.

When they walk, caribou involuntarily make clicking noises with the bones in their ankles. The sound can be heard for a reasonable distance.

In the winter, the caribou subsist almost entirely on caribou moss. It has often been claimed that the antler shovel over a caribou's nose is there to brush aside snow to get at the moss. This old tale should be put to rest as the caribou sheds its antlers and spends the winter shorn of its crowning glory.

Until modern times, caribou hides were favored sleeping robes. The insulating properties of caribou fur are superior. However, caribou hides do not make the best leather. Caribou are often infested with warbles larvae which leave the leather scarred and pocked. If you wish to keep a caribou hide, leave the hair on.

Because of its super insulating properties, it is especially important to get the hide off a downed caribou as quickly as practical. Even opening and cleaning out a caribou from gullet to tail is not enough. With his hide on, body heat diffuses too slowly. Skin your trophy immediately.

There are grand old arctic survival tales about stranded hunters who survived blizzards and killing cold by crawling within downed moose body cavities. Not a bad idea, but I would pick a caribou. He would stay warmer.

This is caribou country. A non-migrating herd lives within the rolling hills most of the year. The herd usually numbers about two hundred head, and a number of excellent racks appear each year. Andy J. Mefford, on the left, is using a .270 Winchester the author built for him. The author, second from left, has his trusty 300 Weatherby. Jerry's rifle is hidden, and Art has slung his 30/06. We lean against a sled that Art was trying out for bringing in heavy loads behind his tractor. The system worked, but it was very hard on the ground cover and left a huge ripped up path behind us. We dumped the sled as soon as the hunt was over.

I hope that readers enjoy these old photographs (and the captions that go along). I believe that each tells something about hunting in those long past seasons, and about those of us who went out for the great animals. Of course, to me, the memories are honey and grow sweeter each year.

New photos are usually of better quality, of course, and a severe problem in assembling material for a book like this, is that back in earlier times few of us carried a camera, and even fewer hung onto their pictures for these many years. When asked, the old timers say, "Sure, I've got some pictures put away some where, I'll see if I can find them." They rarely do.

This book is about hunting, and if beautiful photos are all that is desired, one can turn on the TV and be educated (along with incredibly detailed and colorful pictures) by some young guy who hasn't lived long enough to understand much of what he is exclaiming over—as modified by some production experts who know even less—and edited by another expert who has never shot anything and who feels uncomfortable off pavement. My sentiments on most hunting TV have just been revealed.

Made from modern materials, this huge pack is not as heavy as might be assumed, but I never carried anything that large—excepting a dead animal. This is a good pack, however. It has wide straps that will be easy on the shoulders and not cut in, and there are uprights over which to hook a rifle sling.

Jack McMillin has always been an equipment freak. In 2000, he and I rode our Harleys from Fairbanks to Maryland and Jack had enough stuff hung on his motorcycle to begin a homestead.

On the way, he bought another pair of boots—which made three pair to carry.

Jack is an experienced hunter who was going after caribou and grizzly on this hunt. (He got a fine bear with the .375 H&H Magnum he is carrying.)

As this is written, Jack is the oldest, active duty law enforcement sniper in the United States. He teaches the subject at Blackwater USA, and he mentions how his years of hunting big game have enhanced his understanding of stalking and silent approaches.

Native Alaskans are not trophy hunters. The animals they shoot are most often young and tender—for eating. The native people of Alaska hunt for subsistence, and they can legally shoot just about anything in any quantities they desire almost any time.

Many trophy hunters and non-native Alaskan residents have problems with that program. Most complaints lie in that much of the game shot is fed to dogs (sled dogs), and that natives often do not appear to be the environmentalists pictured on TV.

A classic case that gained public attention some years ago involved a native who shot more than twenty caribou, got drunk and let them spoil, then went out and shot twenty plus more—to feed his dogs.

This treasure turned up among old stuff.

The author bears down on a shot. The caribou never had a chance—maybe.

Note the binoculars slung out of the way. I probably did that to make the photo more dramatic.

The Mag-Na-port recoil-reducing slot just below the front sight can be seen. There is a matching slot on the other side of the barrel. Gases are propelled upward and away at an angle of about thirty degrees from the vertical. The modification reduces kick appreciably and the gases are not blown sideward into other people or into the ground encouraging dust and debris. This Springfield action was always chambered for big cartridges. As the barrel has an integral ramp on it, the caliber could be either a .375 or a .458 in this picture.

Art Troup, Alaskan hunting companion and foreword writer for this and about forty other Roy Chandler books, contemplates a strip of barbed wire that nearly tripped him. The wire was found so far into the timber on the Kenai that one could believe that no human had ever set foot there. One strand going nowhere. Inexplicable.

Chapter
25

WOLVES

This is a book about big game hunting, and the wolf may not really belong in it. Most hunters do not list wolves among Alaska's great game animals. However, it is also difficult to think of wolves as small game or varmints. They are too big, too cunning, too admirable, and too numerous to ignore.

Those who have not seen wolves in the wild probably need a mental adjustment to visualize wolves as they really are. Imagining a large dog does not quite make it. Mature wolves may run to 150 pounds in weight. Their coloration may include nearly any combination of colors. Gray and brown seem most common. A wolf tends to be more narrow in the chest than a dog. His jaws are more developed, and his knees appear slightly knocked rather than bowed, as a dog's do. Even the most expert admit, however, that a wolf *hide* cannot usually be identified from a dog's of the right breed. A very big dog hide can look like an average wolf's.

These days, wolf hunting is limited. As sometimes happens with an animal species, wolves caught the public eye and public sympathy. Bounties were taken off wolves' decades ago, and that alone cut down on serious wolf hunting.

I can remember when Leroy Shebal and some others used to fly out of Fairbanks to hunt wolves on the open tundra. The technique was to fly low, force the wolf to run or cower, then blast him with a shotgun as the plane went by. Later, you landed and skinned out the carcass.

That all sounds a lot easier than it really was. You cannot land everywhere. Unseen lumps and hollows can wreck a light plane in an instant, and in bitter weather there was hard work with your hands freezing. On the other hand, Leroy used to take about one hundred wolves in a two week period. With the bounty at fifty dollars a wolf, the hunters not only had exciting shooting, they made a year's income in fourteen days.

Fierce looking devil isn't he? Do not fear, this wolf is now a mount in the University of Alaska at Fairbanks museum, and has been since the 1960s.

I used my Cessna 170 for hunting wolves, but I never enjoyed it much. I liked the tight flying, but not the hairy landings. I did not enjoy killing animals with the methods we were using. I did it for the money.

I took off the right-hand door and turned the right-hand seat of the Cessna around so that the man shooting rode backwards. I located a wolf, chased it into an area where I could reach it after landing, swept down right on top of the animal, and as he cringed and we zipped over him, the gunner blew him away with a load of buckshot.

When learning, the shooting was tricky. You had to hold way behind the wolf to counter the plane's speed. Usually, the wolf was shot while cowering, but a running animal made the shooting that much more uncertain.

You could imagine wounded animals crawling around down there suffering and unable to get away, requiring a second or even a third pass.

If you do, you are right. Hunting wolves for bounty with an airplane was a mean business, but at $50.00 each, killing a wolf was very profitable, and you kept the hide with one ear removed. Tanning back in those days cost about $8.00 a hide. I could later sell the furs to tourists for about $20.00 each. In an era when a year's work in Alaska might bring in $5,000.00, wolf hunting brought in serious money.

Gordon Haber is the most knowledgeable wolf expert I have ever met. Gordon works out of Mount McKinley Park (Now Denali Park.), and I first met him back in the late sixties and more often in the early seventies. He has studied the park's wolves for at least forty years that I know about. Haber's conclusions on the life styles of wolves were once controversial. Now, most experts agree with his findings.

Gordon has never claimed that his data were applicable to all wolf packs, just to those he studies in Denali. It turned out, however, that most of what he noted did hold for most wolves in North America.

Talking with Gordon is an experience to remember, and his studies are filled with information that often conflicts with our traditional images of wolves. Hunters and trappers often misinterpret Haber's statements because they seem not to agree with their own observations and ideas. I must add that Gordon Haber is not pro-hunting. He is an academic who is interested in wolves. It is virtually unheard of for a North American wolf to attack a human being. All of those stories you have read and heard about (where the wolf-encircled trapper holds a huge wolf pack at bay with his small campfire and clubbed rifle with wolf carcasses dotting the surrounding snow) are imaginative but highly inaccurate.

When times are hungry, a wolf pack breaks into smaller groups to range further in their attempts to find something to eat. They do not band together because the starving would be quicker that way. A wolf pack will normally number about seven animals. Plagued by hunger, wolves may even hunt in pairs or trios.

A wolf pack may temporarily increase in size, perhaps into the twenty animal range, but that only holds until pups break away to create their own packs, or until the food supply gets short. Such large packs are rare.

An additional point that should be mentioned is that the famous paintings from Russia of wolves in hot pursuit of a troika sled shows wolves after the horses, not the humans.

With man's love for the wolf's cousin, the common dog and our insistence that the dog is man's best friend, I have often wondered at our apparently inherent fear of wolves. Traditional children's tales such as "The Three Little Pigs" and "Little Red Ridinghood" start many believing that wolves cannot wait to sink their fangs into our tasty bodies, but if we avoid the wolf as diligently as he avoids us we will see very little of him.

Even the great illustrator, N. C. Wyeth contributed to the bad wolf image when he painted his famous "The Fight for the Peaks," for Scribner Magazine in 1917. The painting depicts a hunter on skis firing his rifle at four attacking wolves. Wyeth later brought the idea home to Alaska with a painting for the Cream of Wheat Company. This painting shows a hunter standing atop his sled swinging a rifle at attacking wolves. The title of the painting is, "ALASKA."

On a Jarvis Creek moose hunt we were all standing around glassing for game. Our rifles were stacked inside the tractor. One of the group said, *"Hey, Art, look at the big dog."*

Art looked and let out a bellow, *"Shoot, you damned fool, that's a wolf!"* The fifty-dollar bounty of the time elicited such a response.

Everybody dove for a gun. The guy who saw the wolf first hauled out a pistol and let go.

That is one (1) wolf pelt being held by the young lady from Fairbanks. Wolves can be very large.

It seemed as though wolves exploded out of every thicket. Later, we guessed there might have been seven of them, but at that instant I imagined dozens.

The wolves must have been hunting in a sort of skirmish line, probably just trying to stir something up. I gather that they had not seen us until the firing broke out. They surely panicked because some reversed their fields a few times before they got it all together and disappeared. The wolves still did best. When the gun smoke settled, our guy had an empty pistol but no wolves. None of the rest of us got a gun into action.

The mark of the wolf. A paw print compared to a common cigarette pack.

I took two wolves on Delta Creek one time. I was glassing an area for bear, and the two wolves came trotting by. I had time to judge the situation, get really settled into a good sitting position, and squeeze slowly. The first wolf probably never knew what happened. The bullet wiped him out at 150 yards. The second wolf turned and started straight away. A going away shot is not any harder than a standing still one. The target stays right in your sights. I held on the back of the wolf's neck and let the bullet drive into his spine. The wolf flipped over and skidded along the tundra, dead before it stopped moving. In those days, that was what we called a fast one hundred bucks.

Paul Barclay with a wolf displayed from an airplane strut

Hunters who take wolves in Alaska these days will probably encounter their trophies about as we did in the above stories. Without an airplane, a hunter who goes out particularly for wolves is more likely to have a long hunt than a successful one.

Here is a hunt that happened this spring. My friend was in Alaska hunting bear with Ray Atkins, the Master Guide from Cantwell. A large black wolf appeared—legal game, and my friend shot it. A nice trophy, but not the end of the story.

It had snowed nearly four feet deep that week, and Gordon Haber's thoroughly-studied wolf pack left Denali National Park in search of caribou. Gordon asked the Park Service to tranquilize the pack that he had studied for forty years and transport them back inside because they would surely be shot. We should remember that the pack, and the generations before those now living, had seen thousands of humans and had never been threatened by a human. Humans were part of their environment and were non-threatening—they thought.

The Park Service refused to tranquilize the wolves, indicating that they were not concerned with individual wolves, only with how many wolves there were in the park (usually seventy or more).

They were dead wrong, of course, and my friend killed the Alpha male (the pack leader). The Alpha female was trapped and shot, and it is doubtful that, although old enough to survive, the pups will find their way back into the park's safety.

Those wolves were not the normal wild animals one would expect, and I think the Park Service performed a disservice in allowing them to be slaughtered. It also ended Gordon Haber's extremely valuable lifelong research, and that should have been avoided. (That from a hunter/writer who is not a wolf-lover.)

Wolf packs have always followed the caribou herds. A wolf may range twenty miles a day hunting caribou, and a wolf is capable of traveling thirty miles a day—day after day. For that reason airplane hunters usually followed the caribou.

Caribou start their northern migration in April. Like the wolves, they cover a comparable twenty miles each day while feeding on lichens and mosses.

Caribou calves are born in June with the size of the calf crop depending a lot on the severity of the past winter. The wolves are on hand for all of this.

Wolves kill for sport as well as hunger. If they can, they pull down more than they need, and they often eat little of what they have killed. A wolf usually starts with a caribou's tongue and then eats the guts before he gets to the regular meat. \When kills are made during starving times, wolves are known to stuff themselves until they are ill and can barely move.

All wolves do not follow the caribou. Some wolves remain more or less in one area. I recall the winter of 1974 when wolves were coming into the city of Fairbanks and killing the dogs that were tied outside and had no chance at all. It happened again in 1977 and at least once during the 1980s.

A study of wolves in Denali Park demonstrated that in the spring much of a wolf's diet consisted of winter-killed animals, meaning moose and perhaps caribou that died of natural or cold weather causes.

Moose and wolves are usually in close balance. Eliminate the moose and the wolves go elsewhere—if there is an elsewhere. Most available Alaskan wolf habitat is already occupied without room for more wolves.

It is interesting to note that more bull moose are brought down in the winter by wolves than are cow moose. The bulls enter the arctic cold drawn and weakened from the rutting season. Some appear almost skeletal. Far from being lords of the wilderness protecting their mates, the bulls' struggle is primarily to eat enough to survive. Exhausted and their antlers discarded, they are easier prey for wolves than are the vigorous cows.

As hunters, we should know nature as it really is and overcome any belief that because a wolf is a predator he is automatically desirable or undesirable. Bambi-ism slips into thinking if we dwell on defenseless calves being pulled down by ravening wolf packs. Man likewise slaughters helpless calves in the name of succulent veal. That is just the way it is.

On the opposite tack, we must not become maudlin about wolves. They are not cute dogs. A wolf is a super-efficient and merciless killer. A band of wolves will take what it can get, whether it is a crippled caribou, a chained up dog, or a flock of sheep.

As part of nature's balance, the wolf has his place, and we should hunt him with due consideration. These days, that consideration is overblown and, unfortunately, we do not take very many wolves. *We do not take enough.*

Weigh these facts. It is accepted that a single wolf could consume twelve moose a year—or thirty-six caribou. Now, if we have, say, 3000 wolves spread across our lands, that could be an entire herd of moose or an intolerable total of 188,000 caribou eaten—every year. Let's hope our wolves find a lot of marmots and field mice.

If you favor the wolves, you will have fewer moose, caribou, and Dall sheep.

Wolves produce litters. Moose produce twin calves and caribou usually have a single calf.

It is believed that the wolf population can remain stable with a 40% annual harvest by hunters and trappers.

If you want more moose and caribou, shoot a lot of wolves.

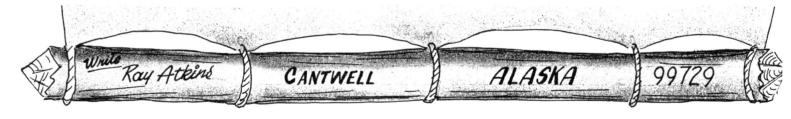

Rick Hyce, featured in full color on the back of our dust cover, is Master Guide Ray Atkin's assistant. The wolves draped across Rick's shoulders were roaming wild only an hour or so before this photograph was taken. Shot as trophies, Rick wears the wolves only to add flavor to the picture—or so we are told. Looks kind of Alaskan to this author.

Chapter
26

Binoculars

Do not leave home without them. Binoculars are as essential to successful Alaskan hunting as is a rifle. I have never known a decent hunter to go afield without his binocs. A sportsman intending to hunt Alaska should spend as much *thought* on his binoculars as he does his rifle/cartridge combination. Some, more wise, spend as much money for their binocs as they do for their rifle.

If you wish to examine pages of photographs of binoculars, gather brochures. This short chapter explains what and how more than it entertains.

There is a general consensus among hunters and outdoor writers that 7 x 35mm binoculars are the best power and size compromise. A hunter's binoculars must be light and compact enough not be annoying. Good 7 x 35mm glasses seem just about right.

A hunter does not carry his binoculars in a case dangling from his shoulder—the way inexperienced lieutenants are prone to do. The hunter shortens his binocular strap and hangs the glasses around his neck. The strap should be just long enough to allow the glasses to go over his head and be raised to his eyes. When not in use, the glasses are tucked into the front of the hunter's shirt or jacket. We all get so used to having them there that they go unnoticed until needed.

Of course, carrying binoculars is secondary to their use. If your glasses are too low in magnification, you cannot distinguish as well as you should. If they are too high, you again cannot see, this time because of the wobble. High power glasses need support to steady them or the images are too shaky to use.

It might be instructive to note that when looking through a telescopic sight, a spotting scope, or binoculars, the human eye can retain its sharpest visual acuity for only a short period. Lengthy staring at an object will always degrade your eyes' ability to examine details. The longer you stare, the less detail you will see. Look away often, roll your eyes, lean back and relax.

Seven power seems about right. The other number in, for example, our 7 x 35mm binoculars explains the size of the big end, the objective end, of the binoculars. The larger the objective lens number, the bigger the lens area and diameter. The larger the objective lens, the more light a lens can transfer toward the eye. Hunters like to speak of that ability as light *gathering,* but no binocular lens *gathers* light. It can only *transfer* light.

Because of their greater light transmitting ability, 7 x 50mm binocs are superior to 7 x 35mm at dusk and dawn. But, the 7 x 50mm is inconveniently large and heavy because of those big objective ends. 35mm is as large as a hunter should select.

Some hunters have settled on 8 x 30mm binoculars as their choice. Those hunters like the extra power of magnification. They accept the slightly reduced light "gathering" ability of the 30mm lens, and 8 x 30s are a bit more handy to use than the bulkier 35mm glasses. Despite an extra power of magnification, an 8 x 30mm can be made small due to those little objective lenses. 8 x 30mm is also a good choice. They are fine up in the sheep and goat meadows where you are little bothered by shadows. They are not as effective as 7 x 35mm when the light is poor.

Because their lenses are genuinely superior, these tiny 8X x20mm binoculars are as useful as any *ordinary* 8X x 30mm glasses I have seen. Lens quality counts! These little binoculars are so compact that a hunter might forget that he has them.

Beyond weight and compactness, and power and light transferal, there are other binocular aspects to be considered.

Weather resistance is a big one. Binoculars that will cloud if they get wet are of no use to a hunter. **Durability** is of utmost importance. Glasses that will not stand rough treatment should never be considered. Binoculars without **coated lenses** to sharpen images are less effective and should never be purchased.

A hunter's binoculars should always be of center focus with finer adjustment for the right eye. There are binoculars on the market that have individual eye focus. They only compound problems of getting on and getting swiftly focused. Center focus is best.

In choosing binoculars, the main effort should be to get the best pair you can possibly afford. Unfortunately, most hunters have never used a top quality pair of glasses. The improvement of clarity and ease of seeing between fair binocs and top quality is barely believable.

When a dealer offers you a pair of glasses costing hundreds of dollars and you know that you can buy a different pair that *looks* the same for less than half that amount, the decision can be tough. But, as a cover does not make a book, so appearance does not make a binocular. Buy the expensive ones. A hunter spends many hundreds of dollars on his gun and more hundreds on his gear. Why skimp on the item that may let him use all of those other things?

It should be emphasized that a rifle-mounted telescopic sight is never a substitute for binoculars. You cannot get by using only a scope. The field of view is not correct, and the scope sight will wear you out if you attempt the necessary hours of glassing.

Nor will a spotting scope substitute for binoculars. A spotting scope of about twenty power is a useful instrument. When you find something you wish to look at very closely for an extended period, the spotting scope on a tripod will do the job for you. However, most of the time you will use your binoculars.

For lengthy and detailed viewing, a spotting scope is the right instrument, but it is not a substitute for super-good binoculars.

When you are ready to buy, do not settle for the first pair of binoculars handed across the counter. You really must test your new glasses. Anyone who wears eyeglasses has noted that no two pairs are alike. The same prescription from the same optician feels different with each pair of spectacles you buy. The same is true of binoculars. I have had top quality glasses that pulled until I felt my eyeballs were well down the tubes.

Take the binoculars in which you are interested outside the store (leave the shopkeeper your wallet or something), and look through them for a half an hour or so. You will spend long, long hours behind those glasses, and they should be right.

When you test your binoculars, the technique is to first see your target—then raise your glasses to your eyes without looking away. [You follow the same procedure with rifle scope sights, by the way.] When your glasses drop in front of your eyes, the object should be there, clear and within a perfect circle without a sense of struggling to see or adjust. Study the edges of your field of view for distortion. With good glasses, there will be none.

Need I add that when lenses are involved it pays to buy name brands? Off-the-wall companies cannot offer you anything that a top company cannot better.

Although I know the above points and many more, they have never stopped me from trying about everything that comes onto the market. Because I am an often-published writer and am known as a hunter and a gun buff, dealers, shopkeepers, and some manufacturers are quite willing that I try their wares. That is satisfying to me as you can well imagine. It means that I have had unusual opportunities to try equipment and weapons that I would never have considered buying. Binoculars are no exception.

As a result, I have gone afield with some weird contraptions hanging around my neck. I have also experienced some genuinely superb glasses whose prices, if I had had to buy, would have brought tears to my eyes.

I have worn any number of 7 x 35mm glasses in the grades that are sold through Sears or a dozen other firms. They are adequate, but not great. I include here the *nautical* binoculars in the same price ranges that are peddled to the yachting fraternity. They are nothing special either. The nauticals were often alleged to be waterproof. Often they were not. Many leaked if the going got tough. Sometimes, they fogged in cold and damp. They all drowned out if dipped in a stream.

I dropped a pair of such binoculars in a stream while drinking. They fell out of my jacket and dangled in the current. They fogged solid and were never any good again. I do not suggest that a hunter should test his glasses in water, but if it does occur, the glasses should be as good as ever after the dunking.

I had a fine pair of pre-WWII Bausch and Lomb binoculars that skidded off a rock and fell a couple of hundred feet. I watched them ricocheting from rock to rock and almost did not bother to go get them. Upon recovery the glasses were scarred and scratched all over and looked terrible, but they worked fine, and I used them off and on for a number of years.

On one long hunt into the mountains at the head of the Wood River, Art Troup found a pair of glasses hanging near an old campsite. The first movement disintegrated the leather carrying strap. From their look, the binoculars must have been hanging there for years. They operated a little stiffly for a while, but the last I knew, Art still used them. Good binoculars can take a whale of a beating. Cheapies may not.

Top-of-the-line binoculars are truly expensive. At this writing, the finest can cost one thousand dollars. Few hunters can dig that deeply into the old money sock, but if you can, you should. Fine binoculars should never wear out. They can be something to use and treasure through lifetimes.

I appear pensive in this photograph taken along the Russian River on the Kenai Peninsula so long ago that no one else was around. Actually, I was irritated by the fire's slow response, and I did not see my partner grab the camera. Sometimes, a cheerful blaze seems almost impossible to generate—Art must have laid this fire!

The reality is that living in the Alaskan wilderness, with hunting and perhaps fishing about to take place, is one of the most relaxing yet invigorating and exciting conditions an outdoorsman can experience. (Well, maybe not the fishing.)

Pensive? Nah, I was as happy as a clam in deep sand.

Chapter
27

Camping

Camping requires a lot of pictures and fewer words. If you really hunt Alaska, you camp. The mountains are unlike the flats, and the soggy areas different than the tundra. The Kenai is never the Brooks Range. There are too many conditions to even attempt to describe, but photographs can.

Hunters from Outside should keep in mind that when we are discussing camping we are referring to Alaskan conditions. Things may be different in many other states. Alaska is still "The Last Frontier," and we have few commercial hunting lodges, and not many residents have hunting camps the way they are set up in other locales.

When you go hunting in Alaska you either hunt the few roads or you go out into the boonies and hunt from camps you or your guide establish. Alaskan hunting usually means tent camping or no tent camping. Rare is the cabin or even a lean-to.

Some of the professional guides have established perfunctory camps pretty far out in their designated areas, and there are some old cabins scattered about, but few hunters can depend on having one for their use.

A snug (well, sort of snug) hunting camp from the 1940s

In the chapter on moose, I described our old camp on Jarvis Creek flats. We had many others in that area, but Jarvis was a special one.

I had a sort of secret place that I really liked and visited on many hunts, but I have not been there in some years. If you look at our map of the Delta Junction area (20D) on page seven, you will see where Jarvis Creek is joined by McCumber Creek. At that stream junction are a number of ancient log cabins. An old hunter/guide used that camp long before my time, and I have forgotten his name, as those who go there now have probably forgotten mine. There are collapsing cabins and some corrals for horses. I was once told that the buildings dated back to when gold was panned and sluiced from Ober Creek and perhaps McCumber.

I never saw color in either stream, but lot of work went into the place. Now, it is tired and sagging. There are such shelters, if you know where to look for them.

A guy called Butch used to have a fine cabin on a lake named Butch's Lake out near Jarvis Creek headwaters. A pair of drunks got careless and burned the cabin down about 1959 or so. Sad loss, it was almost a house.

Mostly though, hunters in Alaska will camp, and that is the best. You can follow the game and not have to hike or ride pointless miles just to get a roof over your head.

Our base camp for goats up on Ernestine Creek was another memorable spot. Mighty cliffs rise all around, the stream rushes at your feet, the game animals are often in view, there are no bugs to speak of, and the only signs of human presence are our own from years past. No distant motors intrude, and few jets leave contrails high above. The animals are as undisturbed as you could ever find them. That all makes for a happy camp.

In the Alaskan Range, fall hunting is noted for really fine days. I think August in Alaska may be the best weather I have encountered anywhere in the world. September gets a little sharper, but is still tolerable. From then on conditions become more rugged.

I have been in the mountains a lot in the first half of October. It can be OK then, but the rest of the month is too cold for me to enjoy. I am not a big admirer of camping conditions in the late seasons.

In my camps, a firearm goes everywhere. Including bathing in a stream.

Despite normally fine weather, things can get rainy and soggy in the Alaskan Range. A wise hunter brings rain gear to his base camp. It is awful to be two days into the mountains and be completely drenched with no drying out place between you and distant civilization.

Even when we go for sheep or goats we always establish a semi-permanent base camp at a sort of central point just off the high peaks. There we leave all of the gear that we do not immediately need.

One year, Stan Thomas and I made a base camp when we were after goats. Then we climbed a too steep mountain and got stuck there. The only safe way down was a full day's hike around the end of the ridges and along the edge of a glacier (which wasn't really safe at all).

We had to sleep out that night just above the glacier. Lordy, it was cold! Stan was a pretty young lad that year. He carried his weight alright, but being the boss I worried about him. Not intending to stay out all night, we did not have a sleeping bag. But, we had plastic bags for putting our meat in, we had gloves, and we each had a military field jacket. Stan pulled plastic bags on like a sleeping bag, and I sort of pushed him under a sloping rock. Then I donned my own bags, which made good windbreakers, and crammed myself against him.

Stan was pretty warm, but I stayed so cold I could not stop shivering. I thought light would never come. We started again in 3 AM pre-dawn and hiked about nine hours the next day getting around that mountain. Base camp looked about the finest place I had ever seen. We pulled shoes off aching feet, washed some of the dirt away, crawled into those wonderfully warm sleeping bags, and flaked out.

I think it was just past noon, but who cared.

This photo is so old even George Nelson (on the right) could not date it. George was 86 and living in a tiny cabin—the one closest to the store at Cooper Landing—in 1973 when I spoke with him about the picture. This was a moose camp on the Kenai near Tustumena Lake circa 1946 or maybe it was much earlier (?).

Sticking to the being cold subject for a moment, I think it is always unwise to go up into really steep mountains without a sleeping bag. At least one bag should be carried for each two people. When the going is cold, you can crowd together and be glad for any body heat that is transferred. Too often I have neglected this rule and have suffered for it.

Once, while looking over some goats out of Haines, I was caught in a sort of whiteout so dense I was afraid to try working my way to lower and flatter ground.

The book says, *"Do not clamber around the crags in thick fog!"* That is sound advice, and I decided to go by the book and wait it out. I picked a seat against a convenient boulder and tried to relax, but the cold mixed with the damp air off the ocean was so intense that I shivered myself to near exhaustion. My packboard contained only a blanket and a couple of rations along with a big Bausch and Lomb spotting scope.

Fumbling in the pack to drape the blanket around me, I discovered an old army candle that must have dated back to World War II. I remembered dropping it in the canvas sack on another trip intending to heat a can of something over its tiny flame.

I wrapped up in the blanket, but the cold leaked in like water through a sieve, and I almost decided to chance the dangerous descent to lower ground.

Then I remembered a trick used by Simon Kenton, the old frontier scout. Poking around for Indian sign, Kenton built a tiny fire and sat with it between his legs with his furs draped over both himself and the blaze. I decided to give it a try using the army candle.

I have used such candles to warm a pup tent, but this technique was new to me. I cut a slit in my blanket and draped it poncho style over my shoulders. Then I got comfortable against my packboard, which was in turn braced against a rock, and lit the candle between my thighs. It worked beautifully. My hands were inside, and as any outdoorsman knows, your face can stand a lot of weather

Ah, a fire, boots drying, wriggling your tired feet. Ecstasy

if you can keep up your body heat.

Those little candles will burn for hours. Mine was sputtering when the mist thinned and I dared to venture forth. The comforting warmth had allowed me to doze, and as the mists moved away I felt rested enough to continue scouting.

One night we were camped on McCumber Creek when a huge wind came sweeping down the mountains. You can expect that when you camp below high notches, but this one caught us about half-ready. The old guide's tent pole snapped off, and I could hear him muttering under the collapsed umbrella tent. Our own army tent was trying to fly off down the creek, and we got out in the cold wind trying to pile rocks on the tent pins and flaps. In the morning I saw rocks stacked on those spots that I could not believe I lifted. It all made for a less than restful night.

I recall Art Troup and I putting up our tent in less than three minutes—where it ordinarily took about ten minutes of fumbling. There was a big rain threatening, and we were determined not to get soaked. There were some other campers (non-hunters) watching our performance that evening. I am sure that they marveled.

I have slept in arctic sleeping bags without a tent down to fifty below zero, but that was not hunting. I was in the army doing arctic testing, and it was survival. I guess we hunters have all slept on rocks, in marsh, on bare ground and on ice, and maybe occasionally in a tree.

Sometmes, mostly in times long past, we have put together almost luxurious safari-like hunts. Those were usually flatland hunts, and the tractor did all the work. Maw Rausch and her friend, Mimi, cared for the camp while we mighty explorers were hunting. It was still tent camping but amid shameful luxury.

Camping, both good and difficult, goes with Alaskan big game hunting, and it is a savage loss when the two are regularly divorced. Despite the wondrous safari hunts, I find it hard to imagine doing much serious Alaskan hunting while returning to cozy shelter each night. I have gone to camps that were a bit too modern for their use, and their luxuries added nothing to the trip and perhaps took a little something away from its memory.

Too many of us who hunt destroy some of our pleasure by working so hard at normalizing the conditions of the trip. We can bring so much of home into the wilderness that part of the adventure and zest of being afield is lost.

I have gone both ways in luxury and hard grounding it. There is no question that efficient gear makes camping comfortable. But, it can also be god-awful constricting. Setting up an elaborate camp can become a major time consumer, as can breaking camp in the morning. Even backpacking can be a monster if you carry a huge load of goodies.

Harking back to our military days, a lot of us know well that when weary enough we will sleep on rocks and be grateful. A hunter's body adjusts. His systems take a big gulp, emit a groan or two, and then adapt. While sporting goods outfitters provide a great service, we ought to keep in mind that we do not need everything in the catalogs.

The freedom *from* possessions can be stimulating. Henry David Thoreau hit it on the head when he wrote that a human becomes a slave to his belongings. We tend to expend more effort and time buying, caring for, and disposing of equipment than we do using the glorious accumulations.

There are now probably more track laying vehicles in use in Alaskan hunting than there are horses. That pleases me. Horses are a pain in the butt. They eat when not in use, and grizzly scent panics them. Bull caribou occasionally get confused and attempt to add a horse string to their harems. Horses roll with packs, get fractious at inopportune moments. They bog down in muskeg, and they love to scrape their packs or the riders' knees against tree trunks. We used to keep horses. We quit as soon as efficient cross-country vehicles were available. What a relief!

Understand this: No four, six, or eight wheel-drive vehicles can make it cross country in Alaska. Forget the balloon tires, dual wheels, etc. They won't work. You have to have tracks! It sometimes seems as if everybody hunting has to try to beat that rule. Occasionally, someone gets by in limited hunting for a little while,

The point of this photograph is not to disclose the hunter's massively muscled physique. The point is to show how untanned Alaskan bodies are. Every Caucasian Alaskan I know (who has shown me his/her body) is snow white. Alaskans do not sunbathe, and they almost never expose their skin to sunlight. It's the climate, not a tan aversion. Goth-inclined teenagers would love to look like this.

but sooner or later they will greatly regret their efforts to avoid the expense of a track vehicle.

The first track laying vehicles we used were army weasels. We tried early tractors by many companies, including common wheeled farm tractors by John Deere and the like. All bogged in muskeg, and most were prone to sinking their front wheels in anything soft. Nothing proved rugged or versatile enough. The early Bombardier tractors were not much good either. The company had some rigs with tracks on the rear and wheels up front like WWII half-track command cars. They were terrible. But, those early models paved the way for the really fine tractor pictured many times in this volume.

Strangely (to my thinking), very few guides and bush-livers have taken to track vehicle transportation. Those who live far out could make their supply trips to civilization pleasant outings instead of the terrain battles that now often ensue. In winter with deep snow? A good track laying vehicle will prance across the country as if it were summer.

It is true that there are places that a horse can go that a tractor cannot. But, they are few. Our tractor has walked out of high country towing a trailer with four moose, a clutch of caribou, and a flock of rams aboard, plus the hunters and their gear. We know because we have done it (see the photos herein). The pack train that could do that would still be in camp when the front end reached the taxidermist.

There is nostalgia attached to horseback hunting. But horses in Alaska are expensive and inconvenient. Even outfitters try to do without them, and for sport hunters, horses are impractical and unnecessary. Forget them. I elaborate further on track-layers and horses in chapters 28 and 32.

In Alaska, what your camp ends up looking like depends on how you transport your gear. In horse days, we did pretty well, but watched weight and size with a jaundiced eye. In this tractor era, we can have big tents, all kinds of camping goodies, and vast supplies of eating stuff in base camps. I feel no longing for the horses. The animals were a necessary evil required to get into hunting country with enough supplies to last a while, and at least a partial means for taking the game out. The tractor does the job better.

When we backpack in it is, of course, another story. Then we watch the load. We figure and calculate to save a few ounces anywhere. I think backpacking is the purist method of hunting.

When you are after big animals of the moose and caribou class your packing *in* is limited by your packing *out* ability. For practical purposes, you really cannot go in more than a couple of miles. A single moose makes ten good, tough round trips, and your personal gear is still in there. Anyone planning on packing a moose five miles is a pretty courageous citizen. That totals eleven round trips, plus the hunting. Or, at least 110 miles of hiking with half of those miles being burdened to the eyeballs. I think that two miles off the road is an absolute maximum for backpackers after big animals.

A caribou camp along a glacial creek. The drum is the spare gas can for the Bombardier tractor. The twenty-gallon drum was sometimes carried on the tractor, but more often it was slung on the front of the trailer, as shown in some photos. Twenty gallons? That is a lot, but we sometimes went long and far. Unlike horses, the tractor never ate or drank when we were not using it.

You can do a little better when hunting goats and sheep. I once backpacked a Dall ram for ten miles. The ram was a good one crowding 40 inches. Obviously an old fighter, his horns were heavy and battered. He had 12 annual rings and slightly broomed tips.

The hunt had been memorable with good weather and abundant game to look over. The ram had been taken on a high meadow up against Mount Hayes. After three days of hard hunting, long glassing, and then more tramping, I was already tired out. The walk out to the Richardson Highway promised to be a lulu. It was!

I cached my extra food with a few odds and ends where I might profit from them on some future trip into the area, and as most of the hike would be downhill, I arranged the bulk of the ram's weight in the center of my back. On flat land or working uphill, I like the weight high on my shoulders, but coming down, such a top heavy load can get ahead of you and cause a nasty tumble.

I removed my pistol and lashed it to the side of the load and hooked my rifle sling over the upright of my packboard.

To hoist such a burden it is necessary to sit in front of the upright pack. The arms are slipped through the carrying harness, the hunter rolls onto his hands and knees, and then pushes himself erect. Once on his feet, the load is totable for some distance. It is the getting up and down that is most exhausting.

I started off down the mountain, finding it necessary to rest every few hundred yards. Later, as I tired, I rested every one hundred steps.

It is difficult to measure pack weight. The longer one lugs, the higher the estimate is likely to become. I suspect I carried nearly one hundred pounds of sheep that day. Great horns still in the head and the always-weighty hide add poundage quickly. Most of the edible meat was boned-out and plopped into the pack. Meat should be low in the load to balance the horns—which are normally at the top of the load. Rain gear, rifle and pistol, plus my basic camping equipment (primarily a sleeping bag) could have jacked the total another forty pounds. Such a pack is no joke. Only a vigorous younger man should even consider it. As the first mile crept by, any meager sense of humor I may have possessed dripped away, and I wondered just why in hell I had taken a sheep so far back in.

Once I held too closely to a streambed and had to retrace steps out of a slick-sided gorge that drained away my energy and left me blown and weary-legged. As I tired I began to fall. Fighting an out-of-balance burden can result in strained and sprained parts. So, I had learned years before to go with the load and land as lightly as possible. But, it became extremely difficult to get up under that pack again and again.

There is only one way to whip a weight such as that ram. You just hang in there and chew away at the distance. But boy, it can hurt!

When I reached the wood line I cut two willow sticks and made an "A" frame for the pack. Thereafter, I could rest without lowering the load to the ground, and my strength began to gain over the exhaustion of the long downhill trek. By the time I reached the highway, I was in better shape than I had been halfway down that mountain.

I hailed a passing truck and got a lift to civilization. I noticed the driver wrinkling his nose a few times. Old sweat and defunct sheep made an odoriferous combination. I paid my way by telling the story of the hunt, but the driver opened the window anyway.

An aerial photograph of that hike does show about a ten-mile walk out to the highway. The long carry felt more like fifty.

A tent fly goes over the tent itself. Flies divert moisture that will eventually work its way through, and it keeps the tent walls relatively dry. Weighs little, and if bad weather drops in, a fly is very welcome. The adjoining photo shows another use for a fly.

I think that if a hunter needs to be told about the advantages of one brand or type of personal camping equipment over another he is not ready for hunting in Alaska. The Great Land is not the best place to learn to camp and hunt. It is more like a graduate course. The beginning hunter would do better to learn basic camping and out of door living before he concentrates on taking the grand animals of Alaska. Still a few reminders might be in order.

Buy the best sleeping bag you can find. Never get a mummy type bag. Not being able to move your feet can get annoying after a while. Why bother with it?

Our tent out at Bolio Lake. No, we did not backpack this load in. The tractor did it. This picture accidentally shows the ultimate boot sole. It is called a Vibram™. All soles will slide, this one slips the least.

Bring along your sleeping pills. The first few nights take one before you sack out. You will not become addicted, and you will wake to a new day rested and ready to tear into the steepest mountains. Incidentally, the great hunter and woodsman, Colonel Townsend Whelen, advocated a sleeping pill. I do not claim discovery.

Bring footgear to wear after daily hunting. Your feet will need rest, but you will still have to hobble around camp. I often carry sneakers to base camp. I do not carry extra shoes to spike camps.

If you have medicine, break it into two packets. One packet stays at base. The other goes with you. Up on the mountain, it is comforting to know that you have reserves within reach. If you really need them, this goes for eyeglasses as well.

When hunting in company, you can carry some things that your partner does not. I *always* have two packets of matches. My partner may not feel the need for extra matches, but I *always* have two waterproof packs. Take no chances on fire starting. When you need a fire, you just might need it desperately.

When Art Troup and I are hunting, we pride ourselves on taking very little. My concessions are to sleeping and lounging comfort. I take an air mattress and my sneakers. On the other hand, I rarely bring a fork or a mess knife. I eat with a spoon and cut with my hunting blade.

I like to keep clean shaven. It makes me feel good. I carry a razor with one blade in it.

Most of my buddies have turned away from coffee. That may sound like an odd thing, but all have stopped smoking, and the coffee seemed tied to the cigarette habit. It is nice not to have to wait while people suck smoke into their lungs and coffee into their guts. Now we are up and gone before most camps have their water hot.

We rarely eat breakfast. We snack along the way. When your feet hit the tundra, you should be off and hunting, immediately. Loaf later on. Wake up while you are moving. Camp time is for evening, not pre-dawn.

As shown in photos herein, I go few places without reading material. I adore lounging in camp on a day off, reading a novel, and escaping from everything. Sometimes on a high ridge I get too tired to enjoy more. It is nice to quit and loaf around, reading a little, and letting time wear by.

Of course, most of my hunts have not been time-limited. On most, I have been able to spend all of the days I desired. If you have flown in on a two week vacation, and your guide is costing big money, you will be unlikely to squander time just enjoying being up here, but remember, in Alaska it does not get dark early during fall hunting seasons. You will have light until ten or after in the evening, and it will again be light by four or five in the morning. Those are long hunting hours, and breaks can be welcome.

I feel genuine sorrow for individuals who have not developed the skills or the habits that allow casual reading. A good book can really fill out a day.

This nylon screen device is called a mosquito bar. Originally designed to go inside an army pup tent, the bar can be used alone in good weather. When the mosquitoes are thick, a hunter would trade his trophy for such a comfort.

Camping on a flood flat—where streams join? Guess they got away with it, but I've seen those rivers rise a foot in a few hours. Their tent pegs should be two feet long to hold in that gravel if a big wind comes through. I would move onto a bank—now.

Bring plenty of toilet paper. Under a photo in this volume is the same reminder. Add this: If you have transportation other than your strong back, change from conventional toilet paper to paper towels. They are tougher.

Carry along spray insect repellent when heading for your latrine, and use it on your bare legs and butt, but avoid the most sensitive of parts. The repellent can burn there. Squat where you have a small tree or limb to hang onto. A back flip into your own pile is disconcerting.

Cooking in the 1970s. Art Troup and the Author

This wilderness-looking campfire was only a few yards from our truck, but we had risked a two-plank bridge that was older than either of us, and we had circled a new beaver pond to make our way through a woods to this spot from which we would enter the mountains via foot. When you leave your transportation for an extended period, you always wonder if some reprobate will steal it. Alaska was once safe in that respect. No one touched others' stuff, including isolated cabins, but safety blew away with the arrival of the hippies after 1965 and later the pipeline from 1974.

The fire seems good. I am sure that I laid it.

Cutters™ is the only insect repellent we can recommend. It is the only brand we use. We have tried them all, believe me. For long lasting, Cutters foam is the most effective. Liquid is next best, and spray is last.

For the hunter, the only backpack to use is the old time cargo packboard. You need a pack to which huge and awkward loads can be lashed. You need an upright to hook your rifle sling over, and you need a frame that can stand violent banging around. The modern aluminum frames rarely measure up. But, if you can find one that does, you will save a lot of weight over the old model Yukon boards. If you are merely hiking, little of this applies, and you can use the almost frameless packs. If you plan on carrying out an animal, my advice is golden.

Avoid the many-pocketed models. What the hunter needs is one big old bag to drop things in. It will be less convenient to locate items, but you will always know which pocket they are in.

You must do this once in a while.

Camping essentials

Chapter

28

The Bombardier Tractor

Behold, the finest Alaskan use, cross-country vehicle this author has ever seen. The three-person cab is homemade (from a WWII era 2-1/2 ton truck cab), but the vehicle itself was built in Canada by the company of the same name. I have ridden this machine to the top of the Granite Mountains. We have roared across the tundra in it. It moves across treacherous muskeg, and we even floated across a small lake on it. Rugged, dependable, and simple to repair, this vehicle is now fifty-three years old *and is still as good as ever*. In all that service, it has never thrown a track. The tractor is powered by a straight, six-cylinder Chrysler engine. The machine can side-hill at an astonishing angle. The tracks apply less than a pound ground pressure, but the metal grousers dig in powerfully.

Art Rausch introduced this vehicle to Alaskan hunting in 1952. It has been the envy of every hunter or guide who has ridden in it or seen it perform. Occasionally, in this mechanized world, something clicks and works just right. This tractor is one of those rare examples.

The US Army tried vehicles like this with one more bogey wheel per side. They were acceptably agile for the military but were too unmaneuverable in tight quarters for an Alaskan hunter's requirements. Our very short model can spin in its own length and wriggle through Alaskan forests as neatly as could a Jeep in the lower forty-eight states.

Tractor

This 1980s photo of the bombardier tractor shows how it looked after more than thirty years of being hammered on too many hunts to count. During the last two years, Jerry Rausch has rebuilt everything, and the old machine is ready to go. The most significant modification was changing the electrical system to 12-volt. The original 6-volt worked fine, but 6-volt batteries are getting hard to find.

Jerry and I speak of loading the tractor on his ancient truck (his father's 1952 Ford that we used so very long ago) and visiting again all of the sites we hunted during decades past. We would not hunt, the plan claims. Well, maybe just a little for the pot. We would simply roam and remember. It is a marvelous scheme for two ancient duffers like us. I wonder if we will do it? That trip should require about two months in the wild country. Next summer sounds perfect to me.

Of course, the military decided to armor plate their tractors, which then required a more powerful engine, and it was quickly discovered that a stronger suspension and drive-train were then needed to carry the armor. Performance fell like a dropped stone, and maintenance skyrocketed.

With astonishment, we watched the Arctic Test Board at Fort Greely destroy the usefulness of their tractors. The experts replaced the steel grousers with rubber pads—so that roads would not be torn up. Interesting idea, but the tractors lacked the great weight of a tank. A Bombardier will even float, and without the grousers digging in, the tracks slid ineffectually in the bush. The tractors became useless even as snowplows. I remember one with a ring-mounted fifty-caliber machine gun mounted on it. In the end, the military rejected the concept with a note that the tractor was not made in the United States and . . .? By then, I was no longer surprised.

The secret to the Bombardier's ability NOT to throw tracks, lay in the factory's unique design. Most track-laying vehicles have tracks with a raised, knife-like ridge included in each track plate. Those ridge rides within a slot in the steel bogie wheels. (See the adjoining sketches.)

Unfortunately sticks and other trash can become jammed in the works hard enough to wedge a track plate out of line, and the track just peels from the rest of the bogies as the tractor moves ahead.

If you build heavily enough, like a tank, the system overpowers obstructions, but on lighter vehicles (the weasels of WWII come to mind) tracks are thrown with disgusting regularity.

Bombardier's answer lay in reversing the system. Bombardier provided bogies that were basically ordinary, rubber-tired, automobile wheels. The tracks were not steel but the rubberized belting that is similar to tire material and is used on machinery (including final drive belts on modern motorcycles). That stuff is tougher than—than anything. In all the years, we have never even torn the edge of a belt. The grousers were made in two parts that were bolted together with ordinary hardware bolts.

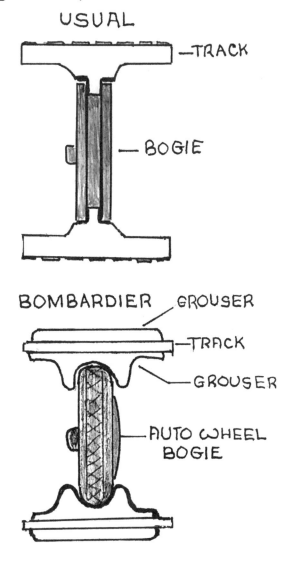

The outer piece of the grouser gripped the earth. The inside grousers sort of wrapped around the bogie's tire and held the tracks/belts in place. You could poke a log in there and, unlike a steel track, the system just twisted and wriggled and went right on. Grousers were replaceable using only a pair of wrenches.

But, suppose a tire was punctured? Patch it. A bogie wheel could be removed as if it were on an automobile. On a trip into Ernestine Creek we had our only such incident and, curse it, our never-tested hand pump failed. So, we patched the leak in the tire's tube, filled the flat with water, and continued.

A number of extra strips of belting have been in our tractor since it was built. Each is an emergency patch about two feet long. The idea was that if a belt ever tore, all you had to do was overlap a patch between two grousers and be on your way.

How could you take tension off the belt tracks so that you would have slack to work with? Simple, you don't even have to jack anything up. That smaller front bogie seen in the photo is also a tensioner. Turn a large bolt and the tension eases. Turn the other way and it tightens. One man can do it all with ease.

I fear that I may approach saturation with all of this how-to material, but that tractor fascinates me. Maybe just a little more?

Note the hand-operated winch out front. Art chose a crank rather than electricity because a need could appear when a battery was down. In theory, the cable and winch could hoist the tractor straight up. We did not attempt to prove that.

In use, three individuals ride side by side inside the cab. The center man is the operator. A hunter can stand comfortably on the rear, beside the engine, with the bar at the back of the cab to hold onto. Jerry and I always chose that spot (one to a side).

A tap on the tin roof tells the driver we see game. In the oldest days, Art would slap on the brakes, and the tractor would rock on its suspension. We would settle down, and Art would use his binoculars through the windshield while Jerry and I leaned across the roof with our elbows braced on the top, binoculars to our eyes.

Man, that was nice. **I want to go back!**

The Bombardier tractor is still ready to go—as it looks in 2005.

The outer-grousers on the tracks can be seen in this closer photo. The author made the Yukon packboard many hard years ago, and it is still in service each fall and spring.

Chapter
29

Fishing for Hunters
By Arthur B. Troup

Among the few personal failings that I will admit to is the fact that, in spite of trying, I have never been able to infect Roy Chandler with a fishing fever. He has watched while I hooked and landed big pike—really big pike. Pike that looked as though they could and would strike at trolled water skiers. I have shown him beautiful lake trout, but his only reactions were to pull his chair closer to the table and get a better grip on his spoon.

A glimmer of hope shines in the distance, however, because Chandler has admitted that _perhaps_ there are a _few_ hunters who might want to, as Roy says, "...*dunk an innocent worm on the end of some damned long pole...*"

Well, so be it. I have been selected to submit a _short_ chapter on the contemplative hunter's optional pursuit. I might add, though, that Chandler's resistance continues to this day.

Fishing in Alaska is found in two extremes: very good and nonexistent. Both extremes are affected by the same conditions: time and location. Allow me to explain.

The Russian river used to be an excellent stream for rainbows. Now it is _not_ a good stream for rainbows, and one would be disappointed in fishing there. However, during the midsummer salmon runs, the Russian is the scene of frantic, elbow-to-elbow tackle-busting, fishing joy. The last time I fished there it was restricted to flies only, and the salmon were taking large, light green streamers fished deep behind several buckshot. They took on the last few curving feet of a downstream drift, and then the action was fast, splashy, and exciting. More often than not the salmon broke free.

Russian River Salmon Madness

It was not always like this. Once a fisherman could find himself alone even at a spot this choice. Now, half of California is in town—and the rest are en route.

Just upstream from the mouth of the Russian on the Kenai River is a sharp curve. The water is deep, heavy, and butts against a bluff as it curves sharply downstream. Salmon rest on the inside of this curve, and I saw their backs and dorsal fins late one might as I headed for the Russian. I stayed there and cast to them. At this point the river is wide and the current on my side was fearsome; it took some doing to reach them. I reached twelve. I kept none. The fishing, in a word, was *superb*! At most other times of the year, *barren* would be the word.

Time then is a significant factor in Alaskan fishing, and one would do well to check in advance concerning the availability of fish, at that time of year, in the area in which one plans to hunt.

If *time* is an important consideration in Alaskan fishing, *location* is equally important. Every stream is NOT teeming with grayling. Some streams, indeed the entire drainage of a large area might be too choked with silt and rock dust from glaciers to support fish life. Jarvis creek for instance, is a beautiful stream in a picture setting, but I do not recall ever seeing anything in it.

Grayling eluded me in that area until Al Remington at Big Delta said, "You want grayling? Come 'ere." We walked to a stream not a hundred yards behind his place, and Al pointed to the tail of a long riffle and suggested that I cast there and let the fly float through the pool below. I did just that and caught two nice grayling. I released them.

The point, of course, is obvious. If one is going to hunt Alaska and would like to fish for diversion or the pot, ask the guide or outfitter in advance; or, if one is not required to have a guide, he should check in advance with persons knowledgeable about the proposed area. Are there fish *where* I will be and will the fish be there *when* I am?

If the answer to both questions is yes, then one can consider what fish will be encountered, and he can plan accordingly. Here, very briefly, are some points to help.

Pike in Alaska can be found, generally speaking, in the southeastern quarter of the state. They are much like pike anywhere and can be caught on plugs, spoons, spinners, and the like. I enjoy catching pike on large wet flies and streamers like big Marabous and Mickey Finns.

Dolly Vardens seem not well thought of in the North. I remain surprised to this day that many people disregard the Dolly, almost as if it were a trash fish. This feeling is predicated, I am told, on the belief that the Dolly is a savage predator on other, presumably more desirable, fish. No matter to me; I like the Dolly because he is not finicky and fights reasonably well.

I once caught an eight-inch Dolly on a four-inch spoon. That seems to bear out the reputation that he is an aggressive predator.

I cannot say how they are in the pan. Plan on small spoons, spinners, and streamers for Dolly Vardens.

The Arctic Char is very nearly everywhere and almost always available. They strike almost anything, put up a respectable fight, are very photogenic, and, like packrats, love bright shiny things. Try a #3 Hildebrandt spoon (gold or silver) with your fly rod or with some shot pinched on your spinning outfit.

Grayling require perfect water that is unbelievably cold. Occasionally, they are found in impoundment type bodies of water, but normally they will be in gin clear, numbing cold water that is moving over stones and gravel.

A nice Arctic Char

The grayling has been to school. He is smart, fast, spooky, alert, and usually a dainty feeder. Scare him and he will vanish. If you have decided to pack along just your fly rod and use it exclusively try a long nine foot leader with the finest tippet you can handle and drift #16s or smaller in sparse gnat or mosquito patterns by suspected locations or actually feeding fish.

Drifting these flies dry you will, of course, see the rise, but, if your drift is wet, look for the characteristic line jump or hesitation as when nymphing.

Spinning with flies for grayling is tough. The plastic bubble required to cast the fly seems to make the fish shy, but if you cast well upstream and are careful to keep the bubble from drifting contrary to the current, you should have some strikes.

I caught, by accident, the largest grayling that I have ever seen. In the late summer of '93 I was fishing for rainbows in a section of the Alagnak River called "The Braids." My lure was an opalescent, salmon colored, costume jewelry bead about the size of a large pea. The bead was threaded onto the tippet and allowed to slide down onto the eye of a bare #6 hook with the barb mashed down. The grayling was in a deep run and took the bead bumping along the bottom on the first cast. Go figure.

Troy Creasy, a guide from Pulaski, New York and King Salmon, Alaska, taught me the bead trick. That grayling was twenty-two inches long and is still swimming—I hope, in the Alagnak.

The moral of the story is clear: many self-respecting Alaskan game fish will take a salmon egg!

A salmon steals my heart. I wish every hunter/fisherman could hook one at least once in his or her lifetime. The salmon learned all that the snook, bonefish, and tarpon learned and then added a grace that he alone possesses. Without reservation, I would suggest to you that if your hunting takes you within the time and location limits of salmon fishing, do it! If you prefer spinning, and the regulations allow any lures, medium spoons produce well; or, if the area is flies only, you can toss them reasonably well using split shot pinched on about two or three feet above the fly. If you prefer a fly rod, you will no doubt have favorite patterns, but I would suggest large, three or four inch egg suckers in pale reds, whites, and combinations of those colors. Fish deep. Use split shot. Silvers take spoons. Kings take eggs. A "Jack" Salmon is an immature salmon that looks a little like a Brown Trout.

Art with a nice King Salmon, perhaps forty-five pounds in weight. Caught with 10-weight rod and line, #30 leader, #20 tippet, double-egg sperm fly. Took an hour and ten minutes. (Released)

One who engages a guide or outfitter for a hunt would not endear himself as the Great Hunter if he arrived with thirty pounds of fishing gear. Your equipment must be minimal. One of the popular, sectioned plastic boxes about 5 x 7 inches should be enough for lures, swivels, snaps, split shot, spinners, etc. Try to match the contents of the box to the anticipated fish. Heavy split shot and large flies and spoons for salmon; tiny gnat and mosquito patterns and several plastic bubbles for grayling; pack plugs for pike and some extra snaps and swivels and some red and white spoons; Dolly Varden will require spinners, streamer flies, and small spoons. If several types of fish are anticipated, then it follows that the lures should be varied. A 5 x 7 box holds an unbelievable amount of gear.

Fly rod or spinning rod? That, of course, is up to individual preference. Even though I dearly love the fly rod, a quality, short sectioned, backpacking type spinning rod is the best "all around" choice. It is tough, and it is easy to pack, light, and not at all unpleasant to use. I use a popular, quality, open-face reel and have two spools of pre-wound line, one 2-pound and 4-pound. A net is nice if it is a collapsible or folding type and can be easily stowed.

I love to catch big pike, big bass, and big salmon, so my fly rod is a 10 weight Browning Diana with a big Pflueger Salmon reel and a 10 weight DTWF salt water floating line. I can cast a sleeping bag with it, but it can still take about an hour to land a big King.

In the final analysis the success of your hunting trip will be measured by the pleasure you receive from it. When the capes are skinned out and the rifles put away, wetting a line can revive tired bones and add to that pleasure. Good fishing…'er…good hunting.

Comments by the author of this tome.

All that Arthur Troup says is accurate, including the part about my unwillingness to fish. I recognize that there must be something in it; enough books and poems about fishing have been written to be convincing. Convincing to most, that is. I continue to find fishing less interesting than taking naps or reading bean can labels.

In truth, I have had some wonderful trips with fishermen—including Troup, but my pleasure was not in holding a rod and staring hopefully at the water. Here is an example of some of the wonderful times we had in earlier days down on the Kenai.

From our base at Delta Junction, it is a hard day's drive to the Kenai Peninsula. We got in and got set up. Art Rausch immediately went fishing. Maw and Mimi organized, and Jerry Rausch and I set up the tents got the firewood and . . . everything else. Some systems never change.

For the next week, Art and Jerry caught huge salmon. They were giant fish, I thought. We weighed none, but Art said many were fifty pounders. Maw and Mimi filleted the fish. They had their smoker ready, and it went into action, and Jerry and I kept it working until we left. They also canned mountains of salmon. We even ate salmon. I thought it was Ok.

My job became driving freezer chests filled with filets packed in dry ice into Anchorage and getting them onto airplanes for the states. The families outside wanted all they could get—for some reason. I got more dry ice and went back to the Kenai.

Even back then I was a writer, and I spent loose time filling pages and exploring around the rivers. Few other people appeared, and except for one airman stationed nearby, no one stayed.

So, it was a great vacation, and I saw some new country. My friends were great as always, and we had other things to eat as well as *fish*. Fishermen use a lot of fancy terminology to describe what they do, but I know how to catch salmon. You get a huge three-pronged fishhook. You throw it in front of a fish and haul it in hard. Sometimes it will stick in the fish, and you get the poor thing ashore. Snagging is against the law, of course, and I would never bother anyway. It's just nice knowing how.

I wish fishing tackle were heavier, had more muscle, looked like it could do something. Then there is all that string, cheez! Boxes and boxes of sharp and shiny little things that are supposed to look alive, or worms, and crawfish, and *eggs*—for what? To catch something that happens to swim by, that I don't want, and the people I try to give it to don't want either?

Fishing is for Art, not for me.

Art Troup is a terrific fisherman. He is as good as they come. Actually, my old friend is good at whatever he decides to try, but at fishing and flying light aircraft, he excels. You should know that that black hat he has been wearing since ancient times was my hat. I put on that beer can hat band. Art lost his and confiscated mine. Ah well, he looks better in it than I did.

Chapter

30

Hunting Knives

Like guns, I seem to have always owned hunting knives, but despite the years of packing assorted blades, I never really began to learn about knives until I arrived in Alaska. At that time, I was sporting a beautiful 6-1/2 inch hunter by Bo Randall of Orlando, Florida. The first time I went out with Art Rausch, the old guide, I showed up with the long Randall dangling from my belt. Art looked at the big blade for a moment then asked, *"What in hell are you, a Mexican bandit?"*

Knowing the fame of a Randall knife and having carried a Randall fighting blade through some of WWII and Korea, I had sudden reservations as to Art's own qualifications as an outdoorsman. As was so often the case, Art was right, and I was all wet. I kept the Randall for many years. It hung with the rest of my extensive knife collection, but I never used it on any continent.

Years before coming to Alaska, I hunted Germany from one end to the other. I noted the small blades used by the proficient German Jaegers, but their game was often small. Did it not follow that bigger animals should require a more hefty blade? In Alaska, I found that it did not.

For the past five decades, my hunting knife has been a Case jackknife with two blades. That is what Art Rausch carried, and in the end so did about everyone who came into contact with him.

If, at the time Art showed me his Case folding knife, anyone would have suggested that I would ever recommend such a blade for everyone, I would have chuckled loudest of all. Cleaning my first moose, I found that a long, heavy blade could not trim neatly around the pelvis to detach all the cords and joints to let the heavy hind legs flop out of the way and to free the tubes leading from the animal's viscera. The thick, wide blade was simply too big. Next, I found that reaching far beneath the immense paunch to free everything for pulling out, the big blade was awkward as well as dangerous. I could never be quite sure where that sharp point was in relation to my other hand, which was also struggling to hold the great mass of guts out of the way.

When I tried to cut through the moose's breastbone I got another lesson. My big knife wedged itself in the cartilage. I could not get through. Art came and did the job for me using his pocketknife. He straddled the animal's rib cage and slid the knife under the sternum and hauled upward with his shoulders. The Case sliced the bone and cartilage cleanly. A few repetitions and the animal was laid open to the throat.

Sharpening time came. I stoned and stoned. Art whipped the small carbon steel blades across his stone a few dozen licks, and he could shave with them. I stoned on into the gloom of night.

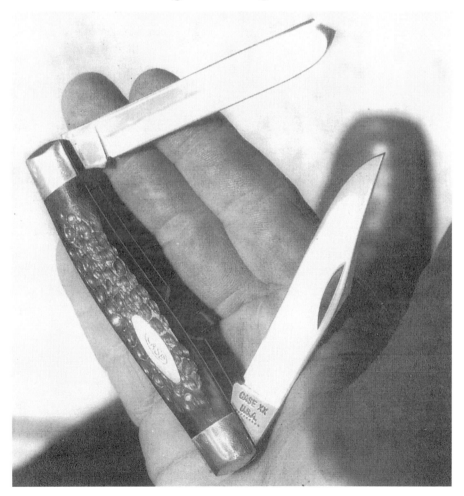

I am well aware that the above facts contrast about one hundred percent with the advice being handed out these days about what a hunting knife ought to be. What I read and hear makes me wonder how much game advocates of huge and menacing blades have actually worked on.

On the other hand, an expert like Elmer Keith does not agree with me. See his letter on page 86.

It may be a case of "Different strokes for different folks," but I think Keith was thinking about hunting in Idaho when he writes of blazing trails back to his downed animals. For Alaska, I am right.

An Alaskan hunter cleans his grizzly hide. ⟶

A belt knife of carbon steel that sharpens easily and holds an edge a reasonably long time is an excellent choice—provided the blade is NOT over four inches long and is thin and without a heavy back strap. I find the pocket knives more convenient, but there is inherent danger in folding blades. *Cold hands inside a huge animal could cause a blade to close and inflict a severe wound; therefore, choose a folding knife with a locking open system or go to a short straight knife.* If a straight hunting knife is preferred, I would recommend a Buck #16. It is the right size although the metal is a touch too hard for my preference.

The author's knife has two blades. The stockman's blunted blade is perfect for running the long incision in the abdomen of a game animal without cutting into the viscera. The other blade is normal shape and is best for trimming around joints and the close work at eyes, nostrils, and lips. Try that with a conventional hunting knife and your mount will look like a Jack the Ripper victim. Either blade does well for slicing away hide, but the pointed blade is best. Gary McMillin of Fairbanks uses surgeon's scalpels for careful trimming. Not a bad idea.

If a reader decides that a pocketknife is his cup of tea, there are certain points to consider. No doubt other companies make knifes equal to the Case, but I stay with that company because using a Case I have never had a hinge pin let go.

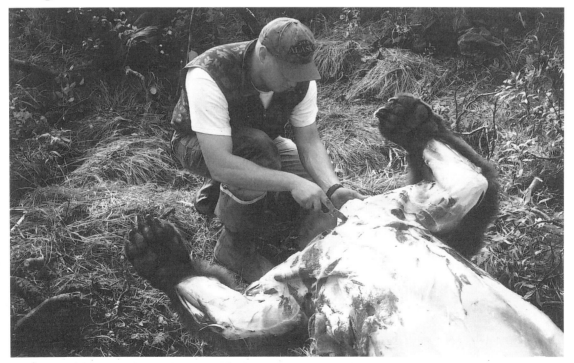

Guide and hunter, Johnny Rhyshek, skinning a *Boone & Crocket* grizzly in the Beaver Mountains.

Big bear, small knife, and that is good.

I have friends who converted to jackknives but chose other brands and had hinge pins bend or break. Such an occurrence is enough to turn a hunter back to straight knives.

I have never had a knife that was satisfactory for both cutting and field sharpening that did not rust if neglected. Conversely, I have never owned or used a knife of the stainless steel variety that I could easily sharpen. I would rather have a knife that I had to sharpen more often than desirable than to encounter one that I had to spend hours honing to get back into shape once it got dull.

Cleaning a moose, I normally sharpen each of the two blades on my Case one time, a little more than halfway through the job.

The sharpening takes five minutes maximum. I could get through an entire animal without sharpening, but halfway through I usually need a breather anyway.

It would be pointless to include a battery of knife photos here. One can buy books on the subject. Suffice to say that most alleged hunting knives look better than they work.

All of the fast and efficient skinners that I know use short thin blades. I do not know one that uses one of those freaky shaped blades becoming faddish these days. We all own lots of weird knives, of course. The knife is close to hunting mystique, and somehow we buy or are given queer ones now and then.

We try them, then store the things along with the other intriguing but less than effective items we gather, like Peruvian ski masks, battery powered hand warmers, and imaginative ammo belts.

Johnny Rhyshek doing delicate work with a scalpel. Around the head a surgeon's touch is needed

There is an argument that claims a heavy knife can be used to smash through thick bone by beating on the back strap with a rock or club. Probably true, but why bother when there is always a point to delicately separate?

A mighty Bowie knife can allegedly be used to cut firewood. Huh! I do not know anyone with hands strong enough to keep a fire burning from wood trimmed by a knife.

The fact is, you cannot even whittle as well with a huge knife as you can with a typical folding pocketknife. I do not suggest that we hunters sit around our fires carving willow wood flutes, but I have made tent pins, and ramrods, and I once made a willow ramp for a lost Model 94 Winchester's rear sight.

It is my solemn belief that if you try a three or four inch long, thin blade on your next big animal (whitetail deer size on up), you will never again carry a short sword. Back about 1960, *Jonas Bros.,* perhaps the world's most famous taxidermists, phrased it as follows:

"A knife is absolutely necessary, of course, but a little bit of thought should be put into the selection of it. Some hunters could do a better job of chopping cane than they could skin out a trophy with the cumbersome equipment that they end up with. A good knife of all 'round skinning would have a blade 3-1/2 to 5 inches long with a fair amount of curve. The author [One of the famed Klineburger Brothers] uses a heavy-duty pocketknife with two blades about four inches long or a sheathed hunting knife with a 4 or 5-inch blade of good steel. A small sharpening stone is handy to carry along."

Choose a top brand knife with a blade of not more than four inches (three inches is better for me). Get a high carbon steel knife that will sharpen. Then take care of it. You will never need more.

When backpacking far from civilization, I carry two knives. One rides in my left shirt pocket, the other in my pack. Both are Case folding knives. If I lose one, I have another, and if I should break a blade (which has never happened), I have three others going for me. How can you beat that?

I belatedly rewrote an earlier portion of this book to note that a photo of Art, Jerry, and me with our sheep (page 173) shows the outline of my Case in my shirt pocket—just as described above.

Herein lies a story. A year or so ago, I received a phone call from the Master custom knife-maker, Ron Duncan of Cairo, Missouri. A friend who likes my books, Tom Andres, had contracted with Ron to make me a super-quality hunting knife.

Ron Duncan may be the best knife-maker in the United States. His blades are Damascus steel. There is nothing finer, and few knife-smiths have mastered the art. Duncan knives are incredibly sharp and strong, and they stay that way. Damascus steel, as Duncan makes it, can be readily sharpened, and the knives are handsome.

Ron made the knife shown here for me. I remain overwhelmed both by Tom Andres's gift and Ron Duncan's skill. What a knife! The blade is a hint over four inches long, which is my maximum, and the grip is effective and good looking.

Even the Duncan-made knife sheaths are minor works of art. Ron's daughter Lacey hand-molds and stitches each sheath to exactly fit each knife's special shape and the new owner's requirements. They are strikingly good looking sheaths, and the knives come free easily. Except for the filler strips that keep the razored edge from cutting through stitching, my sheath is made from a single piece of leather—including the closure strap. More importantly, they hold the knife securely. A knife must never be lost due to a cheap scabbard. That is not a consideration with Ron Duncan knives.

I write this in the fall of 2005, and the Duncan knife is being tested by Fred, Harvey, and Chris Thebes on a sheep and grizzly hunt with Master Guide, Ray Atkins, in the Alaskan Range. The first return comments have been:

"This knife never gets dull. You don't need to re-sharpen it."
"Will you sell me this knife? I need one like it, right now."

[*"No, I will not!"*]

If you need a best-quality hunting knife, Ron Duncan can be reached at (660) 263-8949, or www.duncanmadeknives.com. Duncan is an honest and dependable, straight-arrow man. I like him, and I recommend him.

Art Troup works on a freshly shot rabbit. No, the bunny was not grizzly bait.

Chapter
31

Some Hunting Philosophy

We hunters are often asked, *"Why do you hunt?"*

We could answer, *"We hunt for the meat."* Or, we could say, *"We hunt to thin the herds so that the animals stay healthy."* Neither answer is, of course, complete. Both may be partly true.

A need to hunt is allegedly traced to early man's search for food and is therefore justified as some sort of hereditary instinct. Of a certainty, we hunt animals "because they are there," which is a direct theft from a similar inability by mountaineers to give meaning to their hobby.

Probably, the challenge of the hunt is a primary attraction for genuine hunters. To go into the fields and outwit an animal in its own habitat can be demanding, and the mechanics of the shooting itself can offer immense complications.

We all say that we like being out in the hills, but that hardly explains the desire to hunt while enjoying those hills.

The facts are, it is not easy to explain the thrill and enjoyment of the hunt. It does little good to demonstrate that men have hunted since the world allowed them aboard. Harley-Davidson motorcyclists have a similar problem explaining their avocation. They have a popular T-shirt that says, *"If I have to explain, you will not understand."*

To discuss hunting intelligently, and with reason rather than emotionalism, certain delusions must be dispensed with. The most primary is a belief that natural death among wild animals may be a beautiful demise, merely dropping peacefully into a final sleep within a sylvan glade. Failing abilities to forage or flee expose the old ram, billy, buck, or boar to starvation or death by fang and claw from another species. There are no Golden Years among wild animals. The weak are killed and eaten by the strong. The prime cast out the aged, and death comes to all wild things amid pain, fear and loneliness (if a species can experience loneliness).

The *Bambi Syndrome* that graces wild creatures with all sorts of human attributes such as awareness of family, planned social orders, or respect and care for the aged ignore the obvious fact that when an animal gets old or ill it is in a heap of trouble for which there is no cure but death. Animals have no "Elephant Graveyard" where they can expire in peace. Where man has not eliminated the wolves, wolverines, coyotes and panthers—we must include bears as well, deaths are often violent horrors at the fangs of a carnivore. The rest starve or freeze to death.

If I seem to belabor the agonies of dying animals, it is not without purpose. I reiterate because too many alleged animal lovers refuse to recognize that killing an animal does not cause it "extra" agony. To put it more bluntly, shooting a game animal probably saves it much pain and suffering.

As civilized people, we put our pets to sleep when their bodies or minds decay. Many of the same kindly souls who put old Rex "to sleep" (which we must remember is actually having the old dog executed) blindly ignore the nastiness of natural death in the wild.

A genuine trophy hunter takes only mature animals. Among those that retain their horns throughout a lifetime, a great trophy means the animal has little time left to live anyway.

Few glorify animals more than do big game hunters. The zoo-goers may ogle an animal with unbridled admiration, but the ogler's mind turns away at the next exhibit. The hunter studies his quarry. He knows its habits and its habitat. He savors the hunt before, during, and following the adventure.

Hunters assumed responsibility for game management a century ago. Hunters provide funds and political interest that have resulted in the protection of animals across our continent.

License fees from more than twenty million hunters contribute toward the purchase of public game lands, for stocking programs, and for the salaries of men in the field, such as wardens and management officials.

All do not accept such considerations as justification for hunting. An irate lady once informed me that when I got to hell I would surely be attacked by all the great bears I have killed, trampled by a herd of deceased bull moose, picked to bits by the flocks of ducks and geese I have taken, and severely pummeled by the host of innocent rabbits that fell before my gun. (She did not know about the legions of crows I took during my youthful years.)

Such a series of potential miseries might have disturbed me. However, I soothed my savaged nerves with the thought that while I was undergoing such severe torment, she, in her turn, would be crushed beneath a herd of Black Angus cattle, pecked by a million or so chickens, and gored by a multitude of swine, all of which she devoured with unthinking relish during her life span. I decided I preferred my own suffering to hers.

Surely, stalking, taking a wild animal, eating him, and honoring his memory has merit equal to raising a domestic beast, grooming it for slaughter, then executing it for the table. For any of us to eat meat something must die, and the individual who enjoys a cut of beef, pork, or lamb cannot logically shudder over the activities of a hunter.

Now this is a meat rack to remember. Build your rack strong. Alaskan game is big and heavy. Within a few days, this rack will permanently bend. No problem, the moose meat will be gone by then.

Killing is NOT the hunter's primary pleasure. Killing is a by-product of the hunt—just as the act of killing is not paramount to either a butcher or the steak eater. The shot in hunting punctuates success or failure of the planning and travels, the hoping, hiking, climbing, and perhaps crawling. The shot establishes a victor and a vanquished. It grants an animal a further lease on life or rewards the hunter with food, a trophy, and special memories.

Often hunters are faced with the proposal that we could simply photograph the game and not kill it. Then hunting would be humane and more palatable for those with thinner blood. Photographing, however, is not a substitute for collecting the game. It is easy to say, *"I could have shot him,"* but far too many shots are missed for one to casually claim he could have. You cannot *know* until you have done so.

A perhaps clumsy but understandable comparison of photographing versus collecting an animal might lie in evaluating the idea of photographing a roast beef dinner and saying, *"I could have eaten it."* There is not much satisfaction there.

It is grotesque that in the mores of members of thoughtless animal rights groups we can breed and raise creatures to slaughter for food. I mean cows, sheep, and hogs, and we can husband, butcher, and eat assorted birds such as chicken, ducks, pigeons, and turkeys. But, if a man goes afield and does the same to wild animals he is considered somehow immoral. A man can routinely bash a beef's skull with a sledge and it is all right, but if the same man shoots a whitetail deer he is brutal. A man can slit the throat of a hog, but he is inhumane if he hunts down a wild boar. A man can behead a legion of domestic fowl without recrimination, but he is murderous if he enters the fields and takes pheasant, quail, doves, or partridge. Such attitudes are at least irrational, but they exist and are typical of anti-hunting groups and other poorly informed people.

Then, there are the PETA and Friends of Animals-type people. Their hearts are great and their intentions good, but their incredibly naïve and extremely uninformed pitches sour the guts of those of us who live among and from the great game animals. There are humans who grant equivalency to hogs and humans, fish and humans, and birds and humans. There are others who give animals primacy over humans. In their eyes we must all be vegetarians—although I am not clear on how we would handle the overpopulation of animals that would surely encroach on our plantings.

Extremism is bad on either end of a normal curve. The difference is that we hunters do not attempt to restrict non-hunters, but they are continually after us to change our allegedly cruel and bloodthirsty ways.

Sport hunting has never endangered a species. It never will. There are effective game departments in every state to preclude that happening.

So, how many reasons can we assemble to explain a wish to hunt? I can think of twelve. *I do not necessarily approve of all of them.*

1. For the challenge of finding and taking the animal.
2. As an added reason for enjoying the out of doors.
3. To obtain meat for eating.
4. For enjoyment of firearms (or bows and arrows).
5. As a symbol of manliness.
6. To restrict or protect animal populations.
7. For exercise.
8. For companionship.
9. For adventure (perhaps danger).
10. To escape routines.
11. To collect a bounty.
12. To teach others.

Yes, they have other game in Alaska. This is a blacktail deer shot on Kodiak Island. The imported elk herd on Afognak Island should be mentioned as well, but elk are better hunted in the lower forty-eight.

Chapter

32

Random Thoughts

To eat well on a few days trip into the mountains, pre-make roast beef sandwiches and include compatible servings of thick gravy packed in triple plastic bags. By simply heating the small amount of gravy (which can be accomplished in a corner of a pan held over a candle or the tiniest of spruce twig fires) a satisfying meal is easily and quickly prepared.

Taxidermists use a ploy to "improve" a hunter's goat trophy. They put a fiberglass plug in the hollow horn base and mount the horn a considerable distance further from the skull than it should be. Such mounts do not fool anyone making official measurements, but they do make the horns about ten percent longer, and that is a lot on an otherwise ordinary goat trophy.

A goat horn is measured from the tip to the base of the outer horn. There is a definite ending there, and that point should be right down in the hair of the head, almost on the skull. A taxidermist would commit a lengthening atrocity only with an owner's permission, but it is a mighty poor-spirited hunter that needs to bugger up his trophy with phony additions.

In Alaska, I do most of my practice shooting at rocks in creek beds. Rock shooting is the way I prefer to maintain rifle/pistol skill. In the lower forty-eight such shooting might be hazardous, but in the Great State, creek beds can be hundreds of yards wide with no one else within miles. I am, of course, referring to shooting out to three hundred yards.

Picking interesting rocks at unknown ranges quite rapidly develops skill at estimating range and the holding necessary to make solid hits. It is also interesting shooting. The rocks usually give off a good puff of dust, and the shooter's interest does not sag as it might pumping away at a known distance on a round bull's eye.

I ate a marmot once. The whistling rodents are all over Alaska, and I wondered just how edible they might be. A clean head shot with the old .44 Magnum put a marmot down. Skinned, cleaned, and washed the small animal looked appetizing. We stuffed a few potatoes and a lot of arrowroot dug from along the creek banks into the abdominal cavity; then we wrapped the entire carcass in aluminum foil. The meal baked for hours in the coals of our campfire, and when we finally broke it out the meat fell from the bones. I thought the marmot tasted delicious. The flavor and texture seemed comparable to gray squirrel, and the arrowroot imparted a turnipy flavor that I enjoyed.

In some photos the reader may have noticed that the author carries his rifle on the *right* shoulder and his pistol on the *left* hip. As I shoot ambidextrously there is an advantage or two in having the weapons on opposite sides. Primarily, my opposite side reason is that the butts of the two weapons are not repeatedly striking each other. There is also an ability to draw the pistol without having to swing your rifle out of the way. The rifle is carried slung over the right shoulder because a bolt action rifle is best operated right handed. If I have to go after a bear at close quarters, I sometimes turn my pistol butt forward into a cross draw position. This allows reaching with either hand. I have never needed that small refinement, but if one is doing it, one might as well do it all the way.

No one can learn everything about Alaska and its game, but anyone can add to his knowledge by good reading. Fortunately there are fine books available about hunting in the Great Land. A number of the more difficult to find are listed below. They are worth locating, and they will provide a reader with extensive fact and opinion as well as regale him with interesting and enlightening hunting tales.

The Wilderness of the Upper Yukon
   Charles Sheldon
The Wilderness of the Denali
   Charles Sheldon

A Year Among Sheep at Mt. McKinley
    Charles Sheldon
The Wild Grizzlies of Alaska
    John M. Holzworth
Hunting and Fishing in Alaska
    Russell Annabel
A Naturalist in Alaska
    Adolph Murie
Arctic Wild
    Lois Crisler
The Big Game Animals of North America
    Jack O'Connor

I have never read an article that told me how much ammunition to take with me on an Alaskan hunt. I have worked out my own needs pretty well over the years. Other people may not agree. The old guide carried only what was in his rifle, but I never knew him to need more than one shot per animal. Jerry packed an extra twenty round box in his pack. Art Troup and I usually carry our magazines full but our chambers empty, and the rifle OFF cock. In our favorite pocket are five more rounds. Unless the trip is extended, that is all we take. Lordy, if you cannot do the job with nine or ten rounds…!

When I hunt alone in the mountains I carry an extra twenty round box of ammunition in my own pack. Being alone, way out, changes many things.

Ammunition just stuffed into a pocket is against all of the guidance one reads. After trying belt loops, jacket loops, pouches, and extra box magazines, I am back to loose rounds in my pocket. I have never had them clink at a bad moment (or at any moment), and I have never had trouble with a dirty round. I reach automatically into that right hand pocket, grab 'em all, and in they go, no trouble, no confusion. I guess I will not go on record as claiming that is THE spot to carry extra ammo, but that is my way.

Wind in the mountains can be fluky. Rod Washburn taught me a trick that I use quite often. Before the hunt I fill a squeeze bottle of the nasal spray type with talcum powder. During an approach, little squeezes of the bottle will check even the tiniest of breeze directions. Squeezing a bottle beats tossed up grass or wetting upheld fingers, and it surely stands ahead of our usual condition concerning wind shifts, which is simply not knowing.

A brownie or a grizzly normally fishes by stepping on a fish and carrying it away in his jaws. He almost never flips a fish from the water with his paw, as too many popular painting show.

A neat little gimmick when camping on gravel bars is to fasten your tent rope by tying the rope end around a small stone and then dropping a big rock on top to hold it all in place. Since you cannot get a tent pin to hold in the soil of a gravel bar, you may resort often to this system.

This raises the question of why camp out on a bar? The first good answer is that you can avoid a lot of bugs. You are also close to water, your fire is safer, and you have a flat spot on which to lay your weary bones.

When I am backpacking where I might need a hatchet, I carry a small tomahawk type as shown below. The tool is very light and thin bladed. It slices more than it chops. I recommend a tomahawk of this model for any backpacking hunter.

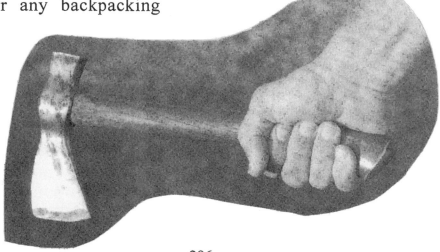

An acquaintance took a charging brown bear at very close range. He mistakenly aimed to hit the bear between the eyes. His bullet struck the brownie in the nose and drove on in to explode the bear's brain. A perfect shot for an instant kill.

In actuality, my inexperienced friend was spared a possible mauling by a ballistic fact of which he knew nothing. If his bullet had been delivered between the eyes where he had intended, the bullet could have ricocheted off the bear's sloping skull, and the brownie might have avenged his instant headache on my friend's tender body.

But, a scope-sighted rifle starts the bullet more than an inch *below* the line of sight. Somewhere down range (about 25 yards or so) the bullet crosses the line of sight and later again drops below it. So, at extremely close range, as my friend's shot was, his aiming point between the eyes compensated and was correct for the bullet still traveling below the line of sight to hit the bear in the nose.

I suppose there are two points to be made here. The first might be that someone seems to look after dumb hunters, but do not depend on it. The second should be that *at point blank range your rifle shoots low*. You should know that and plan for it.

Pistol marksmanship depends almost entirely on sight alignment. Exact sight relationship over the short pistol barrel is critical.

An excellent way to develop sight picture and trigger control is to dry fire your pistol at a blank wall, without a target. This practice eliminates the attention catching bull's eye and allows the shooter to concentrate on his sights and his trigger release.

I often sit in my living room dry firing at my television screen. I can choose a blank area for practice as mentioned above, or I can aim at selected targets on the screen.

An important factor in successful game shooting is to *get off when desired*. There is no slow, timed, or rapid fire in the field, but there are moving targets and perhaps charging ones. Holding and squeezing for interminable periods before the trigger breaks is not practical marksmanship for the hunter. Game too often shifts its position while the perfectionist is struggling with his wobble area and fining his sight picture. The hunter must get his gun up, see the sights, and fire.

A well-lighted TV screen with its quickly changing pictures can provide realistic and effective practice for all of the above for both rifle and pistol. If the shooter loiters on his trigger pull he will be aiming at something different then he intended. Using programs that include big game photography can offer a multitude of angles on actual game.

An Alaskan hunter carrying a bolt-action rifle should have his magazine fully loaded but his chamber empty. When shooting appears close, he should slip a round into the chamber, but not before. Even then, the safety must be on until it is time to aim. The exception to the safety-on rule might be going after bear in the brush. Then there is no time to fiddle with gadgets.

Safety must remain paramount, and a hunter carries his rifle a thousand hours for every hour he uses it. *Cartridges in chambers are not necessary until the last moments, and until then they are bad news.*

If you are going in after dangerous game, and if there is room in the woods or brush, carry your rifle shouldered as if ready to fire but with the muzzle low. If you hold the rifle high, so that you are looking across the sights, your vision is badly obstructed—particularly just below your rifle and your forward arm. Just drop the muzzle fifteen degrees, and notice how your field of view clears up.

Gun cleaning is something I do because I feel it is necessary, never because I enjoy it. I never pamper my guns. I consider scratches and gouges acquired in fair chase as badges of honor. If checkering gets too worn to be useful I have it recut, not for looks, but so that I can get a decent grip on the gun. Cleaning makes my gun function better. I rarely scrub it up for looks.

I once used a rifle for two years in Alaska without even wiping it *off*, much less wiping it *out*. I never had a malfunction, and it shot well. My intention was to determine, as best I could, just what not cleaning a gun really would do. The rifle looked grubby, but I have seen worse that were occasionally cleaned. I do not think I learned much of anything by not cleaning that piece—except that I did not feel confidence in the rifle because I was unsure of how good a shape it was in.

Ordinarily, a hunter cannot conveniently carry along a complete or elaborate cleaning kit. My field kit consists of a rod, I use my worst t-shirt as a rag, and a small can of WD 40. No one needs more. I like the WD 40 because I can spray it on liberally without fear of gumming the works. It gets under moisture, yet I am not trying to grab a grease-slick bolt handle or barrel.

When I go into high country, I sometimes carry an army-surplus cleaning rod that unscrews into a half-dozen pieces. I stick a few rifle cleaning patches and the WD 40 in somewhere, and I am in business. If I need a rag, as mentioned, I use my T-shirt.

Above base camp I sometimes carry the rod, but never anything more. I have occasionally shoved my rifle barrel into a snow bank while clumsy-footing around. Tapping on the barrel and blowing into it while waiting for the snow to melt out does not appeal to my spirited nature. A rod comes in very handy in such cases.

However, I fear that most of my time on the summits I have nothing along to clean out a rifle bore. I would not recommend not having a rod, but I admit to too often ending up that way. When you are laying out a pack to carry all day, it is very tempting to leave out a cleaning rod. With luck you will not need one, but man, is it tough to clamber all the way down to the willow line to try to find a stick long enough to clean out a rifle barrel.

An obvious solution to the above problem is to tape over your rifle's muzzle. (You will see photos in this book of hunters so prepared. They used a single covering of masking tape.) In my military days, we were issued condoms for other purposes, but we used them to blouse our pants and to pull over rifle and machine gun muzzles. A bit of tape does better.

Any rifle used in hunting big game in Alaska should be equipped with a carrying sling. Most of the time your rifle will be hung over your shoulder. Some writers advocate the use of a rifle sling in shooting. I have written that I do not. I have seen a few men crawl into a hasty sling for a shot, but I never felt handicapped because I did not. I DO feel held back trying to shoot moving targets using a sling. My feeling on a rifle sling is that its function is for carrying, not for shooting. A simple sling consisting of a leather strap looped at each end is probably the best. The military type slings that I often end up with are unnecessarily heavy. A sling should not be so wide that it will not grab your shoulder and stay on, but it should not be so narrow that it bites and hurts either. In Europe, where there is more shooting than hunting, 1/2-inch wide slings are encountered. Equipment nuts in our country sometimes show up with slings so wide that they look like cobras. Neither is right. One-half inch slings can be too weak and they can bite your shoulder. Cobra-type slings can slip from shoulders when a rifle is slung because they are too wide to get a grip behind the shoulder point. I believe that a sling 7/8 of an inch to 1-inch wide is best.

Douglas S. Cooper demonstrates how a rifle can be slung over a Yukon-type backboard. Worrying about such a refinement may appear trivial, but as the rifle keeps slipping from your shoulder (and it will), and you are compelled to hang onto the sling, much as Cooper is in this photo, to keep from having the rifle dangle from your elbow for seemingly endless hours, you will wish you had a tall upright to loop over.

That is why I have repeated this advice throughout the book.

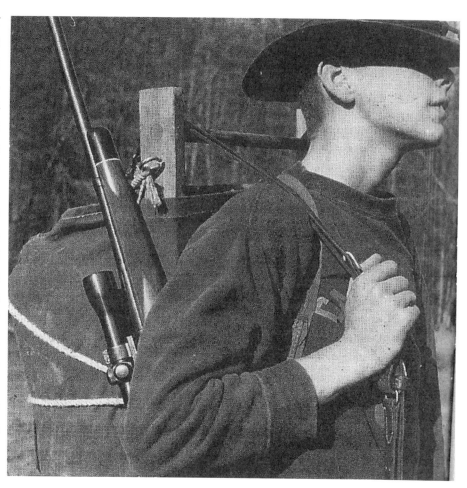

Seventeen of nineteen winners at the Camp Perry National Matches used **Vihta Vuori gunpowder** in their handloads. If you load your own, switch to this powder. It is so superior to the stuff we have been using the last fifty years or so that it is difficult to describe. Incidentally, Federal uses it in their match ammo. The words are pronounced **Veeta Vor-E.**

I find myself embarrassed that every road sign in Alaska has been shot full of holes. As a sportsman I would like to think that men allowed to carry guns at any time, and who do carry guns a lot of the time, would be above blasting directional signs. It appears that is not the case. There is no way that we can blame out-of-state people for doing the sign shooting. There are just too many bullet holes. I do not know a hunter who would shoot at a sign, and I know a lot of hunters. It makes me wonder who these guys are who go around getting kicks out of obliterating metal signs.

I never recall carrying a canteen in the Alaskan range, and only rarely anywhere in Alaska. There is water everywhere. Sometimes it can even be found on the very tops of snow-less mountains. We used to say that any running water in Alaska was drinkable. That was almost true. In the mountains you did not need to worry about pollution, and with springs, streams, even rivers everywhere a hunter could rarely thirst.

About twenty years ago that all changed. Some strange bug got into the water, so we are told, and now no one should drink any of the water unless it is treated. I find that stunning. I suppose the experts are correct. To hell with it. I still drink it straight from the stream anyway.

One of the most enjoyable aspects of Alaskan hunting is that a hunter usually has time to look over his trophy. In other areas, it often seems that a hunter blasts at game only fleetingly glimpsed and probably little more than recognized as legal for shooting. It is nice to locate an animal, stalk him some, look at him a lot, study his horns and condition, and finally decide to take him or let him pass.

Native hunters in Alaska used to take wolves by bending pieces of springy willow with sharpened ends inside chunks of meat. The meat was then frozen. Wolves gulp their food. The wolves swallowed the meat, and as it thawed in their bellies the sharp sticks straightened out and pierced the animals' guts. The hunter followed wolf tracks from his bait until he found the dead animals. Gee, I'm not sure I am glad to know about that.

In all the years I have hunted Alaska I have never encountered a Game Warden or Game Protector while hunting. No Game Department official has ever checked my vehicle along a road or in any way endeavored to examine my license or my game tags. In how many states would a hunter be allowed that much trust and freedom?

The photographs in this book show clearly that Alaskan hunters do not concern themselves with fancy hunting clothes. As the probability of encountering other hunters is remote, the chance of getting shot by another is even more improbable. If you come to Alaska to hunt wear what you like. Dressing as an Eastern deer hunter, however, might prove embarrassing. If you are reading these words ten years after they are written it would perhaps be wise to see if things have changed.

This cold weather boot was perfected in the 1950s. We called them "Mickey Mouse" boots. If the boot is black, it was made for wet snow conditions. If the boot is white, it was built for dry cold—where there was zero moisture. The valve in the side should be opened to reduce pressure during airplane rides. There is a repair patch sewn on just above the pressure valve. I have never found anything better for bitter conditions.

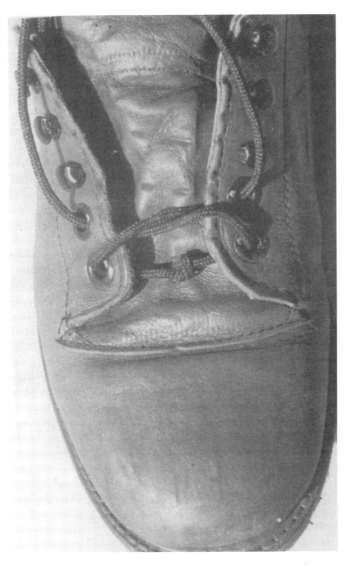

The late great hunter, Finn Aagaard, particularly liked discovering this little bootlace trick. Anyone, soldier or hunter who often dresses in the dark will eventually find one boot lace a mile longer than the other. To keep them even, simply tie a knot at the bottom. When tightening, the knot will be pulled beneath one side or the other and never be seen.

Prepared!

It is the getting up and getting down when carrying a heavy load that exhausts a bearer. If you can find a way to rest while remaining standing, you will be far ahead in the game. Monopods and "A" frames are handy solutions—as soon as you get down to timberline.

A crude "A" frame can be attached to a pack. When the hunter stands erect the feet of the "A" should touch the ground so that the bearer can rest. A normal forward lean while walking will allow the frame's feet to clear the ground.

Using the "A," very heavy loads can be successfully carried without completely exhausting the carrier. The "A" frame system is used throughout the Orient where men still haul huge loads.

A monopod is almost as good as an "A." In this example, the "pod" is fastened outside the double gas can load. This burden is in excess of seventy pounds, but can be handled for long periods by a normally strong man.

This is a wolf and bear trap from the bad old days. Blacksmiths hammered out traps like this mostly in the lower forty-eight, and some came to Alaska along with their owners. It is common to find this type of steel trap with long and sharp spiked teeth as part of the jaws. Reproductions of these traps are being manufactured for "antiquers" these days and are a lousy investment.

Doug Cooper demonstrates how easily a Yukon packboard can be slipped from the shoulders. A pack with a belt or chest harness should be avoided. Slip in and slip out is the best, and the safest, way.

Bob Hirter demonstrates why the author believes a hunting jacket should not have any kind of pocket on the right breast—no matter how Richard Chamberlain dressed in *King Solomon's Mines*.

The author occasionally wears an army field jacket and unless I make certain the right breast pocket is snapped closed, this happens when I dismount the rifle. Incidentally, no loops of large double rifle cartridges on that side of your chest either. (*King Solomon* again.)

A friend of mine is an ardent hand loader. He claimed recently that he had trouble with the animals he hit not falling down. When he finally got an animal on the ground, he examined it closely and found that he had loaded his cartridges so hot, and the bullets were moving so fast, that they cauterized the wounds going through.

(Ah well, every book should have one of those kind of stories.)

Yep, that is a white buffalo calf. We had two white calves, two years in a row, in the Big Delta herd. The cows seemed to recognize that the white calves were different and needed protecting. It was difficult to get a picture of a white calf because the other buffalo formed around it, sort of (crudely) like the bull musk oxen do protecting their females.

Neither calf lasted through a winter. We have always believed that someone shot them for their rare hides. We do not mean native Alaskans. The northern Athabascan Indians have no tradition of holy or sacred white buffalo that I ever heard of, That is American plains Indians stuff.

Of Mosquitoes and Horses (Mules too)

I probably should not write about bugs and beasts of burden because I am unable to be unbiased and what the inexperienced might call fair-minded. I place both the insects and the equines among the undesirables of nature. It is additionally horrible to realize that if you have a horse, you will collect mosquitoes, flies, and black gnats in hordes, swarms, and plagues. Horses in Alaska attract mosquitoes as honey draws bees—only worse. That is bad.

Of course, horses have other really rotten attributes. They panic at bear scent, they panic at lightning, they panic at . . . the damned animals panic at everything. Horses kick at you. They suck in air when you are tightening girths—which means the loads will soon slide under their bellies. They bite. They roll with their packs or saddles, and they try to wipe away their packs and your knees by swiping them against trees. Horses bog down. They tangle in windfalls, they crash through ice, and they regularly break loose and head for home. If you do not have a wrangler on a hunt, you spend most of your time caring for horses.

Horses are very dumb. We are not speaking of handsome and shiny thoroughbreds trotting high-headed and high-tailed through blue grass meadows. Most Alaskan horses are scrub stock raised outside, barely trained, and completely unused to mountains or muskeg. Horses stink, but sometimes caribou bulls are attracted and try to claim an animal for their harem—or something. I always hope the caribou gets the horse, because, I hate hunting with horses almost as much as I despise mosquitoes.

Mosquitoes travel in swarms. There may be none and suddenly they arrive so thick that you breathe them in, and they bite like dragons. Alaskan mosquitoes are not large; there are simply multi-trillions of them—per swarm. You cannot wave them away. They land and stay in place until they are wiped away. Avoid dark and dank stagnant water hollows where there is no wind. At the first step, clouds of mosquitoes can rise from such places. When they rise, flee. There is no other choice.

Even a slight breeze may deter mosquitoes, and the no-see-ums as well. Yep, we've got those miniscule, all jaw-and-fang mites as well. I am sure they are closely related to those dominating Florida. There is a photo I have failed to locate for this book of a man standing on the tundra with his head net raised while glassing (into the breeze) with his binoculars. The picture was snapped from the rear, and his back, sheltered from the wind, is an inch thick with mosquitoes.

I carried four head nets and two mosquito bars in my airplane's survival kit at all times. I also had four bottles of military 100% Deet, which is the real killing agent in the few useful mosquito lotions and sprays. *Cutter's* mosquito repellent is the next best thing to the military stuff. Forget the be-kind-to-the-poor-bugs stuff like *Off.*

When mosquitoes are bad, and they are often simply unendurable, you will sit on the smoky side of the fire with relish, you will wear gloves and keep your ears covered. I have always wondered what mosquitoes eat before I arrived. You will try to camp on ridges where there is often a breeze, and you will still be miserable.

Do not take Alaskan mosquitoes lightly—I never have. Without protection, they could kill you.

Did I mention that I hate mosquitoes?

I do not enjoy bringing up the subject of bow and arrow hunters. I am unwilling to appear even neutral. I am against bow hunting as a matter of principle.

Back in the 1930s, an archer named Howard Hill successfully hunted every game species he could find. The guy was a deadly bowman, no question about it. I avidly followed his adventures. I even knew the justly famous archer Fred Bear a little. Hill had disappeared into the mists of time, when Fred Bear and his pack train of bow hunters marched into our caribou camp on the Tanana River flats one long ago August evening.

Bear and his party of genuine experts were going to hunt Dall rams in the nearby mountains. They pitched camp, ate caribou with us, and swapped yarns at our fire. His party lit out for the high country at dawn. Later, I saw the full curl rams they had collected in *Jonas Brothers, Taxidermists* of Fairbanks. That is the end of my positive reporting about bow hunting.

Before I begin lighting into bow hunters and their terrible (repetitive and interminable) wounding and maiming, I must confess that I am a lousy bow and arrow shooter. Robin Hood would have surrendered me to the Sheriff of Nottingham without regret. As an archer I am pathetic, but it is not my personal deficiency that turned me against bow hunters. My disgust with the sport is based on the lousy shooting and the resulting wounding of game animals that stagger off to die everywhere the sport is condoned.

Through some inexplicable rationalizing, hunters who are ungifted even with a scoped rifle accept that, because they can drill a target at thirty steps with their compound bows, they are qualified to hunt big animals in difficult conditions. So few are bow-capable (the percentage is too tiny to measure) that only proven champions should even consider the sport. The wild game does not deserve to be tormented by poorly directed broadheads, and are too often unrecovered by their clumsy executioners.

Do I exaggerate? In the mountains it is difficult to prove, but lack of skills are demonstrated almost daily on the game hunting farms in the lower forty-eight where bowmen by the hundreds attempt to take animals from buffalo to the smallest of deer.

I have a friend who operates such a business. He curses the archers who regularly leave hogs (wild boar) running about with three or four arrows hanging from them. Licensed bow hunting instructors fail to kill cleanly shot after shot. Sportsmen from sportsmen's clubs try, and they also wound and wound. Clean kills with bows and arrows occur far more regularly on TV programs and in magazines than they do in the hunting fields. Some of these sad sack archers come north.

Consider this actual incident. A client wished to shoot a buffalo with his bow. He solidly hit the standing animal at fifty feet. The buffalo walked away and lay down. The archer moved around and shot again. Once more he hit the bull solidly, but the buffalo got up and charged the shooter who had to be rescued by a rifle bullet. I know where that trophy hangs, and I have heard the story of the kill. Somehow, the backup rifle is never mentioned.

If that were a rare incident, it would not be worth repeating, but that kind of shooting is most common, and that kind of result is even more regular.

For the final time, our game rates better. Bow hunters are not that good, and there should be almost zero bow hunting in Alaska.

If I were asked to name the most grievous error made by Alaskan hunters, I would name the failure to follow through after the trigger pull. That may seem like a minor perhaps improbable error, but looking up too soon ruins more shots than any other listable cause.

I have watched countless hunters, many of them alleged to be experienced, squeeze carefully, then snap their heads up to see where the bullet went. No such movement should occur. Bullets are thrown off course because of riflemen trying to see what happened too soon. The shooter must attempt to remain on his target, holding as solidly as he can right on through the recoil. Not until then should he attempt to look downrange. Check yourself. The error is common.

As I reread the many preceding pages, I see that I have set high hunting standards and have managed to portray myself as quite a hunter indeed. I should modify that image and reduce myself to more realistic status. I will do so by mentioning three blunders that embarrass me to this day. True, I could list pages of errors in judgment and performance over the last fifty plus hunting years, but I lack the humility to do so. These three will have to do.

The first occurred when I was using my long Randall hunting knife to skin and gut my first moose (the 28-incher, see pages 188 and 189). To make the story short, I stuck the mighty blade through the moose's esophagus and pulled on it (blade flat) to raise the innards so that my partner could get at them more easily. Inevitably, the blade twisted and cut through the soft tube and stuck point first in my thigh—deeply into my thigh. What a stupid thing to do, but it had seemed clever until I was stabbed. No major blood vessels were cut, but I packed it in, hiked out and went to the nearest infirmary for a tetanus shot.

The next dopey move that I am willing to mention occurred a few years later. I was on top of a mountain examining a flat area to see if I could land a plane there. The surface looked like ten million dinner plates all stood on end and tight together. Nearly a mile of vertical plates—very unusual; I have never seen anything like it.

I was walking with my rifle slung onto my packboard with my hands stuffed into my jacket pockets. My toe caught on one of the plates. I could not get it over the height of the plate, and I fell forward face first. Unable to drag my hands from my pockets, I landed hard, right on my kisser. Somehow, the wallop did not knock me cold, but the rocks banged up my handsome features and broke my glasses. I wore the bruises and the glasses held together by adhesive tape for the rest of the trip. That was when I learned to pack an extra pair of spectacles into base camp. Darn, I shouldn't admit to such dumb stunts.

The last admitable blunder happened not so long ago. I was explaining our mountains to some folks from flatter lands. I identified a mountain that I had often hunted, by pointing and naming the passes, knobs, and streams while inwardly recognizing that something seemed not quite right. I was finished with my brilliant descriptions before I realized that I was looking at the wrong mountains, and that everything I had just spoken about was dead wrong. (I intended to correct my gross misidentifications, but the conversation turned, and I never got around to it. Those folks accepted all that I, the expert, said. To this day they believe they saw something they were not even near.)

That's it! I confess to nothing more.

As a book ends, more information always appears. For the most part, it is too late, and the photographs and stories must remain unpublished, but I end this tome with just-arrived pictures and a story about friends who always wanted to hunt in Alaska, and this short tale is a bit special.

The folks you see in these photographs have always been hunters. The younger three have safaried in Africa, but until this trip they had never been to Alaska. The old buzzard, Fred, the family patriarch in the white hat, makes the plans and foots the bills for almost everything his family does. The story of this hunt is exceptional because Harv shot his ram at 200 yards with his 7mm Remington Magnum on his first day—a heart/lung shot. Michelle, shot her black bear at 50 yards on her second day—7mm through the front shoulder, and Chris nailed his grizzly (squared 7 feet, plus) with his

7mm at 200 yards while the bear was standing and looking around, a perfect shot through the spine at the front shoulder joint—in the rain on his fifth day of hunting. Master Guide Ray Atkins and Rick Hyce delivered big time about as swiftly as it can be done, and the shooting was one shot each at reasonable distances, as it should be—an enviable hunt and a nice story.

Harvey Thebes with his sheep

Fred and Harvey at the lodge with his ram horns

Michelle Thebes with black bear shot in the Alaska Range

Chris Thebes with grizzly shot near Cantwell Creek, south of Cantwell, Alaska

Chapter

33

In Closing

I wish that I could again experience all of the hunts described in this volume. Almost thirty years ago, I wrote that, even at my desk, I could imagine the bite of cold wind off Saint Anthony's Pass. I could taste the crystal waters of Morningstar Creek and feel the pull of tundra vines across my insteps. I could smell sheep and sense my pulse quicken at the thought. I longed for the high, clear air of mountain country.

I wrote that, as you read, I would be doing those things. My camp would be sheltered from the winds but open to the sun. My rifle would hang close to hand. Water would be near, and there would be meat on the rack. I would smell of sweat and my clothes would be in ruin, but my nose would be clear, my eyes sharp, and my mind one with nature.

All of those things came to be. Glorious have been the years. But, now I am eighty. The hills have steepened. I have implants in both eyes and have suffered one retina collapse, and have had two corneal transplants. My reflexes have slowed, and, of course, I am not strong, as I once was. There are older guys still packing through the mountains, so I may have great hunts remaining. Still, it is often later than we think, and a man is wise to examine his limitations. It would be grand to find another ten years have rolled away with more stories and concepts to include in a later edition of this volume, but it will be another's duty to perform.

The older a hunter gets, the more he will value his memories. I am fortunate. I have many—but I would like to have more!

In Closing

The best thought for closing is the one I used decades ago.

"There is room for you, too, in our Alaskan wilderness. If our paths cross we can share a tale or two. If we never meet, we are already friends through the pages of this book. I guess that alone makes the writing worthwhile."

The author with most of his books and his Harley

Index

A

Acknowledgements: v, vi
A-frame packing: 259
African Rifles and Cartridges: 44-48
Alaska (chapter): 23-33
Alaska, maps: 5-7
Alaskan .450 cartridge: 76-79
Alaskan Hunter: 8, 34, 35
Andres, Tom: 286
Annabel, Russell: 111, 224 295
Arctic Wild: 295, 309
Area 20D: 4,7,
Atkins, Ray: 105, 238, 240, 313
Auto Mag (pistol): 96, 98

B

Background: 34-39
Ballistic tables: 43, 77, 81-82, 95, 155, 175
Ballistics & guns: 40-64
Barclay, Paul: 238
Barnes, Frank: 77
Bear, blue glacier: 152

Bears, general: 6, 30,132-165, 297
Bears, grizzly: (see Grizzly)
Benchrest shooting: 53
Benner, Joe: 96
Best rifle: 74, 75
Big Game Animals of North America: 295
Binoculars: 242-247
Bison: 30, 32 307
Black bear: 30, 135, 150, 151
Black Rapids: 7,
Bolio Lake: 261
Boots: 302, 303
Bowman, Les: 55
Brackenridge: 149
Brooks Range: 14, 32
Buffalo (see Bison)
Bullet penetration: 34, 35, 89
Bullet weight: 44-47
Bullets, explosive effect: 50, 51
Bush flying: 102-107
Butch (& lake): 251

C

Camp Robber (Blue Jay): 39
Camping & camps: 249-266
Caribou: 6, 30, 216-232
Cartridges, the best: 75

Case jackknife: 173, 280-283
Chandler sniper rifles: 68, 69
Chronograph: 50
Chugach Mountains: 31, 111
Chugger's Hunt: 124
Climate: 29, 33
Controlled feed: 161, 162
Cook, Frank: 43
Cooper, Doug: 300, 305
Cooper, Jeff: 95
Crisler, Louis: 295

D

Dall sheep: 6, 30, 166-186
Death From Afar: 56
Deer: 30
Denali firing line: 225
Dillman, Ray: 136
Doc's Hunt: 120-123
Donnely Dome: 7, 197, 198
Double rifles: 87-92
Duncan, Lacey: 286
Duncan, Ron: 286, 287

E

Ebling, Brent: 141
Edwards Brothers, Printers: vi
Elk: 30, 32
Energy: (see kinetic energy)
Ernestine Creek: 120-125, 131
　　174, 251
Expenses and costs: 20

F

Fair Chase hunting: 133
Fairbanks, News-Miner: 93, 94
Feisl, Karl: 202

Fishing: 272-279
Flying: 102-107, 234, 235
Follow through: 310
Fording, use of a pole: 21
Foreword: 1, 3
Fort Greely: 4, 5, 7, 105, 174
Fuller, Bill: 76

G

Game Department: 16, 32
Garrett Ammunition: 78
Georg, Al: 93
Gerstle River: 5, 7, 102
Gessna, Vernon: Front cover
Goat hunting pack: 130
Goats, mountain: 6, 30, 108-131
Golden Years: 13-26
Granite Mountains: 4, 7, 192
Grizzly attack: 140-144, 160, 161
Grizzly bear: 6, 30, 37, 38,
　　132-165
Guilliland, Dyton: 191
Gun Digest: 189
Guns & ballistics: 40-64

H

Haber, Gordon: 235, 238, 239
Harley-Davidson: 35
Hatchet: 296
Herriman, Gary: 203
Hirter, Bob: 306
History: 13-26
Hoecher, Skip: 223
Holzworth, John: 145, 149, 295
Horses: 256, 257, 307-308
Hoyer, Al: 56
Hunting & Fishing in Alaska, 295
Hunting Alaska: 34

Hunting alone: 63
Hyce, Rick: back cover, 241, 313

I–J

Iron Brigade Armory: 68, 69
Iron sights: 65
Ithaca 12 gauge shotgun: 151
Jarvis Creek camp: 213, 236
Johnson, Harold: 76-78
Jonas Brothers (taxidermy): 19

K–L

Keith, Elmer: 66, 83-86, 96, 99, 285
Kelley, Mark: 66
Kenai rifles: 76-78
Kenton, Simon: 254
Kimber rifles: 73
Kinetic Energy: 44-47,
Kinetic Energy formula: 44
Klineburgers: 187, 188
Knives: 280-287
Knock Out blow: 44-49, 52, 53
KO formula: 46
Lean, Charles: 253
Lewis & Clark expedition: 149
Lindsley, Roy: 140
Little, Dunk: 253
Low -Density Dynamic- Equilibrium: 23

M–N

MacKenzie, Sir Alex.: 149
Manowar, finish ™: 71
Mag-Na-Port™: 97
MaGill, (Mac): 120

Maps: 4-6
Market hunting: 15, 16
Marlin, model 95, .45/70: 72
Matching Gun to Game: 56
McCumber Creek: 7, 250, 255
McCutcheon, Steve: 18
McMillin, Gary: 33, 283, 292
McMillin, Jack: 208, 229
Meat rack: 205, 290
Mefford, Andy J.: 222, 228
Midnight sun: 3
Military experience: 41
Mimi: many entries
Momentum, bullet: 44-47
Moore, Slim: 17, 123
Moose: 6, 30, 188-215, 240 237, 238
Mosquitoes: 28, 263, 265, 308
Murie, Adolph: 295
Musk Ox: 31
Nelson, George: 253
Neuls, Leo: 134
New Official Gun Book: 47
Nosler bullets: 49

O–P

Ober Creek: 250
O'Connor, Jack: 18, 66, 73, 111, 173, 182, 224, 295
Offhand position: 61
Old Dog: 124
Orr, George: 149
Oxen, Musk: 31
Page, Warren: 47
Parmalee, Claude: 189
Philosophy: 288-292
Piabola, Ed.: 181
Picatinny Rail: 69

Pistols, An Encyclopedia: 98
Pistol, auto mag: 96, 98
Pistols: 42, 93-101, 297
Pistol hunting: 93-101
Polar Bear: 31
Premier Reticle: 62

R

Ramer, Bill: 53
Random thoughts: 293-307
Range estimation: 59, 60
Rahn, Jeff: 190
Randall, Bo: 280
Rausch, Arthur: many entries
Rausch, Clifford: 177
Rausch, Jerry: many entries
Reading: 117
Rees, Clair: 56
Remington, Al: 274
Rhyshek, Johnny: 127, 185, 190, 226, 283, 284
Rhyshek, Joe: 126
Rifleman's rifle: 64
Rifles for Large Game: 54
Rifles, double: 87-92
Right gun: 74-75
Roth, Brian: 226
Ruger, Bill: 98
Russian River: 272, 273

S

Schmidt Rubin rifle: 61, 62
Scope sights: 18, 22,
Shebal, LeRoy: 233
Sheep, Dall: 6, 30, 166-186
Sheldon, Charles: 294, 295
Washburn, Rodney: 295
Watson, Jerry: 148

Shoemaker, Phil: 71
Shooting ranges: 56, 57, 79-82, 93-98, 158
Sights, iron: 65
Sights, proper: 65-69
Simon, Andrew: 16
Slings: 61, 70, 299
Sportsman's Encyclopedia: 54
Spotting scope: 245
Stebbins, Henry: 98
Stocks, rifle: 70-73
Stock, thumbhole: 71
Sun at midnight: 3
Sustained Yield program: 24

T–Z

Taylor, John (Pondoro): 44-48
Telescopic sights: (see Sights)
The Sweet Taste: 143, 144
Thebes, Chris: 286, 311-313
Thebes, Fred: 286, 311-313
Thebes, Harv: 286, 311-312
Thebes, Michelle: 311-313
Thomas, Stan: 215, 218, 252
Too long stocks: 72
Tourism: 23
Trap, steel: 305
Tractor, Bombardier: 164, 177, 206, 226, 257, 267-271
Troup, A. B: Fwd, 91, 196, 224, 225, 232, 272-279, 287
Trueblood, Ted: 66
Umfreyville, Edward: 149
Vogel, Oscar: 16
Waike, John: 185
Walrus: 30

Weatherby, Roy: 48
West System™ epoxy: 73